STRENGTH IN
NUMBERS

STRENGTH IN
✿ NUMBERS ✿

Population, Reproduction, and Power
in Eighteenth-Century France

CAROL BLUM

The Johns Hopkins University Press
Baltimore & London

•

This book has been brought to publication with the generous
assistance of the Karl and Edith Pribram Fund.

2 4 6 8 9 7 5 3 1

The Johns Hopkins University Press
2715 North Charles Street
Baltimore, Maryland 21218-4363
www.press.jhu.edu

Library of Congress Cataloging-in-Publication Data
Blum, Carol, 1934–
   Strength in numbers : population, reproduction, and power in
eighteenth-century France / Carol Blum.
      p.   cm.
Includes bibliographical references and index.
   ISBN 0-8018-6810-6 (hardcover : alk. paper)
   1. France—Population policy—History—18th century. 2. Human
reproduction—Moral and ethical aspects—France—History—18th
century. 3. Sexual ethics—France—History—18th century. 4. Social
values—France—History—18th century. I. Title.
   HB3593 .B58   2002
   304.6′2′094409033—dc21

2001001521

A catalog record for this book is available from the British Library.

In memory of my husband,
Lauren Vedder Ackerman

CONTENTS

PREFACE

Where does a society look for consensus regarding moral value when the grip of religious authority weakens? In my previous works I traced the galvanizing idea of "virtue" as it appeared in the writings of Denis Diderot and Jean-Jacques Rousseau. I analyzed the uses of virtue as a triumphant political substitute for grace during the French Revolution, one that provided participants with a shared cultural construction and a commonly accepted ideational currency.

In this volume I explore another powerful concept imbued with ultimate moral prestige in eighteenth-century France: populationism. Reproaching the King of France and the Catholic Church for depopulating the nation became an immensely effective arm in the battles of the Enlightenment. A large corpus of works proclaimed there was no higher purpose than to further national demographic progress by any means—including the adoption of new models of sexual behavior.

This corpus contains a few famous texts, such as the celebrated "depopulation letters" of Montesquieu's *Lettres persanes* and Diderot's audacious *Supplément au voyage de Bougainville,* but it consists mainly of a large quantity of lesser-known writings, many of which nevertheless exercised great influence in their time. In these works are formulated projects for increasing France's population by means of manipulating and regulating sexual relations between men and women within the context of one overriding priority, encouraging the birthrate. These texts urge such programs as the reduction or even interdiction of celibacy, the legalization of divorce, the introduction of polygamy, and the elimination of a whole variety of ecclesiastical and legal sexual taboos, even those against violence and incest. Thus a purportedly objective referent, the numerical representation of the nation's population, became the vehicle for a wide-ranging critique of the most intimate details of the citizens' lives as well as a powerful weapon in the Enlightenment's battles against the monarchy and the Church.

The French Revolution permitted these issues to be brought to the table for public debate and legislative action. In the nation's attemp to deal with the realities of regulating human reproduction and its consequences, free from the constraints of absolute monarchy and Catholic intransigence, a new set of dynamics quickly became apparent, the beginning of a change from ardent natalism to eventual prudent Malthusianism.

The story of this vast and varied literature might be of little more than antiquarian interest today were it not for the perspective it provides for an understanding of the tensions in the moral and political thought of the Enlightenment and the Revolution, for the context of the development of new gender ideologies in the second half of the eighteenth century, and for the terms of the arguments about much family legislation during the Revolution.

For better or for worse, populationism in eighteenth-century France drew private sexual behavior into the public arena, judging its worth not according to the hallowed teachings of the Church but on the modern criterion of productivity. The massive propaganda campaign in favor of procreation, in which an emerging nationalism overrode a traditional religion and salvation came in second to natality, was part of the great Enlightenment shift in values from the transcendental to the quantifiable. The application of a statistical measure to human behavior in this most intimate aspect of life permitted condemning or praising sexuality in a radical new way. Marriage itself, the status of women and children, and the transfer of property between generations, perennial areas of tension and dispute both within the Church and between the Church and the civil authority, were cast in a different light by the newly rehabilitated standard of fruitfulness and multiplication.

The reproductive imperative not only served free-thinking philosophes in their wars with both theology and monarchy, but, on a whole different level, as the following chapters show, it also stimulated the open expression of ideas and wishes usually relegated to the margins of literature. The priority accorded to fertility permitted both hostility against the clergy and fantasies about women to be set forth in serious texts, laying claim to high moral purpose. Both groups attempted to respond, the Church by turning the charge of sterility against the accusers at the same time as it embraced the natalist mandate, and women by trying to emphasize the education of children over the mere production of bodies. These reactions in turn stimulated the century's writers to new avenues of inquiry and introspection. "Depopulation delusion," the Enlightenment's "fertile error," demonstrates the power of a widely shared moral conviction not only to facilitate the advancement of social and political ideas but also to generate its own fruitful dynamics of thought and feeling.

ACKNOWLEDGMENTS

I would like to thank the Research Foundation of the State University of New York at Stony Brook, the National Endowment for the Humanities, and the Institut National d'Etudes Démographiques (INED) for their generous support over the ten years of this project. I have very much benefitted from the criticisms and suggestions of numerous colleagues and friends, most especially Jacqueline Hecht of INED, without whose expertise and unfailing assistance this book could not have been written. Christine Théré, Jean-Marc Rohrbasser, Eric Brian, Claude Lévy, Jacques Houdaille, Henri Léridon, and Kamel Kateb, also of INED, contributed much valuable attention to this work, for which I am profoundly obliged, as I am to Patrick Festy, Jacques Véron, and François Héran, who made my stays at the Institut possible. Serge Wazersztrum's generosity in sharing his vast store of bibliographical information about the authors I have treated has been greatly helpful. I would also like to mention my gratitude for the encouragement I encountered at the Cambridge Center for Population Studies, especially from Peter Laslett, Richard Smith, and Anthony Wrigley. I am indebted to Orest Ranum for his help in furthering this project. Frederick Brown and Ruth Plaut Weinreb have been kind enough to read the book in manuscript and to give me the benefit of their good counsel, which I deeply appreciate.

STRENGTH IN
NUMBERS

CHAPTER ONE

The Value of Kings

On n'avait jamais tant parlé qu'on l'a fait depuis quelques années de la multiplication des sujets. Cet objet de politique est devenu de plus en plus à la mode.

J. FAIGUET DE VILLENEUVE, *L'Econome politique: Projet pour enrichir et perfectionner l'espèce humaine*, London and Paris, 1763.

Depopulation and the Royal Person

Louis XIV (1638–1715), King of France and Navarre, was theoretically an absolute monarch. Like his father before him, he was in principle answerable only to God for his stewardship of the land and its people. Keith M. Baker has noted that affairs of government under the royal aegis were referred to as the "King's secret," certainly an alien concept of the head of state from the modern Western perspective. As Baker points out, aside from duly appointed bodies such as the Parlements and the members of the royal council, there was no legitimate channel for questioning or criticizing the administration of the kingdom. Baker refers to "the illegality of open discussion, by unauthorized persons without explicit permission, of matters pertaining to governmental policy or public order. The politics of absolutism was not a public politics."[1] Critical discussion of the sovereign or his policies could result in imprisonment or worse, and, because of his divine character, it was also labeled blasphemy. Pierre de L'Estoile told cardinal Richelieu, minister of Louis XIII, "to be the enemy of my king is to be the enemy of God himself."[2] Evidence of such enmity could be punished, according to Jeffrey Merrick, with a "scale of penalties . . . culminating with the amputation of the incorrigible tongue."[3] Thus there was no legitimate arena for public discussion of governmental policy, although a thriving illicit commerce in pamphlets and other publications from abroad, especially toward the end of Louis XIV's reign, attest to the existence of a viable, if muted, opposition.

I

Much has been written in recent years about the ways in which the monarchy's clamp on the national tongue was circumvented in the eighteenth century, as little by little a "public sphere" was staked out, at first in defiance of the government and then, to a considerable degree, gradually integrated into its operations. As Daniel Roche observes, "The formation of a public space marked a departure from the traditional modes of representation involving the king, the state and its administration, and the traditional *corps.*"[4]

The notion that France was losing population, uneasily endemic throughout the latter years of Louis XIV's reign, became one of the eighteenth century's most effective entrees into, and pretexts for, a widespread, sustained critique of the monarchy and its validating body, the Catholic Church. By the time of the Revolution, the foundations of the absolute monarchy and the Church's moral authority had been seriously undermined by the power of the natalist cause. The ways in which a perception of depleted population in eighteenth-century France was forged into an effective weapon against the entrenched powers of the ancien régime is the subject of the greater part of this study, the remainder being devoted to a sketch of the antithetical movement provoked by "depopulation anxiety," culminating in Malthus's *Essay on Population.*

Concern about demographic decline was not a new phenomenon at the end of the seventeenth century. In the works of both Diodorus Siculus and Strabo (first century B.C.) the transition from Republic to Empire was blamed for depleting the numbers of Roman citizens, and during the Renaissance there again appeared the nostalgic vision of a once burgeoning nation, in this instance often Spain, slowly succumbing to a sterility caused by moral decay.[5] This recurring image of a populous golden past diminished by modern depravity was imbued with new energies in the latter years of Louis XIV's reign, and from that time until the end of the Revolution, France largely believed itself to be, like Thebes under a tainted monarch, endangered by and guilty of a failure to procreate. In fact, the nation's population, far from decreasing during the period, had grown from about 22 million in 1700 to about 28.1 million in 1801.[6] Nevertheless, the educated public's widely shared assumption that the King of France had fewer and fewer subjects carried tremendous weight in Enlightenment controversies.[7] As the common postulate of the majority of eighteenth-century authors, shared by philosophes, physiocrats and Revolutionaries, aristocrats, bourgeois, and popular writers as well as clergy and monarchists, it stimulated and structured the development of numerous aspects of modern demographic, economic, political, and social thought. A number of studies have described the role of France's "fertile error," to use Jean-Claude Perrot's apt characterization of the nation's unfounded alarm,[8] in the intellectual formation of new fields such as statistics, agronomy, and the social sciences during the Enlightenment.[9] As Sylvana Tomaselli comments: "The study of eighteenth-century theories of population growth and decline provides an Ariadne's thread to anyone wishing to make his way into the Enlightenment."[10] While concern about population increase did not originate in the eighteenth century, the unprecedented intensity of the period's valorization of procreation promoted it to the level of a major component of public consciousness in the modern sense. Not only did the perception of the nation's human supply as depleted provide an impetus to scientific and intellectual progress, but it also provoked the government into efforts to modernize its bureaucracy, reform its policies, and mount various defenses against the extraordinarily effective demographic accusation.

In time, those loyal to the throne and the Church also learned the usefulness of playing the population card and wielded it effectively against their common enemies, especially the philosophes. François-Jean Chastellux, by 1772 skeptical about the whole premise, commented: "According to whether they want to praise the government or blame it, repeal old laws or issue new ones, they say: the perceptible diminution of the population, the marked increase in population prove & etc."[11] It is true that "depopulation delusion" should have been laid to rest by the 1770s, with the objectively gathered data published by Messance, Expilly, Moheau, and others, demonstrating the nation's net demographic gain across the century. Chastellux summed up the findings of Messance and Expilly, according to which "the population of France has augmented over the past fifty years by about a twelfth . . . at present [it is] about 21 or 22 million inhabitants."[12]

While the number of Frenchmen had risen, much of the augmentation was due to a rapid drop in mortality which more than compensated for a falling birthrate, the so-called demographic transition, so that while absolute numbers did increase, families in many sectors of the population nevertheless were smaller than in previous generations. Awareness of this trend, coupled with the sense of an increasingly abandoned countryside—two widely shared impressions—kept most people convinced that the nation really was in desperate demographic straits, despite growing statistical evidence to the contrary. Anxiety over dwindling numbers continued to be

expressed and to be used for political advantage throughout the Revolutionary period,[13] although, as I note in chapter seven, demographic anxiety takes on a new form in the late 1790s.

As Michel Delon points out, "the French Enlightenment attempted to
laicize morality, and therefore, oppose the monopoly on virtue claimed by
Christianity."[14] Fear of depopulation provided a high moral ground from
which Church and State could be denounced for weakening the collectiv-
ity. But if a nation's population is in a sense the most public of concerns, the
actual generation of its citizenry takes place in the intimate recesses of private life. Buttressed with alarming statistics about an allegedly plummeting
birthrate, many of the philosophes, encyclopedists, physiocrats, and other
eighteenth-century authors took the opportunity not only to denounce the
government and the Church but to entertain bold speculations about sexuality, writing not as reprehensible libertines but as self-proclaimed champions of a French society in danger of implosion.

The Demographic Rebuke of Louis XIV

The question arises as to why and how Louis XIV was so particularly vul-
nerable to the charge of failing to foster population. To understand the ef-
fectiveness of the accusation, one must consider the peculiar ontological
situation of the Bourbon monarchy under his father, Louis XIII. Cardinal
Richelieu (1585–1642), Louis XIII's minister, had launched a massive publicity campaign, starting in the 1620s, to consolidate the Bourbon claim to
rule France as absolute monarchs. Richelieu authorized hundreds of little
stories and homilies, told in simple language, that presented some piece of
justification for the regime and evidence of its divine sanction. Many of
these simple tales were read from the pulpit, further consolidating the link
between the king and the Church in the minds of the faithful.

The story most central to authenticating the power of the king, the most
polished form of which appeared in Robert Filmer's *Patriarcha* (1680), tells
how God endowed Adam with sovereignty over creation and how all
earthly kings were directly descended from our first father and thus endowed with his authority. The condescendingly childish nature of this
apology for monarchy linked it to the tradition of popular hagiography.
Kings in this account actually resembled God and were invested with a part
of His divinity, in a theory of correspondence that included a third—lesser
but nevertheless venerable—figure, the father of the family. God, king,

father: each ruled over his realm in a mystical union, one patriarchal chief reinforcing and reflecting the prestige of the other two.

However, according to a "religious mystery," the king of France was even more truly anointed than his fellow monarchs; he was God's chosen sovereign. This was demonstrated by his taking communion in the two ways (*dans les deux espèces*—as a priest and as a layman), a unique privilege among crowned heads. In the words of Jacques Cassan in 1632: "Of all the kings who rule in the universe, God chose the kings of France, to engrave on their majesties' faces the most august features and form of his Divinity."[15]

In addition to the imprimatur of the Catholic God on Louis's face, a different, more primitive mystical attribute was also associated with his royal person, as it was with the kings of all European countries, namely his responsibility to guarantee fertility. The ancient connection between the king and the fertility of his land and its inhabitants has of course been amply described not only among Indo-European groups but in cultures around the world. In James Frazier's general formulation: "the fertility of men, of cattle, and of the crops is believed to depend sympathetically on the generative power of the King."[16]

Louis XIV at Versailles would seem far removed from archaic kingship, yet the question of responsibility for national fertility was at the heart of the French monarchy in its very constitutive ritual, the Coronation, during which the Bestowal of the Ring, according to Kantorowicz, indicated that "the king solemnly wed his realm."[17]

The connection between Louis and fertility was an essential attribute of his personal reign as well as his generic kingship. His mother, Anne of Austria, had spent the first two decades of her marriage with Louis XIII unable to become pregnant, whether for constitutional reasons or because of her husband's aversion to heterosexual activity. Her failure to produce an heir to the throne was a source of deep anxiety to the royal couple; the possibility that she might be sent back to Spain in disgrace haunted the court. When, in 1638, Louis XIII announced his intention to consecrate France to the Virgin Mary in hopes that the kingdom be at last blessed with issue, he requested the prayers of the whole nation. The birth of Louis XIV, called *Dieudonné*, seven months later, was considered a miracle and occasioned religious celebration throughout France. His own ascendance to the throne, some twenty-three years later, coincided with the birth of his only legitimate son and heir, Louis dauphin. Louis XIV, even more than other French kings, was the ambiguous symbol of an anxiously desired fertility and the fear of its absence.

In principle, the ultimate objectives of Louis's royal attentions were two: the nation's wealth and its population: "[A Prince] could never see his cities become too rich or his provinces too densely peopled," he wrote in his instructions to the dauphin, "because he knows the art of making both their numbers and their opulence serve the glory and the well-being of his kingdom."[18] A kingdom both well-populated and prosperous was essential to the achievement of full glory for the king of France. The rather enigmatic motto Louis XIV chose for himself, "Nec pluribus impar"—literally, "he is not unequal among [or because of] many [people]"—is interpreted by Pierre Goubert as signifying "He is above the rest by reason of numbers," defining his monarchical prestige as dependent on a numerous population.[19]

In 1661, at the beginning of his personal reign, Louis was probably justified in his pride of numbers. France's population is evaluated at having been superior to those of England, Spain, and Sweden. In short France was the most populous state in Europe and, by Louis's stated standards, he was thereby a uniquely successful ruler. It has been shown that French military success was largely dependant on its numerical superiority from 1661 until the 1690s.

Thirty years after assuming full responsibilities Louis XIV was still on the throne, but the situation of the kingdom had changed. Although public criticism of the monarchy or the State was not permitted, a number of texts, either unpublished but privately circulated or published abroad, attest to what observers considered the diminution of both the nation's wealth and the numbers of its citizens. Louis's pursuit of glory had repeatedly led to war, which brought loss of life and disruption of families. Crippling levels of taxation imposed on peasants and workers to support his military ventures diminished the already marginal existence of many in the French countryside. The expulsion of the mainly productive Protestants by the Revocation of the Edict of Nantes further damaged the well-being of the kingdom. The marquis de Mirabeau commented that this revocation was "responsible for the departure of 300,000 individuals, among the most productive classes of the nation."[20] The adoration Louis XIV had enjoyed at the beginning of his reign was replaced more and more by disappointment and anger.

In 1694 the archbishop Fénelon (1651–1715), to some degree protected by his high ecclesiastical rank, dared to admonish Louis XIV, reminding the monarch of his sacerdotal duty to protect the well-being and population of the nation: "Sire ... your people, whom you should love like your children, who have been up until now so devoted to you, are dying of hunger. The cultivation of the earth is almost abandoned, the cities and the countryside are depopulating."[21] By reminding Louis that agriculture was declining in France and that "the cities and the countryside are depopulating," archbishop Fénelon was using his authority as Church dignitary to reproach the king on the grounds that the sovereign was responsible to God for knowing the state of his people and for seeing to their well-being. No official reception of the letter was noted by the king, and Fénelon was exiled from Versailles to his archbishopric at Cambrai in 1697.[22]

Fénelon's desire to make Louis XIV aware of the decrease in the number of his subjects in order to reverse the decline, without getting himself imprisoned or worse, was shared by one of France's most respected military figures, Sébastien Le Prestre de Vauban (1633–1707). A renowned military engineer and *maréchal de France,* Vauban had traveled widely in France, as the king was less and less wont to do, witnessing firsthand the suffering of the peasantry, the deserted villages, and the uncultivated fields that announced the nation's debilitated state. The plight of the kingdom preoccupied him over a period of twenty years. His efforts to bring the condition of the nation to the king's attention are contained in three texts: *La Méthode générale et facile pour faire le dénombrement des peuples* (1686), *La Description de l'élection de Vézelay* (1696), in which he details how his method of compiling a census was applied to a specific region, and the *Projet d'une Dîxme royale* (1707).

These writings, although ostensibly dealing with the problems of census-taking and tax revenues, are clearly motivated by Vauban's desire to see the sufferings of the people alleviated. Unlike the Christian context of Fénelon's admonitions, Vauban's focus was on the collection and interpretation of statistical data at the service of national self-interest, objectively represented. After explaining his "easy and simple method" of accumulating information, Vauban recommended that it be applied by provincial administrators: "This method is very necessary for the *Intendants des Provinces* ... the more so since of all the means of realizing population growth, cultivating the land well and making it pay result in the greatest service possible to the king and to the State ... it would make the needs of the provinces clear as day."[23]

Note that the goal was to make "the *needs* of the provinces clear as day," so that they could be met, not the *resources* of the provinces, so that they could be bled. While Vauban used the language of divine right, it was at the service of a different ideal, namely improving the welfare of the people. In a letter to Hue de Caligny, he reveals his strategy clearly, suggesting that "a little notebook" be prepared for the king, "where he could always find his accounts . . . in view of repopulating the country, since princes without subjects are nothing more than inconvenienced private individuals . . . let's just keep this between ourselves."[24]

Probably under the influence of Vauban's ideas, a government inquiry was launched in 1694, described by Jacques Dupâquier and Eric Vilquin as a "real census."[25] At first its purpose was to determine the needs of the nation during the famine of 1693, but it was quickly used in order to initiate yet another tax, the oppressive *capitation*. Vauban's "Méthode" was reprinted in 1707 as part of his magnum opus, the *Projet d'une Dixme royale*, proposing a reform and simplification of the tax system which would have relieved the overly burdened peasantry and imposed obligations on the tax-exempt privileged elites.[26] He sent his plan for the tax reform to Louis XIV in June of 1700. The sovereign did not respond. During the following years, Vauban added a proto-statistical section to his argument and included various pleas to the king in which he described himself as motivated only by the desire to increase the glory of his sovereign. Vauban reminded Louis that his prestige rested on the quantity of Frenchmen, quoting, all in capital letters, a fundamental axiom of monarchy: "THE GREATNESS OF KINGS IS MEASURED BY THE NUMBER OF THEIR SUBJECTS."

The king still made no reply to his loyal old maréchal's admonitions, and Vauban took the exceptional step of having the book printed, bound, and sent to his friends at court and in Paris, thus recasting his advice to the monarch into criticism of the monarch. The book was condemned by the *Conseil privé du Roi* to be ground up for pulp, as it contained "things contrary to the order and custom of the kingdom."[27] Vauban delivered a few last copies to friends and his confessor to show he had done "nothing against his conscience" and died (30 March 1707).

A few months later there appeared the revised edition of another work, much influenced by Vauban's ideas: Pierre le Pesant de Boiguilbert's *Détail de la France ou Traité de la cause de la diminution de ses biens, et des moyens d'y remédier*. In this work and its *Supplément*, Boisguilbert delivered an impassioned denunciation of the financiers and the tax system they administered, accusing them of destroying the French peasantry, the mainstay of the population. Like Vauban,[28] Boisguilbert saw the depopulation of France incarnate in the physical sufferings of the poor, brought about by ruinous taxation and the devastation of war. He challenged the king: "Must you await peace . . . to save the lives of two or three hundred thousand creatures known to die of poverty every year, above all the children, not even half of whom can live long enough to make a living, either because their mothers have no milk, for lack of nourishment or overwork."[29] This work, like Vauban's, was seized by the government and destroyed.

Despite the official condemnations of Vauban's and Boisguilbert's writings, they were repeatedly reprinted in numerous editions. Although Saint-Simon claimed that Louis XIV was so curious about his subjects' lives that he hired legions of spies to uncover secrets everywhere, "in public places, in private homes, in society, in the intimacy of family life and liaisons," and regularly had extracts of personal letters read to him,[30] Louis appears to have invested considerably less energy in getting to know the situation of his miserable peasantry. The *Grande Enquête* of 1697, compiled for the instruction of the dauphin, did not appear to have engaged his attention.[31] A remarkable number of people remote from the throne did sustain serious interest in the numerical evidence of France's distress in the years following Vauban's work. According to Pierre Goubert, "after the publication of Vauban's *Enquête* of 1697–1700, what is called public opinion (a few thousand more or less informed individuals) seemed to become passionate about what was not yet demography."[32] Michel Bernstein estimates that "an astonishing 27,000 to 33,000 copies of the two texts [Vauban's and Boisguilbert's] were sold between 1695 and 1713."[33]

Not only were these writings widely read, but collections of demographic data taken from various earlier attempts at census enumeration were published by a Parisian book-dealer, Saugrain, under the title of *Nouveau Dénombrement du royaume*. Including data from the *Grande Enquête* and other sources, these publications enjoyed considerable popularity as well, undergoing a number of reprints in the 1720s.[34] It seemed that more and more people were making an effort to understand the nation by means of mathematical representations of its population.

While efforts to motivate Louis XIV into reforming the tax system, or subsidizing the renewal of agriculture, or renouncing his war efforts had come to little in the closing days of his long regime, the impetus given to the gradual development of a "public sphere" of knowledge about the State was to have enormous consequences. Eric Brian points out that the French king "in principle, did not need to account for his power before his fellow citizens, he had no mandate other than divine right. This is the double constraint that connects numbers and their publication from the second half of the seventeenth century through the following century, if a figure is established, its public diffusion mortgages the consecrated authority of the monarchy. Thus censorship and census come together."[35]

Anxiety about the condition of France's population, objectified by statistical representation, went from being the preoccupation of a few specialists to a common cultural given, a shared mentality among the educated at the end of Louis XIV's reign. A new value had been posited in the moral sphere, providing the matrix for the development of sophisticated demographic science as well. This new value was the constant referent in such moral-political controversies as those over the role of luxury in the economy, the agricultural projects of the physiocrats, the legitimacy of the slave trade, the regulation of the commerce in grain, and numerous other issues.

In 1721, however, a work appeared that made a radical and original use of depopulation anxiety, opening up new avenues for the powerful vehicle of public demographic apprehension. Toward the middle of a brilliant and racy new epistolary novel, Charles Louis de Secondat, baron de la Brède et de Montesquieu's *Lettres persanes,* there appeared a group of eleven brief letters devoted to depicting the catastrophic demographic devastation not merely of France but of most of the world, spawning, among other progeny, a vast literature devoted to ideas about repopulating the nation not only through governmental and fiscal reform but also through "moeurs," by restructuring Christian marriage to maximize the reproductive capacities of sexuality.

Montesquieu's conceit met with a success of which the author could scarcely have dreamed, and its consequences shot off in directions remote from the preoccupations of Fénelon, Vauban, and Boisguilbert, as well as, in all probability, those of Montesquieu himself.

CHAPTER TWO

Montesquieu and the
"Depopulation Letters"

Si l'on a dessein de faire une censure des livres les plus dangereux que les Impies ont mis au jour, je prie qu'on n'oublie pas les Lettres persanes.
ABBÉ GALTIER, *Les Lettres persanes convaincues d'impiété*, 1751.

Montesquieu published *Les Lettres persanes* anonymously in 1721. Although he was not the first author to synthesize two fashionable literary currents of the period, the epistolary novel and the oriental tale,[1] into a new genre at once cerebral and libertine, the success of his work went far beyond that of his predecessors. The vastly amusing, divertingly subversive correspondence between the Persian traveler Usbek, the wives and eunuchs of his seraglio in Ispahan, his young friend Rica, and assorted other acquaintances is interrupted by a group of eleven more sober letters devoted to a description of depopulation, its effects, causes, and possible remedies. This little epistolary essay was to reformulate the depopulation question raised by earlier authors, indicting a whole new set of authorities and institutions for depleting the number of citizens. Montesquieu's novel was set in the period between 1711 and 1720, a decade in France's demographic history marked by dramatic famine and epidemics. As Jacques Dupâquier has shown, "the crisis of 1709–10 in two years provoked a rise in mortality of 66%, a drop in marriage rates of 40%, a drop in the birthrate of 15%."[2] The year 1719 witnessed another wave of death, and in 1720 plague in Provence became epidemic and catastrophic. Thus both the period in which the novel was set and the time of its publication were experienced by the French public as moments of unstable and alarming population depletion.

The proposition that France was losing inhabitants was central to Montesquieu's political and cultural arguments.[3] It informed the cases against despotism, Catholicism, and colonialism that he was to elaborate in the *Es-*

prit des lois (1748). Yet depopulation's first and most spectacular appearance, in the *Lettres persanes,* concludes by evincing a subtext that ultimately challenges the validity of populationist thinking.

In the tendentious little epistolary demonstration of letters III–22, buried in the novel, Usbek and his friend Rhedi discuss the evidence for global, continental, and national demographic decline, as well as the political and cultural causes to which Usbek attributes it. In fewer than twenty pages, Montesquieu presents a series of brilliantly formulated assertions concerning the central importance of numbers in the evaluation of government, the responsibility not only of the monarchy but also of religion, specifically the Catholic Church and Islam, and of colonialism in increasing or diminishing population, and a final description of the appropriate role of the government in determining the numbers of its citizenry.

As Jean-Claude Perrot has summed up Montesquieu's role in the depopulation debate, "the power and longevity of the French quarrel is explained by the seduction that Montesquieu's arguments exercised on those who wished to reform the monarchy" and, it should be added, many other institutions of the ancien régime as well.[4]

Part of the fascination exercised by these letters, however, lies in the shifting, twisting, sometimes apparently self-contradictory movement of Montesquieu's argument, as one brash demographic assertion after another seems to throw into question the authority of those preceding it. Perhaps an observation from his *Pensées* may help to explain his baroquely enticing but mystifying technique. He compares the text to a *machine* and warns that apparent self-contradictions may not be so in reality: the reader sees wheels going in opposite directions, he comments, and thinks the "machine" is breaking down, but he is mistaken because it is actually moving toward its desired end, "It keeps going [and] these pieces, which at first seem to be destroying each other, unite to achieve a concerted goal."[5] In the same way that Montesquieu's famous metaphor of the "secret chain" has been read as a way of understanding the novel as a whole,[6] the trompe l'oeil of the "self-destructive machine" offers an entry into his rhetorical strategy in the population letters.

The group of eleven letters begins with Rhedi's sweeping question: How is it that the world is so thinly populated compared to what it once was? First he invokes a metaphysical hypothesis: "How has Nature lost the prodigious fecundity of earlier times? Is she already in her dotage and has she fallen into a stupor?" (1:296). Rhedi launches into a description of the entire globe, everywhere afflicted by the same devastating dearth of human inhabitants, compared to the thriving nations of earlier times. Italy contains scarcely more than the debris of its former self, Sicily has nothing left but volcanoes, Greece has only a hundredth of its earlier masses, the lands of the North are "sadly depleted," Poland and Turkey have almost no one left, and America has only one fiftieth of the people who once lived there; in Asia, under the Turk and the West, barely a few stragglers are to be found of the throngs ruled by Xerxes and Darius. Egypt and Africa are equally afflicted, and, as Rhedi sums up his sad inventory, the earth "is depopulating every day and if it continues, in ten centuries it will be a wilderness," repeating his belief that an "internal vice" seems to be devitalizing human nature. It must be noted that China is not mentioned in this catalog of demographic delinquence, and, as we shall see, its absence signals a grave problem for Montesquieu and will continue to do so for many of his disciples.

Usbek's response, in Letter 113, evokes the long and perilous history of human life on earth, frequently menaced by plague, flood, and other disasters "which have more than once brought humanity to within a hair's breadth of its demise." He ends his letter by promising Rhedi that, besides these physical causes of population loss, he will explain the "moral ones that have produced this effect" (1:298). The following letter begins with Usbek artfully reformulating the problem. Cutting to his main argument, he shifts from discussing the "world" to concentrate instead on the former Roman Empire. The causes of depopulation are not to be found in Mother Nature's senescence after all, it seems, but in the great changes in mores, or *moeurs*, attending the collapse of Rome.

Christianity and Islam, the two great religions that replaced the cult of the Roman gods, have each in its own way severely reduced the fertility of the peoples under its sway. Islam, by permitting polygamy, and Christianity, by forbidding divorce and demanding clerical celibacy, have effectively transformed the mighty torrent of Rome's masses into a desultory trickle.

Usbek indicts Islam for the approval of polygamy found in the Koran, along with a supposed injunction placed on the Muslim husband to keep all his wives satisfied. From the lofty considerations of Nature's mysterious loss of procreative energies in the previous letters, Usbek swiftly descends to the somewhat comical plight of the sexually depleted polygamous husband, "like an athlete condemned to give combat without relief, but one who, soon weakened and overwhelmed by his initial fatigues, finds himself ... buried under his own triumphs" (1:300).[7]

The pious Muslim, according to Usbek, is more exhausted than satisfied by all his wives, concubines, and slaves, and the evidence of his collapse is the paucity of his offspring. "It is quite ordinary among us to see a man in a prodigious seraglio with but very few children," Usbek confesses. Not only is the patriarch depleted, but his wives and other female dependants are frustrated, the eunuchs needed to guard them are a loss for the purpose of procreation, and both Constantinople and Ispahan would have died off completely had not their sultans regularly been bringing in fresh subjects from elsewhere.

Usbek's amusing denunciation of his religion's unrealistic demands on a Muslim's virility is actually his autobiography, as we learn later in the novel. The reason Usbek cannot go home again is the same reason that his whole harem has produced but one child: Usbek cannot meet the libidinal demands of his women.

The letter, however, does not end on this note of erotic flippancy. Instead, Montesquieu suddenly brings up a consideration of another order, the connection between slavery, commerce, and population. He asserts that whereas Islam kept slaves from both reproduction and gainful employment, Rome permitted slaves to engage in business and eventually buy freedom so that vigorous new families were founded to replace "the old ones that were destroying themselves. "The more men there are in a state," Montesquieu concludes, "the more commerce flourishes," and conversely, commerce contributes to the multiplication of men. Thus liberty of procreation is endowed with an economic value for Montesquieu, the free circulation of goods and money and the free circulation of reproductive energies combining to produce "abundance and industry" (1:302).

Usbek turns his critical eye from the abuses of Islam to those of Christianity in the following letter (116), denouncing the depopulationary tendencies of the doctrine of indissoluble marriage. Another subtle rhetorical shift takes place in this letter, for in eighteenth-century Europe it is only Catholicism that absolutely insists upon the interdiction of divorce. However, Usbek, the guileless foreigner, does not distinguish between Catholic and Protestant, preserving the sweep of his antithesis between Islam and Christianity, the two "heirs of Rome." By prohibiting divorce, Usbek claims, Christianity (that is, Catholicism) not only robs marriage of its charms, it also hampers the accomplishment of its ultimate object, the procreation of the human race. Human feelings are not taken into consideration, says Usbek, and in forcing two people who no longer care for each other to remain together, "they do as the tyrants did who had living men bound to dead bodies" (*l'on fit comme des tyrans qui faisaient lier des hommes vivants à des corps morts*, 1:303). Montesquieu is using here a metaphor found in Pierre Charron's *De la Sagesse* (1606), but where Charron had specified that the tyrant was wont to "bind the live [man] to the dead [woman]" (*attacher le vif avec la morte*), Montesquieu attenuated the gender bias, without, however, eliminating it.

Unhappily married Christians, in Montesquieu's view, had to contemplate not only a lifetime of despair but also the prospect of a disagreeable eternity, since married couples in Paradise, according to Christian doctrine, are reunited in perpetuity after death. Usbek cannot quite grasp the meaning of marriage among the Christians. Whereas other peoples view it purely as a contract, for Christians "it is an image, a figure, and something mysterious that I do not understand" (1:304). Usbek's reference to a "contract" in this context is somewhat disingenuous, since, according to the novel, some of his own wives were purchased and none would seem to have consented to the marriage. The "contract," then, would have been made between Usbek or his proxy and the father or legal master of the bride. That "mysterious" something Christians bestowed upon marriage was of course its nature as a sacrament, which introduced a spiritual element into the exchange of women. For a woman to be lawfully wed in post-Tridentine France, it was necessary that she pronounce the word *yes* before witnesses, a crucial recognition of some minimal level of female autonomy.[8]

While Christianity is bemused by its obfuscating sacrament, Usbek advocates taking a utilitarian view of marriage, with population growth as its goal. If divorce were possible, women would pass from one man to another, and each husband "would get the best to be had out of them along the way." In fact, says Usbek, in an intelligently run state, "if, in a republic like Sparta . . . it were established that husbands change wives every year, an innumerable population would be born" (1:304). In this letter, under its veneer of insolence, Usbek has proposed a radical reordering of priorities: population growth, a quantifiable phenomenon, is accorded a value superior to the prestige of holy matrimony. At the same time, the male quest for pleasure is redirected toward marriage.

From his criticism of the prohibition of divorce, Usbek moves on to denounce the second great cause of "the depopulation of Christian countries": the great number of "eunuchs" they have among them. He is referring, of course, to the celibate clergy, and again, while he speaks of Christianity in general, only Catholicism continues to demand vows of chastity of its clergy. By characterizing celibate priests and monks as "eunuchs," Montesquieu is establishing an audacious parallel between the castrated slaves of Usbek's own harem and the servants of the Catholic Church, a comparison that could hardly fail to offend the faithful.[9]

The most telling rhetorical thrust of the letter, however, concerns the relative population advantages of Protestant versus Catholic nations, as Montesquieu turns his attention to the reproductive differential within Christendom. Remember that in 1710 England's population probably numbered fewer than 5 million, whereas France boasted about 22.5 million citizens.[10] Montesquieu envisages, however, that the Protestant nations, without the handicaps of clerical celibacy and the economic drain imposed by Church-owned property, were outreproducing the countries where Catholicism was established. "It is certain" says Usbek, "that the Religion gives Protestants an infinite advantage over Catholics. Protestant countries must be, and really are, more populous than Catholic ones" (1:306). Population, agriculture, and commerce are mutually dependant phenomena, flourishing or languishing together, and therefore, in Montesquieu's view, clerical celibacy inevitably leads to a less numerous population.

While Montesquieu was wrong in 1721, his prediction had been largely realized by the end of the century, as England's population had risen by 38.8 percent while France's had grown only by 13.4 percent, although many factors besides indissolubility and clerical celibacy contributed to the difference in ratio. On the whole, according to J. Dupâquier, the share of the French population in the European ensemble, "approximatively 18.3% in 1700, will descend to 17% in 1750 and 16.2% in 1800."[11]

Turning to the rest of the world, Usbek depicts Africa and America as systematically depleted by the slave trade. Petty chieftains sell their people to European slave traders to be shipped off to America, where they perish. This negative analysis of the *traite noire* will be developed into one of the major arguments against both slavery and colonialism in the *Esprit des lois*. Usbek also condemns the lethal effects of forced labor in the mines, voicing the criticism of exchanging living men for lifeless metal that Rousseau will develop so eloquently in the *Discours sur l'origine de l'inégalité*.[12]

The weak link in Montesquieu's theory, despotic China's burgeoning population, threatened to undermine his system and indeed became the subject of intense debate later in the century between such authors as Voltaire, Linguet, Rousseau's disciple the abbé de Mably, and Quesnay,[13] the apologist for Oriental despotism. In letter 119 Montesquieu offered an explanation of how certain peoples escaped the general laws affecting population growth. The Jews, the ancient Persians, and the Chinese, according to Usbek, reproduced mightily although their circumstances were not favorable to procreation, because in each case they held to some idiosyncratic belief that moved them to make maximal reproductive efforts. In China, where families are inspired by ancestor worship, "each person is impelled to augment the family, so submissive in this life and so necessary in the world to come" (1:308). Jews and Persians were also pushed to multiply by particular dogmas that offered theological encouragement to parenthood. Montesquieu concludes the letter by contrasting the demographically helpful beliefs of these "Oriental" peoples with the destructive primogeniture (*droit de l'ainesse*) established among Europeans, that unfortunate preference for first sons which diminishes the chances of reproductive success for younger siblings. He ends the letter with the surprising assertion that European primogeniture is undesirable because "it destroys that which produces all opulence—equality of the citizens" (1:309). Thus is the word *equality*, associated with the concept of wealth, introduced into Montesquieu's brief thesis on world depopulation, in this way posing the population problem in a new framework.

In the next three letters, the last of the group dedicated to population, Montesquieu moves beyond religion's role in the numbers of peoples and elaborates yet another order of explanation. In this new model, he divides the world into different types of government, explaining the relative density of population according to the style of political organization each group has adopted. This explanatory structure in some ways contradicts Montesquieu's fundamental theory of ecological determinism and is equally difficult to reconcile with his preceding Muslim-Christian dichotomy or the subsequent procreative division between Catholics and Protestants.

Montesquieu begins this new discussion by describing "countries inhabited by savages" as relatively underpopulated, basically because of the hunter-gatherer system of subsistence. The savage's reluctance to engage in labor keeps numbers sparse, as does the recourse to abortion among savage women. The main thrust of the last three depopulation letters, however, is aimed less at the inadequacies of indigenous peoples and more at what Montesquieu now labels the great underlying cause of modern world depopulation: colonialism. Climate, which this current theory would seem to

have invalidated as the active demographic agent, makes a surprising reappearance in these pages. Rather than ascribing any particular demographic
characteristic to a given geographical area, Usbek offers a different theory:
it is the act of *moving* from one ecosystem to another that has a baleful influence on human life, leading to illness and high mortality. The air of a
given region is charged with particles of dust, according to Usbek, and individuals, being physically accustomed to the atmosphere of their own
country, suffer and frequently perish when transported to another climate.
For this reason, colonialism is, with rare exceptions, disastrous in demographic terms, and "sovereigns must not imagine they can populate large
countries by means of colonies." Having recourse to an organic image employed by Thucydides to explain the fatal consequences of the Sicilian ex-
pedition, Montesquieu compares an empire to a tree whose "over-grown
branches suck all the sap out of the trunk and serve only to make shade"
(1:311–12).

Since, according to Montesquieu, those men sent from Europe to col-
onize the New World both leave an irreparable void behind them and fail to
thrive in the Americas, colonization leads not only to a decline in the
numbers of citizens at home but also a failure to be fruitful and multiply
abroad. He particularly condemns the Spanish for their additional antidem-
ographic policy, the extermination of natives. "We have witnessed a people
as numerous as all those of Europe put together disappear from the face of
the earth at the arrival of these barbarous men, who seemed to have no
other role in discovering the Indies except to demonstrate the ultimate in
cruelty" (1:312). Montesquieu's denunciation of colonization on demographic grounds therefore had three components: that native peoples were
exterminated, that colonizers' emigration emptied their native lands, and
that colonists failed to multiply in their new homes. The first two items of
the indictment appear irrefutable. On the other hand, the third accusation
was belied both by the historical record of earlier times and by the statistical
evidence of population increase in the Western hemisphere in the eighteenth century, as other writers of the period were aware. In Richard Cantillon's *Essai sur le commerce en général*, for example, written contempora-
neously with the *Lettres persanes*, he put forth the famous and sinister
dictum that men "multiply like mice in a grange" if subsistence is adequate,
unfamiliar dust notwithstanding.[14] Thomas Malthus pointed out in 1798:
"It has been universally remarked that all new colonies settled in healthy

countries, where there was plenty of room and food, have constantly increased with astonishing rapidity in their population."[15]

In the last of the depopulation letters, 122, Montesquieu spins his explanation of the demographic differences between peoples in yet another direction. It is not religion, not climate, not idiosyncratic belief, not colonialism, and not foreign dust that distinguishes the densely from the sparsely populated lands of Europe, but rather the political system. Republics like Switzerland and Holland, despite their naturally unfavorable terrains, are yet the most populous because their inhabitants enjoy freedom and equality, which lead in turn to opulence and population growth. In nations subjected to arbitrary power, however, "the Sovereign, the courtesans and a few private parties possess all the wealth while the rest suffer in extreme poverty" (1:313).

Montesquieu's desire to bash despotic governments with the demographic club immediately raises an obvious objection, namely that poverty and numerous progeny are not mutually exclusive. The great fertility of many impoverished peoples would seem to undermine Montesquieu's economic connection between despotism and population decrease. It is at this point that he raises what is perhaps the most crucial question of the population letters: What, exactly, is the connection between good government and the quantity of citizens? Is Vauban's dictum, "the value of Kings is measured by the number of their subjects," really true?

"What good is it to the state to have this number of children languishing in poverty?" Usbek asks in the conclusion of the last population letter, finally challenging the validity of the numerical weapon that he has used so skillfully against the monarchy, Catholicism, Islam, and colonialism. Children born into direst poverty never flourish, says Usbek, and to the extent that they reach adulthood it is as damaged human beings, incapable of leading productive lives. "Men are like plants, they never grow well if they are not well cultivated: among the poverty-stricken the Species loses and sometimes degenerates" (1:314).

Montesquieu illustrates this degeneration of the species by the example of France, where a government that does not care to raise "men like plants" condemns whole generations to "poverty, starvation and illness" (1:314). The population letters of the *Lettres persanes* end on this note. The swooping, swerving intellectual trajectory of the eleven letters takes the reader across centuries and continents, but the final destination is eighteenth-century

France and the final judgment is as negative as those of Fénelon, Vauban, and Boisguilbert in regard to a government that fails not only to encourage abundant procreation but also, most pointedly, to see to the well-being of its children.

Montesquieu's conclusion points in the direction that many eighteenth-century thinkers will follow, attempting by numerous means to improve the well-being of France's citizenry. The following chapters explore the abundant consequences of his other populationist ideas: the effect of celibacy, the demographic disadvantages of indissoluble marriage, the connection between polygamy and population, alternate forms of sexual union, and, finally, the emergence of a new recipe for fruitful marriage.

CHAPTER THREE

Celibacy

From the Grace of God to
the Scourge of the Nation

Sans le célibat des prêtres, on aurait aujourd'hui quatre millions de Français de plus, à prendre seulement depuis François I.
ABBÉ CASTEL DE SAINT-PIERRE, *Ouvrages politiques*, 1733.

Quand on n'a ni femme ni enfant, peut-on s'inquiéter jamais?
ALEXANDRE-GUILLAUME MOUSLIER DE MOISSY, *Le Célibataire détrompé*, 1770.

Miracle de l'hymen! Dans l'amoureux ébat, Nous servirons l'Eglise, & le Trône & l'Etat. BENJAMIN BABLOT, *Epître à Zulmis*, 1776.

After the unprecedented success of Montesquieu's *Lettres persanes*, the word *celibacy* became a popular battle cry, endowed with great aggressive energies in the depopulation debates throughout the eighteenth century. Blaming the nation's alleged demographic decline on a celibate priesthood became a favorite freethinker's conceit, offering the ideal rhetorical stance from which to castigate Catholicism. Although, as Jacqueline Hecht has shown in a recent article, celibacy actually played a vital role in the homeostatic regulation of population in early modern Europe, this mechanism was largely remote from the mental horizon of those engaged in the propaganda wars of the Enlightenment.[1]

Varieties of Celibacy

In the last decades of Louis XIV's reign, before Montesquieu sounded the demographic alarm, the word *celibacy* had encompassed certain sets of ideas, traditional and time-honored but isolated from one another and often at odds.[2] One definition of *celibacy* signified the chastity and self-sacrifice of those taking religious vows; another referred to the condition of

certain other heroic unmarried individuals; a third included all those who
were unable to marry for financial or other reasons; confirmed bachelors,
whether self-indulgent, sexually opportunistic, or given to "unnatural practices," constituted yet another category, as did single women, whose often
unenviable plight differed in a number of aspects from the situation of their
unmarried male counterparts.

The conviction that France was losing population introduced a whole
new register of alarm into the traditional discussions of celibacy. The old
Catholic suspicion of carnal pleasure for its own sake was recast and imbued with a nationalistic raison d'être in the push for a higher birthrate.
Like a couple whose conjugal life is marked by spats and kisses, natalism
and Catholicism repeatedly embraced only to come to blows during the
eighteenth century. Jack Goody has provided an explanatory structure for
one aspect of the seeming anomaly in Catholicism's simultaneous valorization of chastity and progeny. He shows how, in the interest of inheriting
from those among the faithful who died without direct legitimate issue, the
Catholic Church had, over the centuries, pursued a consistent policy of opposing practices that could enlarge the pool of potential heirs: "adoption,
concubinage, plural marriage, widow remarriage (including the levirate). It
does not seem accidental," he observes, "that the Church appears to have
condemned the very practices that would have deprived it of property."[3]
Viewed within that model, celibacy, whether clerical or lay, coincided opti-
mally with the Church's policy of acquisition.

In the eighteenth century, however, these tenets of Catholicism were
challenged in the name of demographic imperatives, which the Church itself eventually endorsed. Throughout the Enlightenment two contradic-
tory mandates competed for moral ascendancy: the spiritual value of religious vows of chastity and obedience to Church dogma in sexual matters
versus the newly declared primacy of population. By the end of the century,
a vast array of other celibacy-related issues had been indicted as well.[4]

Religious vows

For complex historical, social, and undoubtedly psychological reasons, as
well as the self-interest described by Goody, the Catholic Church had traditionally upheld a scale of moral value that placed chastity at the summit.
While marriage, even with procreation as the object, was better than burning, according to Paul, nevertheless it represented a major step down from
the perfection of the elect who refused any compromise with the flesh. Ac-

cording to Saint Ambrose, writing in the fourth century on the advantages of virginity: "The women who get married trade their freedom for a price & devote themselves to servitude. The condition of slaves is to be preferred on this account."[5] In the following century Saint Augustine defended Christian marriage against the extreme asceticism of the Manicheans and the Gnostics, but he nevertheless viewed it as, at best, a necessary compromise. He explained that the command to "be fruitful and multiply" really referred to the "advancement of the mind" and the "fulness of virtue," holding that without original sin, God would probably have permitted man to procreate in some other, more seemly way, "like bees, without intercourse."[6] He firmly stated the relative merits of marriage and chastity: "it is better and holier, from all points of view, not to go looking for corporal descendants but to stay free in perpetuity from any conjugal tie and to submit spiritually to the only spouse, Christ." For the whole Church, according to Augustine, "is espoused as a virgin to one Man, Christ" (145).

From the papacy of Gregory VII (1073–85) on into the early modern period, those in religious orders were not permitted a conjugal alliance that might undermine their principal loyalty to Rome.[7] The Council of Trent (1563) rejected arguments for permitting priests to marry, claiming that "the introduction of marriage in the clergy, by turning the affection of priests toward their wives and children and thus toward their families and their countries, would detach them at the same time from their dependance on the Holy See," and further, "that the liberty to give wives to priests . . . would destroy the whole Catholic faith,"[8] a statement to be read in both political and economic terms. The public discourse of Catholic apology, in any case, insisted that men bound by vows of chastity, spiritually purer and less constrained by earthly ties, could claim a moral status superior to that of ordinary humans.

Of course the challenge to this point of view became central to the Reformation. The Protestant struggle against religious vows included references to procreation from time to time, as in Luther's comment that "we cannot be other than what God wanted us to be. Children of Adam, in our turn we must leave children." As much to the point perhaps, he exhorted his followers to marry for political reasons as well: "Even if one has the gift of remaining chastely celibate, one still ought to get married to spite the Pope."[9]

On the other hand, for some women religious celibacy had long seemed to offer a particular kind of advantage: freedom from reproductive servitude. "In the eyes of the most engaged primitive Christians, the woman's role in reproduction—her sexual duty and her pangs of child-birth—symbolized slavery, whereas virginity could represent liberty," in the words of Elisja Schulte van Kessel.[10]

The seventeenth century saw the continuation of the Reformation's struggles over clerical celibacy. Urbain Grandier, curé de Loudun, produced a little work in 1634 titled *Traité du célibat des prêtres*. Grandier argued against celibacy, describing it as a "foundry exhaling the vapors of adultery, incest, fornication and sacrilege that soil the spouse of Jesus-Christ [the Church]." According to Pierre Bayle's account, Grandier was condemned to be "burned alive with the manuscript he composed against the celibacy of priests, and his ashes thrown to the winds," a sentence executed in the spring of 1634.[11]

The noble Venetian [Louis] Luigi Cornaro, whose popular work translated into French as *L'Art de conserver la vie des princes . . . et la santé des religieuses* was published the following year, was much more fortunate an author than Grandier, his tract being reprinted seven times between 1635 and 1735.[12] The positive Catholic value attached to chastity and the total indifference to population still proclaimed prior to the eighteenth century is strikingly illustrated in Cornaro's work, according to which sexual desires were planted in human beings by the Tempter himself and it was the Christian's duty to combat them. Cornaro defined nuns as exemplary soldiers in the war against the instinctual life: "Nuns . . . are a sort of *militia*, who, within the walls of a fixed camp, wage battle against the Enemy of the Human Race and overcome him." Thus, desire was the work of Satan and efforts to surmount it were acts in defense of a collectively beleaguered humanity. "No other religion, whether Jewish or pagan ever had this kind of Militia, or even thought of it," Cornaro claimed, "since they paid attention and respect to fecundity and to the Propagation of the Species. This glory and this ornament were reserved to the Christian religion alone, which has for its leader Jesus Christ, the flower of virgins and the only one to be born of a Virgin Mother" (210). Thus celibacy was seen as heroic virtue in terms of man's primary goal, eventual salvation, while populating the earth was specifically labeled an irrelevant consideration.

In reality the convent served other, more mundane purposes as well in the economy of Catholic families under the Old Regime. Aside from harboring those with authentic religious vocations, the cloister was the place to send unmarriageable daughters. If a young woman's parents could not provide a dowry, or if the family's matrimonial strategy involved concentrating resources on one daughter and sacrificing the others, or if a girl was mentally or physically impaired in some way, the convent doors resolved any number of family problems by enclosing such daughters definitively, *tamquam vere mortua*, "as if they were dead."[13] While it was technically possible to have vows of chastity rescinded by special papal dispensation, such reversals of fortune were rare.

Despite the Reformation's stand against chastity vows, religious dedication to celibacy was not unknown to the Protestant world either. To take but one example, the Camisards, Calvinists from the Cévennes expelled from France at the end of the seventeenth century, established themselves in England, where they exercised an influence over James and Jane Wardley, founders of a new cult, the Society of Believers in Christ's Second Appearing, or Shakers. In 1758, one of their followers, Ann Lee, a poor blacksmith's daughter, led a small group of Shakers into a renunciation of marriage, finally moving to America, where she established the sect as celibate in 1774. Preaching that "the marriage of the flesh is a covenant with death and an agreement with hell,"[14] Mother Ann Lee made thousands of converts of both sexes in New England, Shakers who shared communal dormitories in total abstinence from carnal relations until their sect gradually dwindled away in the twentieth century.[15]

Leaders of Mankind

Those arguing from a more secular perspective often took a dim view of marriage and the family as well, holding that although certain men of genius and achievement had been husbands and fathers, domestic life was not really conducive to accomplishing great things. It was best suited, in the words of the seventeenth-century moralist Pierre Charron, "to those who have more body than soul."[16] The eminent theoretician of natural law Samuel Puffendorf (1632–94) held that man in general has an obligation to enter into marriage "when a suitable opportunity occurs," except for "anyone who has the temperament to lead a chaste life as a single person, and feels that he can achieve more good for the human race or his country by not marrying than by marrying, especially when there is no fear of a shortage of children."[17] In 1778, Jean-Baptiste Moheau was still able to extol the merits of the exceptional men who declined the matrimonial knot, from whose ranks issued "acts of the greatest courage, an indifference to their own lives, generous feelings that seem to raise a man above the level of humanity. It is mainly to celibate men," he insisted, "that we owe master-pieces of the mind and inventions in the sciences."[18]

Younger Sons

For most families with property, not only the very rich, it was customary to ensure that at least some of their descendants enjoyed the same standard of living as themselves by marrying off one child advantageously rather than arranging financially and socially mediocre marriages for all.[19] According to Richard Cantillon, this was primarily an aristocratic habit: "The children of the French nobility are raised in affluence; and as ordinarily the largest part of the fortune goes to the eldest, younger sons are not anxious to get married, they live mainly as bachelors, either in the military or the cloister, but rarely would one find them unwilling to marry were they offered heiresses and fortunes."[20] Mme de Verzure commented in 1767 that the *droit de l'aînesse* applied to the prosperous bourgeoisie as well, who "only permit their oldest son to marry,"[21] an observation repeated by numerous authors. Unmarried younger sons from properted families had a certain range of choices precluding marriage, including religious and military careers. Another possibility was the status of *abbé*, which also required celibacy but usually permitted a relatively untroubled worldly existence.

The Poorest

Poverty kept many men from taking on the responsibilities of families they could not support. Envisaging a penniless future, the poor unmarried man, according to Louis-Sébastien Mercier, pictured his children "weeping from want, [they] are better off not existing than on the city streets where they come into the world without an inch of land."[22] Poor young men often became domestic servants, while the least well-off villagers were limited to unmarried existence often attenuated by recourse to prostitutes, to "maraîchinage" (sexual encounters between young people short of intercourse), and even to group violence against unprotected girls.[23]

Libertines and "Nonconformists"

On the other hand, for some men, especially those in the upper classes, celibacy was perceived not as a privation but as a liberty to be enjoyed, decried, approved, or envied depending on one's point of view. While some elite social positions required a consort, by and large the bachelor suffered little social prejudice; his financial well-being was often superior to that of his married peers, and though he had no wife he typically managed to console himself with those of other men, if he was so minded.[24] For the so-called libertine, an unfettered *vie sentimentale* went in tandem with unconventional ideas. Madelyn Gutwirth traces the association between sexual and intellectual libertinism in the eighteenth century, pointing out that the rake's "idea of sexual freedom is the form freedom itself assumes for the pre-Revolutionary eighteenth century, still enmired in the rigidities of its social and gender structures."[25] From Molière's Don Juan to Laclos's Valmont, the free-thinking man about town was perceived to cut a figure in the world, and even if he were subject to gossip, the doors of the best houses were rarely closed to him on that account.

Obdurate bachelors engaging in all kinds of nonprocreative sex technically fell under the heading of "celibates" as well. As Michel Foucault and others have shown, the rigid taxonomy of individuals according to sexual proclivities was only beginning to form during the eighteenth century and through much of the Enlightenment. The behavior of "sodomites" and "pederasts" remained an "utterly confused category." An awareness—largely antagonistic—that some men preferred unspecified "acts against nature" to fruitful matrimony was frequently expressed in natalist literature of the period.[26]

Male "celibacy," therefore, could signify those who could not marry because of financial or other social reasons and those who would not marry because of promiscuity, egotism, or unconventional sexual habits, as well as those who did not marry because of religious vows.

Single Women and Widows

Celibacy "in the world" did not have the same significance for women as for men. Among the propertied classes, where a woman's *état*, her status, reputation, and economic well-being, almost invariably depended on her father, her husband, or a religious institution, the unmarried secular state left the majority of women in a kind of desperate limbo.[27] Ineligible for most types of gainful employment, under severe social pressures to restrict her movements in the public space, and with her sexuality under constant negative surveillance, the unwed woman from a family of even meager means was a disturbing anomaly best resolved by the cloister. According to Mme de Verzure, women "are born the slaves of prejudice; they must marry

or become nuns. Staying single is not made for them unless they take perpetual vows. Most of them would be happier if they could just remain single. If she does not get married, she is the slave of a million conventions.
Celibacy is not for her a state of liberty; as long as she is young she has no
place in the world."[28]

An occasional rare female voice emerges from this period, asking
whether unmarried women could not simply be allowed to remain at large.
These authors take pains to apologize for their audacity in daring to express
themselves in print. They petition for an obscure corner of the world where
women could live quietly in retreat, outside the constraints of matrimony
and the convent walls. Gabrielle Suchon, an unfrocked nun, managed the
rare feat of eluding both marriage and an edict of the Dijon Parliament returning her to the cloister. In a curious little work, *Du Célibat volontaire ou
la vie sans engagement,* published with official permission in 1700, she pled
for "neutrality," or a "third way." She preferred celibacy because an unmarried woman was not obliged to "put up with the ill treatment of a husband
. . . his suspicions and jealousy," nor, perhaps more pointedly, did she need
"fear an invariably painful change in his feelings." Suchon is careful to point
out that the unmarried are useful to society in that they contribute to the
family lives of their brothers and sisters, help raise orphans, and are
uniquely able to devote themselves to charity and the public good. As for
the obligation to "people the world," Suchon still could state, at the very beginning of the eighteenth century, that "it no longer applies, because the
human race has multiplied so much that there is no more reason to fear . . .
a lack of men," a supposition that will be rarely aired after the publication
of Montesquieu's *Lettres persanes.*[29]

L.-S. Mercier, among many male observers later in the century, took no
such benign view of upper-class unmarried women, claiming that since
they have "no duties, they have no right to usurp the consideration and respect due to the mother of a family, surrounded by her children."[30] More
sympathetic was Simon-Nicolas Linguet, who painted a somber picture of
the near-ostracism of single women: "Isolated, without support, they have
no consideration in society, subject to the most severe censure, pursued, in-
spected in their slightest activities, they can only avoid scandal by the most
excessive privations." Should a girl permit herself to be seduced, Linguet
goes on, the consequences can be dire; she may be put to death if she bears
a stillborn child without having informed the magistrate of her pregnancy.

If she avoids that fate, she faces the choice between "the cloister and infamy." Without private means, she almost certainly will be reduced to prostitution. Such women "die on the dung-heap, treated like nature's lowest excrement," according to Linguet's bleak scenario.[31]

Arlette Farge presents the picture of working-class women in Paris, for whom settling down was a necessity. She points out that although the working girl's life was materially deprived and her labors endless, she enjoyed much more freedom than did the rigidly corseted daughter of the more prosperous classes. She discusses Mercier's admiration for the indomitable Parisian "grisette" and his assertion that since she had no dowry to offer, her marriage was more fertile because it was based on love rather than calculation.[32] In fact, as Antoinette Fauve-Chamoux has shown, more and more young women were leaving the rural villages of their birth and traveling to cities in order to seek employment as domestics as well as a husband. Since "a number of these migrant females do not succeed in finding a spouse, either in the country or in the city, the preindustrial urban agglomeration is characterized by numerous women alone who earn their own way. This concentration of adult women without husbands, along with the phenomenon of domestic service, is a fundamental characteristic of the old cities of Western Europe."[33]

Widows presented a special problematic case, since an ancient traditional prejudice against remarriage was coupled with a Catholic insistence on the marriage sacrament as an eternal bond, discouraging what was referred to as "serial polygamy."[34] The Church's disapproval of marriages after widowhood was enforced by numerous folk customs, which persisted into the modern period and subjected the remarried to various types of collective abuse.[35] "Almost everywhere," according to Jean-Paul Marat, the remarrying widower "is punished by ignominy, by rigging him up with two distaffs and marching him through the streets on the back of a donkey." As Goody and others have shown, not only had the Church early broken with ancient Israel by condemning leviratic marriages from the seventeenth century on, but it also came down increasingly hard on all remarriage.[36] When widows did remarry, they were subject to a number of laws governing their residence, inheritance, and the status of children born of the first marriage as opposed to those of subsequent unions. The preferable solution, from the perspective of traditional Catholic thought, was discrete retirement behind convent walls.

Philosophy versus Celibacy, 1721–1748

With Montesquieu's depopulation letters, the whole subject of celibacy was cast into a different light, as the secular value attributed to population was rhetorically pitted against the ecclesiastical virtue of chastity. Montesquieu had lumped celibate clergy together with the castrated eunuchs of Islam's harems, all useless beings in terms of propagation. While eunuchism had been associated with following Christ since the inception of Christianity,[37] it had signified a voluntary offering up of sexuality to achieve a state of spiritual election, not a surgically imposed deprivation. Montesquieu's daring witticism could hardly have been more offensive to the Church.

Celibacy, presented in a strictly utilitarian perspective, had no perceptible product: its results were purely negative in terms of society as a whole. In addition to the faulty economic and social policies that were depopulating the Kingdom, in Montesquieu's argument, an antiquated religious prejudice was sapping the nation's fertility. France, as a Catholic nation, was losing her national edge against the Protestant countries surrounding her.[38]

Jacqueline Hecht has shown how a certain impatience with clerical celibacy was already being intermittently expressed before the eighteenth century, evinced most notably in the promarriage edicts promulgated by Colbert in 1666 but also perceptible in such writings as those of the unfortunate Urbain Grandier as well as Philippe de Béthune, Gui Patin, Pierre Bayle, and H. Morin.[39] It was with Montesquieu's splendidly successful brief against depopulating vows of chastity, however, that the theme became widely appreciated and utilized, as one after another the philosophes and their followers took up the cry, denouncing the Catholic Church for its unpatriotic infertility, pitting the interests of the King of France against those of the Kingdom of God. In Eric Walter's words, "The indictment of clerical celibacy joins forces with a populationism which, since Colbert, invokes 'la raison d'Etat' to accompany the project of secularizing the Church, putting an end to its fiscal privileges, its proprietary power and its political influence."[40]

The abbé Charles-Irénée de Castel de Saint-Pierre (1658–1743) was one of the first to take Montesquieu's sarcasms and reshape them into a serious plan. In his *Observations politiques sur le célibat des prêtres*,[41] he claims that ecclesiastical celibacy was neither a historically consistent point of Church discipline nor essential to the Christian faith. The abbé then asks what the advantages would be of letting priests marry, and he answers: population.

"If forty thousand curés in France had eighty thousand children, as these children without doubt would be the best raised, the State would gain subjects and decent people, & the Church would gain believers." He goes on to discuss the function of the priesthood in terms of its utility, calculating that since the Reform, clerical celibacy had cost France four million citizens, representing "a considerable amount of money, if what an Englishman says is true, that a man is worth more than nine pounds sterling to the State"[42] (3:607). This direct national bookkeeping of human beings, regarded not as children of God but as objects of financial value to the nation, emphasizes how the criterion of population as financial asset could be used to preempt the Augustinian value placed on chastity. J.-C. Perrot comments that "in these texts, sparkling with pre-Benthamite precocity, money has become the general standard that measures private and public life."[43] Castel goes on to recommend that negotiations be undertaken between the Kings of Catholic countries and the Vatican to lift the barriers against religious marriage.

In 1734, expressing admiration for Castel's analysis, J.-F. Melon proposed that the minimum age for taking religious vows be raised to twenty-five years, in order to discourage immature choice of vocations and reduce the population toll of monachism. He warned the King that "peoples of the North," unhampered by a celibate clergy, were about to overrun the nation and that the interests of the monarchy demanded an end to wars of conquest so the economies could be spent to "favor marriages, help the fathers of large families, see to the upbringing of orphans and abandoned children. This would fortify the State much more than making conquests."[44]

Around the same time, Richard Cantillon was circulating the manuscript eventually published as the *Essai sur la nature du commerce en général,* in which he saw the issue from a different perspective. It was not the chastity per se of the clergy that had a depopulationary effect so much as the lands they occupied, which might otherwise be used to support useful citizens. Likewise, the mendicant orders, while they did not waste land, constantly bothered ordinary working people with their demands. Cantillon denounced celibacy as a waste of *productive* rather than *reproductive* forces; in either case, however, the result was a declining population. "Experience teaches us that the states embracing Protestantism, who have neither monks nor mendicants, have become visibly more powerful," he commented, again sounding the nationalist demographic alarm against Britain and the Germanic states.[45]

Voltaire restated the point with his customary irreverence in his *Diction-naire philosophique* the same year (1734): "I believe that England, Protestant Germany, and Holland are proportionately more populated [than France]. The reason is obvious: in those countries they don't have any monks who swear to God to be useless to humanity."[46]

Around 1735, a widely-circulated, influential, clandestine manuscript, the "Testament de Jean Meslier," which, according to Voltaire, was being sold "for eight gold Louis in Paris" (xlvii–xlviii), pronounced the Catholic deni-gration of sexuality one of the "Three principal Errors of Christian moral-ity." According to the radical priest Meslier, the error "consists of con-demning as vices and as crimes worthy of eternal punishment, not only the acts, but also the most natural thoughts, desires, and affections of the flesh,—the most necessary for the conservation and the multiplication of the human race."[47] In his introduction to Meslier's *Oeuvres*, Roland Desné discusses the importance of Meslier's militant atheism and the influence it had on the philosophes, who extracted parts from the work, shortening, editing, and even falsifying the document, but eventually launching it as "one of the first bombs hurled at *l'infâme*" (lxvii).

A few years later, in 1737, Voltaire took up the cause of reproduction as a stalking-horse for another related battle, that for the rehabilitation of the passions, in a segment of his *Discours en vers sur l'homme* entitled "Sur la Nature du plaisir." Voltaire, of course, does not purport to attack Christian-ity from the position of an atheist but rather from that of a Deist, a believer in God who is appalled at what religion has done to his Deity. The Chris-tian believes he is pleasing God by mortifying the flesh, but, says Voltaire, it is God who endowed us with the capacity for pleasure in order for us to do what pleases Him.

> Whether 'tis the prick of lust,
> Or sweeter still of love,
> Prodding you to procreative deeds,
> A merciful God adds vital pleasure to your needs.

The Christian God, on the other hand, Voltaire remarks, could be com-pared to a jealous Muslim husband who surrounds himself with sterile eu-nuchs.[48] Although Voltaire was skeptical about France's alleged depopula-tion, the usefulness of the premise was often much too good for him to pass up.[49] The taunting, suggestive provocations he tossed in the direction of the Church provided an impudent leitmotif to the more earnest pronouncements of serious natalists and added new dimensions to the century-long demonstration of the destructive energies of wit.

L'Esprit des lois

In 1748, a quarter of a century after his *Lettres persanes,* Montesquieu returned to the subject of celibacy in *L'Esprit des lois,* "Laws in their Connection with the Number of Inhabitants" (book 23). The first chapter bears the significant title "Men and Animals in Relation to the Multiplication of the Species," alerting the reader that human reproduction would be considered in its quantifiable, biological, and political, not its spiritual or theological, dimensions. After this sober beginning, Montesquieu quotes a long passage from Lucretius, apostrophizing Venus, "mother of love!," in praise of the irresistible powers of sexual desire to "populate through the attraction of pleasure,"[50] thus continuing the erotico-pragmatic line of argument laid out by Meslier and Voltaire and derived from early Protestant thinking.

Montesquieu goes on to comment, erroneously, that while female animals "have a constant fecundity," in the human race, "propagation is troubled in a thousand aspects, by their way of thinking, their character, their passions, their fantasies, their caprices, their notion of conserving their beauty, the burden of pregnancy, worries about a too numerous family" (2:683). Having attributed barriers to fertility to women's vagaries, Montesquieu turns his attention to men and their responsibilities in marriage. He does not in the least sentimentalize fatherhood, as authors in the following decades will do; instead he apparently approves the observation that since paternity is always more or less putative, marriage is simply the means by which society declares which man is to be assigned responsibility for a particular child.[51] Socially acknowledged marriage then serves the essential purpose in a state of protecting its children. Irregular liaisons, promiscuity, and prostitution do not produce stable offspring, and, hence, "public continence is naturally united with the propagation of the species" (2:684), an observation that announces a utilitarian rather than religious rationale for sexual morality, one that will enjoy wide acceptance throughout the eighteenth century and be quoted repeatedly as axiomatic.[52]

In this work, a somewhat more circumspect Montesquieu attacks clerical celibacy in a less outrageous way than he had done in his youthfully audacious *Lettres persanes.* Instead of calling the clergy eunuchs, he lays out in a few paragraphs a sober but nonetheless devastating critique of Christianity's alleged effects on population since the time of Constantine. Affirming the influence of the principles of religion on the propagation of the human race (2:706), he goes on to evaluate which beliefs have been beneficial and which have not. In the former category he includes the religions of the Jews, Muhammadans, "Guèbres" (Zoroastrians), and the Chinese, whereas that of the Christian Romans, he claims, is opposed to reproduction. One can almost feel the tension in the author's mind, drawn between the wish to treat religion respectfully and stay out of trouble and the compelling appeal of an impudent aphorism. He describes how, little by little, the natalist ethos of Republican and Imperial Rome, as exemplified by the Papien Laws, was replaced by the Christian priority accorded chastity. Despite his aforementioned respect for "public continence," he cannot resist the kind of observation the Church found so objectionable, namely that Christians "never ceased preaching continence, that is to say, that virtue most perfect because by its very nature it will be practiced by very few people" (2:706).

Where "celibacy predominated, marriage could no longer be honored," Montesquieu concluded, throwing an unconvincing sop to the clergy by claiming to criticize only the libertine celibates, not the ecclesiastical kind (2:707). Further along, in line with his theory that the hotter the climate, the more ardent the inhabitants, Montesquieu comments that celibacy does more harm in southern countries than in those of the North, hastening to add that "these reflections concern only overly-extended celibacy, not celibacy itself" (2:740). Such nods to Catholic sensibilities, in the midst of his long thesis on the structural causes of falling fertility and the destructive economic effects of Church property (book 25), did not fool the opposition.

Reproduction: A Right and a Duty

In 1748, the same year Montesquieu's magnum opus was published, Fr.-V. Toussaint (b. 1715), friend and collaborator of Diderot,[53] published *Les Moeurs,* a work taking a light, slightly ironic tone toward the issues of the day, more reminiscent of the *Lettres persanes* than *L'Esprit des lois.* Toussaint interjects population concerns into moral issues, à la Montesquieu, and he not only criticizes celibacy but also states as a principle that "whoever is so constituted as to be able to procreate his fellow being has a right to do so and must do so. This is the voice of nature."[54] The phrase sums up the emerging ideology of values, conflating "natural rights" and civic responsibility into one blanket imperative that denies the validity of both Catholic teachings and ecclesiastical discipline: a construction dubbed "Nature" both confers reproduction as a *right* and commands it as a *duty.* The work was refuted by several defenders of the Church and condemned by the Parlement de Paris to be burned by the executioner.[55]

In 1758 a curious affair attracted Paris's attention and brought the wrath of the police, as a priest attempted to escape his vows and marry, publishing his intentions in two small volumes entitled "The Advantages of Marriage, and How it is Necessary and Salutary for Priests and Bishops Nowadays to marry a Christian Girl." Melchior Grimm recounts in the *Correspondance littéraire* that this book as well "was burned by the executioner, by act of Parliament. The author was thrown into the Bastille and when he came out . . . he married a Christian girl."[56] Both the book's existence and the reaction it elicited speak for the increasing attention paid to the problem of clerical celibacy. The public continued to be indignant at that old Reformation scandal, the Church's refusal to permit the clergy to marry while at the same time numerous priests were known to keep concubines or to frequent prostitutes.

Taking a different tack, the chevalier d'Eon de Beaumont also declared that the clergy were celibate not to their glory but to their shame, reiterating Montesquieu's derisive reference to castration, in the hope that "eventually it will be possible to persuade men that it is more glorious to be useful to the King and to one's country than to be a voluntary *castrato*, useless to the world and often even useless to religion."[57] Referring to Halley's calculations of population in Breslau in 1693, he estimated the waste brought about by convents for women. "If the hundred thousand girls in convents or consecrated to celibacy had gotten married, they would have given on the average two children each during the course of their lives—that makes two hundred thousand children who should have existed."[58] It was not only priests, nuns, and monks who were a drain on the nation but especially abbés, "that sort of amphibian so common in France, dressed in black, neither ecclesiastic nor secular" (*Les Espérances*, 62–63). Abbés were denounced not for being voluntary castrati but for wriggling their way into respectable households and causing mischief, which has a negative impact on domestic peace and hence proper propagation. Eon de Beaumont claimed that population literally formed "the riches and the strength of Empires" as he too put himself to the task of ascertaining exactly how much it cost France to permit religious celibacy within its boundaries. The nation, he decided, was poorer "than it should be in the present year by the sum of 332,4000,000 (sic) livres" (*Les Loisirs*, 278). Even allowing for the extra zero, it was clear that for Eon de Beaumont an equivalency between men and money, both subject to strict accounting, could be set forth to challenge the Church's authority. Vows of chastity were a source not of spiritual riches but of demographic and economic bankruptcy.

Jean-Jacques Rousseau, like the chevalier d'Eon, felt that chastity vows were actually prescriptions for cuckolding husbands. He comments in a note to *La Nouvelle Héloïse:* "Imposing celibacy on a body as numerous as the clergy of the Roman Church is not so much forbidding them to take wives as ordering them to make do with the wives of others."[59]

A translation of Robert Wallace's influential discourse on population, re-iterating Montesquieu's assertion that antiquity was more densely populated than the modern world, was published in 1769 along with David Hume's more skeptical take on the alleged decline. Wallace affirmed the primary responsibility of religious vows for the woeful state of the world: "Nothing has done more harm to the population than the opinion long-held by the Church, that celibacy is preferable to marriage."[60]

The *Encyclopédie*, Allies, and Enemies

In general, populationist concerns provided a constant theme throughout the *Encyclopédie*, appearing in a great number of entries, such as: "Abun-dance, Agriculture, Annuities and Life Expectancy, Political Arithmetic, Celibacy (Diderot), Colonies (Saint-Lambert), Commerce, Community, Competition, Political Economy (Rousseau), Foundlings, Miscarriage, Farmer [tax] (Quesnay), Foundations, France (Jaucourt), Geneva (Rous-seau), Grains, Man (Diderot), Hospital, Hôtel-Dieu, Industry, Laborer, Luxury, Manufacture, Marriage, Environment, Monastery, Moravians, Population, and Taxes."[61] The basic question dividing contributors to the *Encyclopédie* was the one signaled by Montesquieu at the end of the depopu-lation letters: whether the government should directly prod natality per se, or whether its responsibility was to increase the well-being of the nation as a whole, leading eventually to an increase in population. Quesnay stipu-lated that population was dependant on the relative prosperity of the na-tion. The government "should not be involved with the multiplication of men but with the multiplication of wealth . . . population growth depends entirely on the increase in wealth, the employment of men and the employ-ment of riches."[62] This emphasis on prosperity was essential to the political program of the physiocrats, a necessary link in their argument urging lib-eral government policies toward agriculture. It did not necessarily have much connection to demographic realities.

Most of the *Encyclopédie's* abundant populationist commentary routinely denounced chastity vows and confirmed bachelorhood as assaults on patriotic procreation. Diderot begins the entry under "Célibat" by quoting selectively disparaging arguments from Morin's *Mémoire sur le célibat* of 1713,[63] in which the author traces the origins of priestly chastity in Egypt, in China, and among many other peoples of the earth, demonstrating along the way how inconsistent and how very far from monolithically coherent the Catholic position has been. Diderot summarizes Castel de St. Pierre's calculations of the demographic damage inflicted by an unmarried priesthood and calls for its reform, concluding with praise for Montesquieu's illumination of the connection between chastity vows and demographic decline. The references at the end of Diderot's passage send the reader to "marriage," "monk," "vow," and "virginity."

The whole idea of "virginity" (s.v. "physiologie") is treated with mordant sarcasm by the chevalier de Jaucourt, who labels it an extravagance invented by men who want to claim exclusive rights over everything in nature and have transformed purity of heart into an attribute of the body: "it is this kind of madness that has made a real thing out of the *virginity* of girls." He goes on to detail the fearful superstitions surrounding female virginity in various societies—the barbaric methods employed in some primitive cultures to preserve it, including female subincision, as well as the ritual defloration performed by priests among other peoples. It is impossible to destroy these "ridiculous prejudices," says Jaucourt, because "the things people enjoy believing will always be believed, however unreasonable they are" (35: 799).

This angry and contemptuous blast is immediately followed by a second "virginity" entry, this one dealing with the historical and ecclesiastical aspects. The tone abruptly changes, and we are treated to a history of Catholic vows in typical encyclopedic style, emphasizing that the cloister was a relatively recent development, not an inseparable given of Christianity. Even the patron saint of Paris, the chaste Ste. Geneviève, according to Jaucourt, lived her whole life "in the world." Jaucourt ends his entry by quoting a pope who declared that no woman should be forced to take vows against her will (35:800), a precept that was not, of course, necessarily observed in pre-Revolutionary France. This technique of creating startling juxtapositions, such as the one between a nun taking a chastity vow before a Catholic priest and a daughter of the bush having her labia sewn shut by a tribal priest, was one of the *Encyclopédie's* most effective tools in realizing

Diderot's ambition of "changing the ordinary way of thinking" (s.v. "Encyclopédie").

Jaucourt first describes the monastery (s.v. "Histoire ecclésiastique") as having become a "public expense, oppressive and clearly resulting in depopulation; it suffices to look at the Protestant and Catholic countries. Commerce is thriving in the ones while monasteries are killing the others." The reason that Spain, according to Jaucourt, was so decimated compared to its former thriving state was "above all the quantity of *monasteries*" (22:105). The second entry, supposedly dealing with the "jurisprudence" of monasteries, actually concentrates on the tangled political battles within the Church over the control of monastic institutions and their financial assets (22:105–6), highlighting the fiscal rather than the spiritual side of monachism.

The subject "homme" (s.v. "politique") starts off with a militaristic population manifesto: "Man's value is in numbers; the more a society is numerous, the more powerful it is in peace-time, the more redoubtable in time of war. A sovereign will thus occupy himself seriously with the multiplication of subjects" (17:682). J.-F.-H. Collot, Minister of War (1716–1804), explains under "invalides" that "France lacks factories for the manufacture of men. We must make marriages, multiply them, encourage them. The King should establish a program to marry off those receiving pensions," including disabled former soldiers, who even if otherwise incapacitated could still "serve propagation" (17:802). Collot offered to direct the program personally.

Jean le Rond d'Alembert, Diderot's collaborator in editing the *Encyclopédie,* offered an "Eloge de M. le Président de Montesquieu" at the beginning of the fifth volume (1755), in which he fulminated against the Church for its sinister chastity vows, "as if Christianity had as its aim the depopulation of society by recommending the perfection of celibacy" (5:lxxi).

The most famous and influential of the encyclopedic philosophes, Voltaire and Diderot, never ceased drawing ammunition from the anticelibacy arsenal throughout their careers. Voltaire, even while casting doubt on the proposition that France really was depopulating, refused to forgo the useful accusation of unpatriotic priestly sterility, deploying it predictably whenever the occasion seemed appropriate. In his *Dictionnaire philosophique* of 1734, Voltaire assumed a moralistic posture toward the clergy, who, in his view, were not really chaste at all but rather misguidedly wasting their procreative potential: "It has often been observed that nocturnal pollutions are frequently experienced by people of the two sexes who are not married, but much more often by young priests than by nuns, because the temperament of men is more dominant. One concludes from this that it is a great folly to condemn oneself to these shameful acts, and that it is a type of sacrilege by holy men to thus prostitute the gift of the Creator and to renounce marriage, expressly commanded by God himself."[64]

"The best government," Voltaire remarks in his *Diner de Comte de Boulainvilliers,* "is without doubt the one that allows only the number of priests that is [absolutely] necessary . . . the one where priests are married."[65] The inference that spiritual matters were properly subordinate to considerations of public policy perfectly sums up anti-Catholic populationist thinking. In his *Conte philosophique, L'Homme aux quarante écus* (1768), for the most part concerned with the economic abuses of the regime, Voltaire urges reducing the number of monks for the purpose of demographic increase.

Population could be used to attack targets other than the Catholic Church as well. For example, in Voltaire's "Raisons pourquoi le nouveau monde est moins peuplé que l'ancien," the primitive peoples of America, whose virtues his rival Rousseau so often vaunted, were rather snidely depicted as procreatively deficient, at least in part because of their fondness for pederasty, "a passion that reverses the laws of human propagation" (*Essai sur les moeurs, Oeuvres,* 12:383). Voltaire was well-informed on demographic issues, and while populationism appears in a polemical sense throughout his works, it is used more instrumentally than as an end in itself.[66] Pushing the birthrate was never a cause close to his heart in the same way as, for example, religious tolerance was. However, the sheer pleasure of turning the moral tables on the Church by insisting on the antiutilitarian dimension of clerical sexuality was one he indulged in without stint.

Of all the philosophes, it is only Diderot who seems to have sincerely attempted to synthesize his natalist principles with the realities of paternal responsibility. He is the most consistent of the philosophes in the generation following Montesquieu when it comes to castigating celibacy and embracing the cause of procreation as at once a national mandate, a powerful weapon against the Church, an element in the rehabilitation of the passions, and his own personal mission.[67] A constant preoccupation with claiming moral authority by embodying the virtuous *père de famille* haunts his public writings, from his two bourgeois comedies to his correspondence with Catherine of Russia. He prefaces a letter of 1774 to the Empress, for example, by theatrically situating himself as paterfamilias. "It is from the bosom of my family that I have the honor of writing to your Majesty," he grandly informs her. E. Walter points out that far from annoying his aristocratic Russian correspondents, this "staging of the thinker's private life, this display of the most intimate familial feelings . . . is what impressed the great lords of Saint-Petersburg and contributed to the Philosophe's paradoxical sacralisation."[68]

Frequently inveighing against his brother, the chanoine Didier, for his election of priesthood over fatherhood, Diderot never tired of insisting on the moral duty and paternal pleasures not merely of engendering children but also of raising them. His recognition of the postpartum aspect of paternity put him in a minority among eighteenth-century natalists, whose populationism tended to go no farther than higher birthrates.

In his *Religieuse*, written in 1762 and published posthumously in 1796, Diderot targeted the convent specifically for its demographically deplorable effects. He brought up the heavy artillery in this novel, announcing dramatically that "taking a vow of chastity is promising God the constant infraction of his wisest and most important law."[69] With his persecuted heroine, Sister Suzanne, who, unlike Gabrielle Suchon, did not succeed in having her vows rescinded and was doomed to spend her life as a prisoner, Diderot gave human flesh and drama to the question of religious celibacy. Like Montesquieu's sterile harem, Diderot's convent kept women behind bars, channeling their sexuality into infertile practices such as lesbianism and masturbation. In as much as Diderot was committed to his position that all human activity springs from two great instincts, "[one] for the preservation of the self and [the other] for the propagation of the species," he depicted such nonreproductive sexual behavior as strictly fallback mechanisms in the absence of reproductively appropriate partners, as Voltaire believed, or pretended to believe. Diderot's Sister Suzanne wonders why Christ needs to wed "so many mad virgins," and, appropriating Montesquieu's metaphor, she asks how society can tolerate convents: "Will they never feel the necessity to close up these pits where future races plunge to their destruction?"[70]

Diderot's most developed and idiosyncratic treatment of the questions is to be found in his *Supplément au Voyage de Bougainville*, where, as I discuss in chapters five and six, he finally elaborates his great synthesis of maximal patriotic fecundity, religion, sexual liberty, and family responsibility.

The Conceptual Gap: 1770–1789

Starting in the early 1770s, both the reality of French reproductive life and its representations in literature and art began to change, but the directions in which they were evolving were, at least apparently, antithetical. On the one hand, as Jacqueline Hecht points out, "from 1770 on . . . until 1789, we witness . . . the beginning of the demographic revolution with the progress of contraception."[71] On the other hand, the discourse of ardent natalism really starts to heat up during these years, so that the gap between theory and practice, between public populationist rhetoric and private birth control, grows ever wider in the decades preceding the Revolution.

As the disparity deepened between words and deeds, the Catholic Church was increasingly blamed for not having followed the lead of the reformed Churches. P.-H. D'Holbach, encyclopedist and forthright materialist, called the Catholic Church the "enemy of public good, opposed to healthy policy." The Church seemed, according to him, to be guilty of lèse-population not inadvertantly but by design, having "formed the project of depopulating the universe: it attaches who-knows-what perfection to *celibacy*, when a man refuses himself the pleasure of producing his fellow-being the Church calls it merit."[72] The learned Italian Ch.-Antoine Pilati di Tassulo drives home the moral conflict peculiar to Catholic ecclesiastical celibacy: "The Catholic religion . . . preaches virtue, but by giving celibacy a great preference and numerous advantages over marriage, it depopulates all the countries where it is established. One must distinguish between the religion of the Gospel and the one invented by wickedness and superstition. The first does not destroy population, it is the second that has that effect."[73]

Pilati's comment is typical of the assumption, widely accepted in the 1770s, that Catholicism brings about depopulation and represents a degraded form of Christianity. Particularly notable is the equation Pilati assumed between "virtue" and demographic success, a sign of how successfully, at least in some circles, moral value had been wrested from theology and pressed into the service of fertility.

Fortunato-Bartolomeo de Felice (1723–89), renegade priest and prominent editor, publisher, and philosophe in Switzerland, devotes thirty pages (compared to the nine in Diderot's *Encyclopédie*) to Gabriel Mignard's article "Célibat" in his 1778 compendium of moral, social, and political concerns, *Le Code de l'humanité*. Unlike the ironic cross-referential technique of Diderot's encyclopedic treatment of the subject, the structure of the

Swiss article is systematic and straightforward, as was possible in a Protestant state. The author traces with scholarly precision the history of the concept of celibacy from antiquity, illustrating the principles that "the number of subjects constitutes the strength of the State [and] that debauchery and *celibacy* destroy morals and population." The fall of Rome was directly attributable to "the citizens annihilating themselves by the effect of debauchery and their contempt for marriage," he claims, contradicting Montesquieu's notion that Christianity was responsible for the collapse of the Empire. Felice's article argues forcefully for a married clergy, repeating the utilitarian argument that "the priest as father of a family would be more useful to more people than the man who practices celibacy." As François de Capitani notes, Switzerland's population went from about a million at the end of the seventeenth century to 1.7 million at the end of the eighteenth century, a 70 percent rate of increase compared to the roughly 20 percent experienced in France, although the connection, if any, between this phenomenon and clerical celibacy is not clear.[74]

In the 1780s, schemes to improve the birthrate in France became more pragmatic and specific, while at the same time they were increasingly used to buttress other, extraneous causes. One of the most popular solutions was the proposal to abolish the dowry, thus presumably permitting men to make their marital choices on the basis of fruitful sentiment rather than sterile economic considerations. "When the Woman brings the Man no dowry but her Virtue and her Charms, both sexes will be better off . . . there won't be so many bachelors" claimed François de Menassier de l'Estre, *Avocat au Parlement*. Louis-Sébastien Mercier sounds a more apocalyptic note the following year, protesting that "beauty and virtue have no longer any value for us unless a dowry backs them up, there must be a radical vice in our legislation, since men dread putting their signatures on what ought to be the sweetest of contracts!"[75]

The anonymous author of *Moyens proposés pour prévenir l'infanticide* proposes to abolish both slavery and monachism, putting monks to work instead of slaves and making use of ecclesiastical property to raise children. "No more will these burning hot countries be invaded, their men purchased as slaves. Hateful, odious commerce, it's revolting both to one's reason and one's humanity," he protested. Instead, since "the capacious buildings devoted to housing monks, surrounded by agreeable, salubrious gardens, are inhabited by useless men who enjoy immense revenues while living in a state of deep inertia, would it not be better to give these men back to society, which needs hands to help it sustain itself, and should not their income and housing be used for the lodging and support of orphans and pregnant women?"[76]

Echoing Cantillon's perspective, this kind of multipurpose proposal, putting to good use not only the potential productive and procreative capacities of monks but also their income and properties, was voiced with increasing frequency in the 1780s, heralding the Revolutionary legislation that would, for a time, not only permit but pressure priests, nuns, and monks to marry, as well as facilitating the State's appropriation of ecclesiastical property.

In the years preceding the Revolution, the language employed to denounce celibacy became increasingly harsh, the proposals more Draconian, and the recourse to violence more frequently invoked. Grouber de Groubent de Linière (1739–1815) chose a particularly sinister passage from Scripture, "omni arbor quoe non facit fructum bonum excidetur" (Matt.7:19) as epigraph for his tract, *L'Antimoine* (1787). Grouber claims that "be fruitful and multiply" was "the first order the first man received from the Supreme Being," an express command straight from the Divinity, "precise, formal and not subject to any interpretation whatsoever." Continence or chastity "must be considered states of reprobation," and individuals professing them are "murderers of themselves and their posterity" and must be stopped, according to Grouber.[77]

Not everyone, however, accepted the notion that depopulation was due to religious vows. The marquis Victor-R. de Mirabeau (1715–1789), for example, insisted that neither celibacy nor the other frequently denounced sources of demographic disaster—war, navigation, colonialism—"is causing the current depopulation, on the contrary, most of these things tend to *increase* population. It is the decadence of agriculture, on the one hand, and the luxury of a small number of inhabitants on the other, that withers in the root the seed of population."[78] Elsewhere he approvingly paraphrases R. Cantillon's famous dictum about men multiplying "like mice in a grange"[79] if there is adequate subsistence, substituting the word *rats* for Cantillon's *mice* and conjuring up what for many readers might be a nasty vision of pullulation and pollution. To Mirabeau however, the rodent-ridden structure was not so much a revolting image as a positive metaphor for the procreative potential of the human race.

While Mirabeau was a great natalist, unlike many other authors he did not give marriage per se first priority. He was opposed to the custom of marrying daughters of poor but noble families to well-off bourgeois. The German nobility showed better judgment in cloistering such women, he claimed, rather than permitting mismatches, harmful to society, because it is essential that "each person be attached to his like, and each class preserve its principles unalloyed" (180).

David Hume was typically skeptical about the role convents played in depleting the nation, grasping the notion, as so few others did, of their role in maintaining the homeostasis of the population by pointing out that in ancient times, "every great family in Italy, and probably in other parts of the world, was a species of convent."[80]

Depopulation Refuted: Moheau

On the level of demonstrable evidence, the most formidable defense of Catholicism against the depopulationary charge came from what was called "political arithmetic," seen especially in the works of the abbé Jean-Joseph d'Expilly (1762, 1770, 1780), Louis Messance (1766, 1768), Fr.-J. Chastellux (1772) and Jean-B. Moheau (1778),[81] in which France's alleged depopulation was rudely challenged. Eric Brian comments: "Expilly, Moheau and Messance attacked a tenacious prejudice; they were intent on demonstrating the inanity [of the depopulation thesis] by a strategy of observations and calculations."[82] Jean-Baptiste Moheau took issue not only with the belief that France was demographically diminished but also with arguments that the Catholic Church exerted a negative influence. In his *Recherches et considérations sur la population de la France*,[83] he claimed that critics of religion were deliberately abusing statistics to discredit it. "For several years now people have been denouncing religions a great deal . . . they have been represented as harmful to the population," he noted. To be sure, he went on to say, the Catholic Church was an essential support of the monarchy, while at the same time it furnished a moral curb for the conscience of Kings. "We cannot disguise or ignore the disadvantage that results for the population of France from sacerdotal and religious celibacy," he acknowledged; however, "we can say with confidence that prejudice and hatred have always exaggerated the anticipated destruction of humanity resulting from vows of sacerdotal celibacy" (243, 245).

Moheau, among the first to provide serious statistical evidence on the subject, demonstrated that, in any event, the proportion of *religious* celibates to the general population was negligible: one-seventy-fifth or one-eightieth.[84] In a letter to Condorcet of 25 September 1778, however, he claimed that "in France, including children, more than half the human race is in a state of celibacy," thus labeling religion only a minor factor in the marriage rate (536). With Moheau, the factual aspect of the debate moved into the emerging field of demographic statistics while the polemical side continued unheedingly to batten on its own rhetorical success.

Luxury

The abbé Charles-André-Alexandre de Moy, in his "Address to the King" of 1776, agreed with Mirabeau that *luxury*, not religious vows, was to be blamed for reducing French procreation, but his reasoning disregarded economic factors to concentrate on the moral causes of the century's allegedly debilitating lay celibacy. It was the wish to produce an impression of opulence in the world that led so many families to hire armies of liveried servants, most of whom were obliged to stay single. "Is it not luxury," he asked, "that buries under the trappings of pride these troops of motley slaves wrenched from the countryside whom it rarely permits to reproduce? Is it not [luxury] that generates and perpetuates that celibacy one can only regard as a theft from society or an outrage against nature when it is not a sacrifice to the Divinity?"[85] Moy's reasoning demonstrates why the Catholic argument was not the easiest to sustain: if it was accepted that reproduction was at the summit of the scale of human values, and that those refusing its call to duty were derelict, it was tricky to claim that the very same refusal to procreate was a *virtue* if made in the name of God. Could the same act, or more properly the same inaction, be at once a "theft" and an "outrage" and a demonstration of piety? Two different systems of moral meaning clashed in the matter of population: a Catholicism à la Cornaro that professed indifference to the "propagation of the species" in the name of virginal purity versus a Catholicism that had climbed on the century's populationist bandwagon.[86]

The relations between demographic alarmists and the King had evolved in a number of ways since Vauban had uttered his dire warning to Louis XIV. Moy, speaking for a Catholic view that held corruption to be the cause of depopulation, congratulated the new King in 1776 on the elevated moral tone he had brought to the monarchy, informing the young Louis XVI that: "the title of Restorer of Morals is the finest that can be conferred on a Monarch. YOUR MAJESTY, SIRE, obtained it as soon as he took the affairs of state in hand." It is an irony of fate, in this context, that Louis XVI, devoted husband and devout Catholic, should have been for so long unable to consummate his marriage. To reign impotent over a nation ever more obsessed with procreation was not the least of the crosses that would be his to bear. Even those who did marry, according to Moy, were infected by a taste for luxury and display that undermined their natural parental impulses. "Is it not [luxury]," he asked, "sullying even the sanctity of the nuptial couch, that decides for the two spouses the number of children whose caresses they will receive, and that shows them in the conjugal knot nothing but an association of pure personal advantage?" (2–3).

Melchior Grimm, editor of *La Correspondance littéraire,* while on the other side of the century's battles on most issues, joined abbé Moy in condemning the lower natality brought about by luxury and its concomitant inclination toward small families. "The number of inhabitants diminishes in direct proportion to the growth of luxury, because luxury makes children burdensome to their fathers, and maintains in celibacy an infinite number of men who prefer to live comfortably and alone than with a family that would reduce them to basic necessities. Without counting the fact that a man only thinks of marriage when he is sure of procuring and leaving to his children the same affluence which he enjoys, luxury even obliges fathers to take precautions against the excessive growth of their families."[87]

Stripped of Grimm's moralizing, this reproductive strategy was, in Jacqueline Hecht's words, "typical of pre-Revolutionary France." She points out that "the concern for preserving for oneself and for one's children at least the *same* standard of living contributed, by means of the postponement of marriage, and, in certain circles of society, by voluntary birth control, to adapting, to some extent, demographic growth to the possibilities of subsistence and employment."[88] Richard Cantillon was in the minority of eighteenth-century commentators in presenting this thinking nonjudgmentally, pointing out that men in all social strata avoided matrimony if their offspring would not be in a position to live at least as well as they. Most would gladly marry, according to Cantillon, "if they could count on a support for their families as they would wish: they would feel they were wronging their children if they raised them only to see them fall into a lower social class."[89] For most authors, however, the preference for ensuring a comfortable style of life rather than producing the largest possible number of children was increasingly and virulently denounced as morally reprehensible.

So-called celibacy in marriage, an ambiguous phrase that seemed to have been used to mean some form of birth control, probably coitus interruptus, or, alternatively, avoidance of conjugal relations altogether, became a favorite target of populationist writings.[90] From serious tracts to poetic effusions, the proto-Malthusian "married celibate" was depicted as a menace to the nation and a monster around the house. In his ode "La Population et la Beauté" (Paris, 1764), André-Hyacinthe Sabatier accused prudent husbands of putting pride before procreative prowess:

> Useless husbands, how cruel you are.
> Of just one son you'd make a star.
> To see him rich you embrace half-hearted,
> And the Desire of Nature ends up thwarted![91]

Women too were wont to draw the line at just one child. Mirabeau describes the flighty wife who gives birth to her first child, a daughter. The midwife remarks that the next time she'll have a son. "Oh, as for that, excuse me," the new mother replies, "the job is dreadful & and I don't feel like sacrificing myself for my posterity. I already love this little girl & I want her to be an heiress."[92]

The number of domestics employed by the rich, usually drawn from the provinces and attired in the livery of the household, was a source of prestige. Household servants, however, were by and large not able to conduct their private lives according to their own desires. According to J.-P. Gutton, "Domestics are not permitted . . . to marry without their masters' consent, under penalty of losing their wages, to be donated to the neighborhood's poor."[93] Unless such permission was granted, servants' family life usually had to be postponed until very late, frequently eliminating their contribution as breeders. Yet at the same time, as Sara Maza and others have shown, women servants often had great difficulties resisting the sexual advances of their employers and fellow servants.[94] The offspring of such unions were frequently abandoned; Bernos reports that in a study of unwed mothers in Saint-Rémy-de-Provence, 93 percent were servants.[95] A few authors, like Louis Messance, defended luxury and those it employed, claiming that the "rich man is useful to those he hires for the sake of his luxuries . . . he augments the number of consumers and therefore the number of inhabitants." The imprudent man who throws his money around, on the other hand, is soon bankrupt; "they attribute this to luxury but it's only madness that ruins fools."[96]

Moheau favored government action limiting the number of servants, which he estimated at about one-twelfth of the nation and which he

1. "L'Amour européen" (love European style). Bibliothèque Nationale.

termed "particularly harmful to population." Whereas Voltaire thought the number of priests should be restricted, Moheau remarked that "it would be advisable for the number of domestics to be ascertained and for limits to be placed on their multiplication."[97]

Nobody took this argument further than the Marquis de Mirabeau in his *L'Ami des hommes*. For Mirabeau, agriculture and those trades essential to it took first place in importance, whereas other industries used up resources while contributing little or nothing to population. The use of horses for transportation appalled him, for example, because each horse consumed as much food as four men. Therefore every rich man's carriage drawn by a spanking pair represented eight people who would never be born. He proposed a varying luxury tax on horses, the lowest for farm animals and the highest for carriage horses.[98] He was particularly incensed that France was still covered with forests where the privileged pursued the hunt and that the gardens of the rich produced only useless flora. If all those woods and flowerbeds could be dug up and turned over to the production of wheat, according to Mirabeau, France could accommodate more vast throngs of citizenry. By the same token, in cosseted households, "women servants each have their own room with their own fire, their own light" (1:15), again wasting valuable resources. Instead, the land growing trees for wood to heat servants' rooms could be planted with wheat, feeding more mouths for the nation. Under Mirabeau's reform, a servant in the dark and cold of a winter's evening could console herself that she was helping to resolve France's population crisis.

To Georges-M. Butel-Dumont (1725–88), on the other hand, it seemed to be strictly the government's fault that so few families were being founded. In his *Théorie du luxe* of 1771, he ruminates on the monarchy's responsibility to force citizens to take on the responsibilities of family life, an urgent task since "there have never been as many celibates in the kingdom as now, they constitute more than half of humanity." He buttresses his assertions with what purports to be objective evidence, a table of five cities showing the numbers of married and unmarried inhabitants. He was not alone in demanding that the government intervene in the lives of its citizenry to punish those who remain unmarried. Ange Goudar (1720–91) insisted that "if it is illegal to commit suicide because that means robbing the Fatherland of oneself, it should be all the more so to stay single [because] each citizen is obliged to contribute his work to the duration of the general population and . . . his share in its perpetuation."[99]

From midcentury on, many writers expressed their conviction that luxury further undermined the nation's reproductive capacities by insidiously sapping male virility. The foppish *petit mâitre,* in his silk britches and wig, perched on a little gilt chair and wearing more make-up than his hostess, was unlikely to father a vigorous family. Molière had popularized the stereotype in *Les Précieuses ridicules,* and such individuals were frequently a source of hilarity in Marivaux's comedies as well, but, under the influence of the "intellectual terrorism of the day,"[100] the bejeweled, mincing marquis of comedy was soon seen less as a joke than as a sinister portent of France's demographic deterioration, as more and more authors began to equate luxury with the loss of virility.[101]

Laurent Withof, in his *Dissertation sur les eunuques*, took the "luxury-equals-sterility" equation literally, citing the tragic example of the ancient Scythians, who fell into the luxurious habit of going "on horseback, [thus] becoming incapable of the duties of marriage. Hence these unfortunate men, attributing to some god's anger what was the effects of their own bad behavior, started wearing women's clothes and occupying themselves with women's work. But the poor people and those who had to go on foot, fortunately deprived of these baleful conveniences of opulence [horses], did not suffer the same disability."[102]

So a taste for comfort led to a decline in population, whether dramatically, as in the case of the emasculated Scythian horsemen, or more subtly, through the "softening and unnerving of the male sex." For not only were overdressed, effeminate lounge lizards unlikely to propagate, but, perversely, those men too fond of expensive adventuresses were also falling down on the job as paterfamiliases. "Libertinage," "incontinence," or indulgence in sexual luxury, proclaimed the anonymous author of *L'Homme en société* (1763), "kills millions by preventing the propagation of the species." The solution was to force women whose favors could be bought, from the dearest courtesan to the cheapest prostitute, to inhabit government-run brothels and to subject them and their customers to public shame. Thus with "scandalous commerce banished from society, opulent persons will be forced to marry and have children, which will populate their class."[103]

Grimm, Moy, and a host of others denounced the taste for luxury as responsible for prompting couples to avoid having children, whether by means of prolonged breast-feeding, coitus interruptus, abortion, or "unnatural" sexual practices. According to the abbé Jacques-Joseph Duguet, "Anything opposed to fecundity, even if it's only the wish, is criminal and degrades marriage, as for all the more reasons are sterile pleasures." As for père Féline, he warned his readers that "the Lord punishes sentiments unfavorable to population."[104]

"Luxury," "celibacy," and "celibacy in marriage" formed a sort of diabolic trilogy, the object of endless fulmination. Cerfvol conflates the three in a statement typical of much eighteenth-century propopulation propaganda. Because of luxury, he claims, "Nowadays we see celibacy has become the favorite condition. Even in the conjugal bed it opposes the progress of population."[105] Like abbé Duguet and so many others, the Protestant minister Philippe Dutoit-Mambrini lumped masturbation and coitus interruptus together as twin vices, equally reprehensible because equally sterile. In his *Code de l'humanité*, F.-B. de Felice (1723–1807), not normally an intolerant commentator, utters the direst judgments on the subject: "Onanism is opposed to the natural destination of sperm . . . the one who engages in it becomes his own murderer. Still more criminal is the [onanism] committed in marriage."[106] The voice of the Church and the voice of philosophy are for once in harmony, more and more insistently condemning those who prefer their comfort and pleasure to the propagation of the species.

Jean Blondel (1733–1810), charged with the redaction of the criminal code, went so far in the campaign to rehabilitate libido as to claim that "the action most agreeable to God is the one tending to the propagation of the human race." It was the poor, however, who engaged most wholeheartedly in that blessed act, whereas the rich, wallowing in luxury, "besides the attention they pay to not letting themselves go with the temptation to fulfill the duties of matrimony and the care they take to have only a small family . . . even take it upon themselves to [abort] their wives."[107] This last inclination, according to Blondel, was particularly marked among financiers.

The marquis Jean-François de Saint-Lambert (1716–1803), philosophe, poet, and contributor to the *Encyclopédie* (s.v. "Luxe"), published a long poem in praise of both agricultural and marital procreation in 1764. Following the line of Voltaire, Montesquieu, Meslier, and Blondel, he insisted on the Providential role of pleasure in prodding men into insemination. His tone, however, unlike Voltaire's, was in the newly fashionable, rhapsodically sentimental mode, asserting that man does not need money to be rich: "His children are his happiness, they are his fortune. If one wishes to see him happy, submit him to the chains of matrimony."[108]

The Sterility of the Military

Besides "conjugal onanism" and a preference for luxury, another factor in French life was destroying population: the military. While Moheau demonstrated that the population of France was not really declining, he nevertheless expressed concern that various portions of society were not propagating as they ought. The unfortunate situation of the military had a particularly depressing effect on French population, according to Moheau. In France under the ancien régime, married men were usually not conscripted into the armed services, and officers traditionally remained single until their retirement and often after.[109] Since soldiers were paid a bare subsistence wage and frequently moved from one assignment to another, they were effectively disqualified from the marriage market. Moheau estimated that a fifth of unmarried (presumably male) adults were single because of their status in the military. He speculated on the economic advantages of permitting soldiers to marry and providing a small subsidy to those who did, even of offering them rewards for the birth of children. He put forth another suggestion that is more startling for the modern reader, although it would enjoy great success in the remaining years of the eighteenth century. This proposal departs most markedly from the individualist current of the century's thought and is a direct expression of utilitarian doctrine applied to people: "Could the State not take hold of all the children [fathered by military personnel] and make soldiers of them? Obligated in advance by the nourishment they would have received from birth, would not the children of the nation's most handsome men conserve the beauty of the race? Born in a tent or in a barracks, their first clothing being rags from uniforms, would they not quickly absorb the military spirit and could the nation expect to have any better defenders?"[110]

Moheau goes on to imagine the mothers of these little soldiers, caserned in one place and thus able to work and support their offspring. He concludes with a suggestive question about increasing the progeny of the armed forces: "Would there not be many other means, many other doubts (sic) to propose, if it were permitted to entertain doubts on certain subjects?" (290). One is tempted to wonder whether the redundancy of "doubts" in this sentence is intentional or whether the first "doubts" should not have been rather a more positive word, such as *program* or *plan*. Perhaps the redundancy betrays Moheau's reservations about the necessity for soldiers to be married in the strictest sense, as the maréchal de Saxe and others suggested (see chapter four), in order to reproduce. In any case, supporters began to trumpet plans to lighten the marital burden for soldiers for natalist reasons.

Vincent de Gournay, *Intendant du commerce* from 1751 to 1758 (celebrated for an aphorism he apparently never pronounced, "laissez faire, laissez passer"), believed deeply in the importance of work, insisting that the nation that had at its disposal the greatest quantity of labor was in reality the strongest. Gournay and the group of economic thinkers in his entourage (including Montesquieu's son, the baron de Secondat) saw society divided into two classes, the productive and the others. Gournay placed the military in this latter category for their failure either to produce or to reproduce.

Reproduction was a civic obligation, both religious commentators and freethinkers increasingly agreed, one to be accepted regardless of personal inclinations. "The first duty of a citizen," according to Moheau, "is to accept the yoke of marriage, and one of the greatest services he can render to society is to augment the number of individuals composing it. Married people form the most useful class of citizens because they serve reproduction and because the children are hostages they give the fatherland, so that all the ties that can bind a sensitive soul tie them to their native land" (98).

"Yokes," "service," "hostages," "ties," "bind,"—Moheau's choice of vocabulary would seem to indicate a less than felicitous view of domestic life, and, indeed, he entertains little optimism concerning parenthood as a rationally attractive venture. "Reflection and calculation would never lead to the propagation of the species," he comments, emphasizing the need for moral support within the society to encourage the self-sacrifice of individuals electing parenthood (271).

An occasional other voice was to be heard expressing a certain pessimism about the attractions of having children. Mme de Verzure, for example, agreed with Moheau, claiming that only the uneducated were simple enough to burden themselves with the woes of reproduction. "The populace of both sexes [among the poor] are inclined to marriage because fortunately they are not very reasonable,"[111] she observed. Meanwhile Moheau insisted on the importance of various gratifications children provide their parents as spurs to parenthood. "It is also necessary that the attachment and the subordination of children form a perspective of happiness for the parents' old age: these feelings are the result of mores" (271).

In the Cause of Parenthood: Drama and Poetry

Diderot emphatically agreed with Moheau; his bourgeois drama about the rewards of parenthood for the elderly, *Le Fils naturel* (1758), ends with the patriarch invoking "Heaven that blesses the children by the fathers and the fathers by the children." His other sentimental comedy, *Le Père de famille*, is equally insistent on the centrality of fatherhood, while in the *Epitre dédicatoire* he reminds the Princess of Nassau-Saarbruck that, unless women were good to their children, the day would come when, turning into "wrinkled children themselves, they will beg in vain for the tenderness they never felt."[112] Stanislas Leszczynski, discussing the emotional bonds of marriage and the family, felt that fathers' efforts in raising their offspring were repaid in some way by "the pleasure of seeing their own existence reproduced and prolonged, reclaiming a part of it from death."[113]

The theme was continued in a number of plays in which the man who avoids family life becomes a sad object lesson in the results of selfishness, as in Mouslier de Moissy's *Le Célibataire détrompé* (1770), Dorat's *Le Célibataire* (1776) and Dubuisson's *Le Vieux Garçon* (1783). This last drama movingly depicts the old boy's regrets when, once his salad days are over, he finds himself without progeny.

Starting at midcentury, another strategy was used by various authors attempting to fuse the erotic urge and parental responsibility into one big libidinal gratification, a synthesis which, if properly brought off, would resolve the issue of celibacy all by itself. How could family life be depicted as a source of erotic satisfaction? Jean Blondel solemnly lectured libertine bachelors: "You believe that the wedding is the funeral of pleasure, but you do not know [conjugal] pleasure, and the one you are familiar with is unknown to virtuous spouses."[114]

But no one went as far as the doctor Benjamin Bablot, *conseilleur du Roi* (1754–1802), in the effort to endorse parenthood over celibacy for demographic purposes. In his *Epître à Zulmis sur les avantages et les obligations du mariage* (1772, 1782), rather than depicting conjugal life as an immense burden citizens needed to be encouraged or even forced to shoulder, he embarked on a truly prodigious effort to imbue marriage and family life, in the service of patriotic populationism, with the erotic energies usually reserved for libertine fiction. Bablot begins with a somber depiction of a nation suffering from a terminal failure to procreate while at the same time churning out ever greater amounts of prose in praise of virtue: "What kind of century is this where people have never been busier with idle speculations about the means to better humanity's lot?" "Friend, our modest ancestors who came before, / Spoke less of virtues and practiced them more."[115]

Bablot objects to the assumption that pragmatic self-interest could contribute to the regeneration of the state. "Do they imagine they can uphold, even fortify, the worm-eaten pillars of a State nearly in its death throes through lessons in egotism? [an interesting appraisal of France in 1772]— that they can destroy and dry up, down to the very roots, the causes of the greatest of all scourges of Empire, *depopulation?*" (6). No, not lucid self-interest but the sexual drive itself will repopulate the State abundantly, according to Bablot, if only this drive can be properly channeled. His work is divided into six parts, the titles of which resume a whole amalgam of eighteenth-century Catholic monarchical reaction and progressive thought in regard to population increase:

1. In praise of marriage.
2. The indispensable duty of women to nurse their children.
3. The horror inspired by the filthy pleasures of a debauched bachelor.
4. The contempt deserved by modern philosophy.
5. The only study for young people—the Holy Bible.
6. Parents must never force their children's marital choices.

The body of Bablot's work is a long poem in which he purports to describe his courtship, marriage, and eventual procreation with Zulmis. He expresses the fear, at the beginning of the poem, that the steamy scenes he is about to describe might inflame the imagination of chaste readers. He decides, however, to run this risk because of his mission to attach ideas of pleasure to the marriage bed rather than the extraconjugal chaise longue.[116] Bablot's wife, Zulmis, is depicted in this remarkable poem as a passive partner in her husband's enthusiastic reproductive efforts. She is so docile that she does not even speak, expressing herself exclusively by glances. Bablot assures his beloved that he will never practice the coitus interruptus so popular among less virtuous husbands because, for him, pleasure and paternity are but one:

> Dear Love, most tender Spouse,
> It's you I long to satisfy.
> You'll never see me, struggling to get free,
> Leaving you high and dry.[117]

The Church Fights Back: Philosophes and Men of Letters

The Church was not slow in launching its counteroffensive. Montesquieu was the target of Abbé Galtier's *Les Lettres persanes convaincues d'impiété* (1751). "If one wishes to censure the most dangerous Books that the Impious have ever put out, I ask that the *Lettres persanes* not be forgotten," he began. Galtier suspected that Montesquieu's "taste for what he calls the *propagation of the species*" was nothing but the pretext of a lascivious temperament. "A man who would make a virtue of changing wives every year must find a Religion that elevates Virginity above Marriage really strange," he remarks. Were the men making such arguments even really to be called men? "These souls of clay cannot rise above the earth. They talk of nothing but propagating the species and what tends to populate the State. They would like to metamorphose men into stallions."[118]

The *Dictionnaire anti-philosophique* rejected the basic premise of both the philosophes and the demographers, namely that the fate of humanity here on earth was man's most essential consideration, reasoning, not incorrectly, that to make that concession to materialism was to lose not merely the battle but the war: "The irreligious philosophes! Wanting to make [men] terrestrial citizens, fixing their laws and their minds uniquely on the temporal progress of the human race, this is a project worthy of a Pagan Republic . . . the monstrous chimera of Materialism opens the door to all the vices!"[119]

The Church's most brilliant defense was not dismissing as irrelevant the "temporal progress of the human race," already a lost cause, but rather a vigorous lunge at the philosophes' own vulnerability. Celibacy was responsible for depopulating France, it was true, however it was not at all the celibacy of clergy taking chastity vows but rather the depraved, licentious, immoral "celibacy" typical of libertine philosophers.

The abbé Thomas-Jean Pichon (1731–1812) suavely accepted at face value Montesquieu's lip-service to clerical celibacy in *L'Esprit des lois*. According to Pichon's *Mémoire sur les Abus du célibat*, the Church too was opposed to celibacy—the "dishonorable" kind. To abolish it he urged the establishment of a graduated "tolerance tax" to be levied on the unmarried, the proceeds to be used to help fathers of large families and to raise abandoned children.[120] Père Guillaume-François Berthier (1704–1782), reviewing Pichon's work in the *Journal de Trévoux*, approved the plan, expressing his hope that "this odious celibacy, the fruit of libertinage, luxury and a so-called Philosophy—as much an enemy of the State as of the Religion,—will finally be proscribed or at least so heavily taxed that greed will accomplish what honor, virtue and the love of public good have been unable to produce."[121] Thus the Jesuits took up the populationist banner, branding luxury, libertinage and philosophy as deeply "dishonorable" and highly taxable agents of France's allegedly plunging population.

Another abbé, Ch.-L. Richard (1711–94), produced a half dozen works between 1773 and 1779, lacing into hommes de lettres and charging them with falsifying the effects of an unmarried clergy and ignoring the pernicious influence of luxury. In the abbé de Moy's *Discours*, the author, equally incensed at the diatribes against the clergy, reflects on the need for religion to use rhetoric as cunningly as its enemies. "Perhaps we live in a time when the study of literature is indispensable for the pastors of souls. You have to rise to the tone of your century. Where the apologists for vice are literate [lettrés], the apostles of virtue had better become so too. Let us speak, write, seduce the way they do and we too will have disciples."[122]

Defenders of the religion agreed that it was rank injustice to blame religious celibacy at all for the declining population when the *real* cause was the failure of intellectuals, philosophes, and other hommes de lettres to take on the responsibilities of family life. Ange Goudar accused the writing classes not only of lack of patriotism but of murder, proclaiming that "almost always a philosophe is a bad citizen" and should be dealt with severely. In Goudar's view, the bachelor should be punished by being denied "public employment or appointment," his taxes should be doubled, and "any unmarried man of letters should be excluded from the Academy and from becoming a University Professor."[123]

Jérôme Pétion de Villeneuve, in his natalist tract, *Essai sur le mariage* of 1789, had nothing but contempt for those who used their intellectual pursuits as a dodge for their bachelorhood. "Men of letters do not wish to get married because of the cares of domesticity. Frivolous pretext! Anyway, all the minute details of domestic life are the wife's responsibility. The man scarcely casts a glance at the whole business."[124]

Dr. Louis-Joseph-Marie Robert chided the Enlightenment's "men of letters" particularly for their delinquency as procreators, claiming that "they were the first to take up a habit [masturbation] that Diogenes found so agreeable that he was astonished it had not become more fashionable."[125] Whether murderers, onanists, or simply egomaniacs, intellectuals found that the accusation of nonprocreative behavior could be lodged against them as well as the clergy.

The charge of being "bad citizens," too preoccupied with pronouncing judgments on men and institutions to be bothered with the responsibilities of family life, was especially aimed at the encyclopédists. Diderot, Voltaire, the Chevalier de Jaucourt, Jean le Rond d'Alembert, Jean-Jacques Rousseau, and Saint-Lambert, as well as many other contributors to the *Encyclopédie* and friends and collaborators like Melchior Grimm, took a tone of moral superiority in regard to throne and church which never failed to enrage pious monarchists. François-V. Toussaint loved goodness so much that he claimed he was "inflamed with Apostolic zeal for virtue, I wish to make my readers virtuous," while S. Linguet assured his readers: "I feel myself burning with love for the human race when I take up the pen."[126] Such assertions were typical of the grandiose posture reformers typically assumed in relation to society. Turning the accusation around to accuse "philosophy" itself of demographic delinquency became a particularly popular weapon in Catholic hands.

Natalists as Nonbreeders

The philosophes, it is true, for all their talk about virtuous propagation, did not present an admirable parental profile.[127] In J.-L. Flandrin's words, "Which of these philosophes was the father of a large family? Which one did not, one way or another, sin every day 'against nature'?"[128] Of the major figures, only D'Holbach, Helvétius, and Diderot were married with families, and though it was mainly Diderot who spoke publicly of his domestic life with enthusiasm, in his letters to his intimate friends Sophie Volland and Grimm, he often complained bitterly about his pious, ill-tempered wife and her stultifying influence on their daughter, Angélique.[129] D'Alembert never married, and neither did Grimm, Jaucourt, Voltaire, Saint-Lambert, Fontenelle, Linguet, nor of course did the abbés Raynal, Morellet, Lenglet du Fresnoy, or Galiani. Abbé Castel de Saint-Pierre, who had proclaimed the clergy's duty to marry and propagate in his *Observations politiques sur le célibat des prêtres,* always kept, according to Jean-Jacques Rousseau, "a servant girl of an age to make [babies] and slept with her every Saturday . . . he believed he owed the public an accounting of his prolific virtue."[130] André Lefebvre, who provided three articles on child-rearing and two on morality to the *Encyclopédie,* was a bachelor. D'Amilaville, who wrote the "Population" entry for the *Encyclopédie,* was separated from his wife but had a long liaison with Duclos's wife, Jeanne Catherine de Maux, before she had an affair with Diderot. Ange Goudar did eventually marry his mistress, Sara, but they had no children and, after relieving her of her financial assets, he abandoned her. Mirabeau did have a family, but the "Friend of Man" had obtained *lettres de cachet* against both his son, Honoré Gabriel, comte de Mirabeau and eventual Revolutionary orator, and his wife, the marquise de Mirabeau, while arranging for his eldest daughter, Louise de Cabris, to be locked up as well.[131]

Grimm, for all his professed scorn for men who stayed single out of a taste for luxury, was for many years the lover of his collaborator Louise d'Epinay, wife of a rich farmer-general, and, according to Alan Kors, Grimm led a life nearly as sumptuous as his royal patrons. "By 1771," notes Kors, "he was seeking advice on how best to invest some 186,000 *livres.*"[132] The opulent bachelor Saint-Lambert, whose poem *Les Saisons* included lyrical panegyrics of frugal conjugal happiness, enjoyed a fifty-year liaison with Mme d'Epinay's rich sister-in-law, Mme d'Houdetot.[133] The Chevalier d'Eon de Beaumont, who so urgently demanded that celibacy "no longer be a respectable state . . . from now on it ought to be more honorable to have a wife and six children than a carriage and six horses," was in public, as well as private life, a self-proclaimed virgin who wore women's clothes.[134]

In a letter of 1765, d'Alembert wrote to Voltaire, expressing his wish to leave Paris and live in the country. He complained about current rumors concerning a marriage between him and Julie de l'Espinasse. "You must judge . . . that I am a long way from getting married, although the gazettes are talking about my wedding. Oh my God! What would become of me with a wife and children?" Voltaire replied with a cheerful exhortation to outbreed the enemy for the cause, regardless of his marital status: "My dear philosopher, if you had gotten married you would have done very well; in not getting married, you're not doing so badly; but one way or another, make some d'Alemberts for us. It's an infamy that the Frérons are pullulating while the eagles have no little ones."[135]

Voltaire himself, who had praised God in his *Discours en vers sur l'homme* for "the pure ardor that puts an adored spouse in your arms," was long content with the adored spouse of another man, M. du Châtelet, until she died giving birth to a child conceived in the arms of Saint-Lambert.[136]

The bachelor Rétif de la Bretonne, on the other hand, although not a member of the philosophes' group, was an indefatigable populationist moralizer, denouncing voluntary celibacy as "the greatest of crimes." From lower-class origins than the dominant literary groups of the day and the only important French writer from the peasantry in the eighteenth century, Rétif, unlike some others, lived his natalism, not permitting his single status to get between himself and fatherhood: "When I wrote the *Pornographe* my senses were too susceptible [*accensibles*] for me not to fall sometimes, and since I was always tender, even with whores, the most jaded among them became pregnable. Thus at the end of 15 to 24 years, I had rendered about sixty of these poor creatures mothers, in this way saving them, through love and nature, from brutal debauchery and uselessness."[137]

Even Benjamin Bablot, among the most rhapsodic of all procreation propagandists, confessed, in a note to a new edition of his *Epître à Zulmis* in 1782, that the sincerity of his familial effusions had been questioned on account of his own refusal to get married. "Certain funny guys maybe find me pretty funny myself, since I enjoy preaching the happiness of marriage

. . . [and yet] the state of matrimonial inertia I'm living in has not yet given me any clear ideas about it."[138]

The disparity between personal behavior and natalist pronouncements (of which only a small sample are quoted in these pages) is striking. Is it merely a matter of ordinary hypocrisy, of writers latching onto a popular cause for propaganda purposes while ignoring the message in their personal lives? It cannot be denied that ideological opportunism played an important role in the professed populationism of many nonreproducers.

Yet an evolution in mentalities was occurring across the eighteenth century, and a more complex set of dynamics came into play as well. As the fin de siècle approached, it became increasingly apparent that men of letters, themselves accused of reproductive negligence, were interiorizing the very pressures to procreate within the marriage bond that they had contributed to generating. According to his autobiographical writings, Jean-Jacques Rousseau's shame over abandoning his children began only after his behavior had become public. Before this moment, he says in 1768, he saw no harm in his refusal of paternity, but as soon as the scandal broke he felt not guilty but ashamed.[139] By the 1770s and 1780s, a whole series of famous writers (and apologists for procreation) were marrying the mothers of their so-called natural children. Beaumarchais married Marie-Thérese de Willermawlaz, the mother of his eight-year-old daughter, Eugénie, in 1775. "Any man who is not born horribly wicked ends up being good . . . when he has tasted the sweet happiness of fatherhood!" he claimed in his preface to *La Mère coupable.*[140] Choderlos de Laclos, who after *Les Liaisons dangereuses* dreamed of writing a novel that "would popularize this truth that there is no happiness except in the family,"[141] married Marie-Solange Duperré, the mother of his son Etienne Fargeau, in 1784. Would these writers have felt the need or the urge to convert wild oats into family life a half century earlier? Diderot's constant fear that feckless adventures among the philosophes could be used to belie their principles is significant in the evidence it provides for a philosophic *prise de conscience* concerning reproductive responsibility. The increasing adoption of "family values" at the end of the century appears to have been both the effect and the ongoing cause of successful propaganda.

CHAPTER FOUR

Divorce, the Demographic Spur

On tremble de serrer des noeuds qu'on ne pourra plus jamais rompre.
FR. DE TOUSSAINT, *Les Moeurs,* 1748

Législateurs français . . . songez qu'une institution qui tend à augmenter
le nombre et la fécondité des mariages, à garnir vos campagnes de labou-
reurs et vos frontières de soldats, est nécessairement une des meilleures
institutions politiques. ALBERT JOS. HENNET, *Du Divorce,* 1789

The Crisis of Marriage

While the possibility of legalized divorce was not up for public discussion
at the end of Louis XIV's reign, authors had long depicted the institution
of indissoluble marriage as disastrously unsatisfactory. One classic description of its shortcomings is that of Pierre Charron (1541–1603). He characterized the immutable conjugal bond as:

> a harsh and overly brutal captivity, in as much as one person is unduly at-
> tached and subjected to the whims of another. When people are ill-assorted
> and have made a bad bargain, when they have gotten more bone than flesh,
> they are miserable their whole lives through. What greater iniquity and in-
> justice would be possible than this: for an hour's nonsense, for an honest
> mistake, made without malice, often in obedience to the wishes of others, to
> be condemned to perpetual punishment? It would be better just to put a
> rope around your neck and throw yourself in the ocean head-first and get it
> over quickly, rather than spending forever in hell.[1]

While Charron's description may have been unduly bleak, it is not difficult to understand why so many French marriages were unhappy. In the
seventeenth and eighteenth centuries, couples above the poorest levels of
society wed mainly for reasons of family and fortune, their choice usually
dictated by others. The most generous financial arrangements and the most

2. "Le Lendemain des noces" (the day after
the wedding). Bibliothèque Nationale.

prestigious family name usually took precedence over the inclinations of
the interested parties, particularly among the propertied classes.[2] Olwen
Hufton points out that throughout Europe, the poor working-class men
and women over the age of consent enjoyed a degree of freedom in their
marital choices that was forbidden to their social superiors: "Parental control diminishes, in most countries, the lower one descends the social scale."[3]
Better-off young women had little to say in the choice of a prospective
spouse, even less than their male counterparts.[4] To the extent that personal
libido played a role in marriage, it was often that of an older, experienced
man, who chose a much younger woman on the basis of her carefully protected purity. The comte d'Antraigues deplored matches in which "a priest
dares to order a timid young girl, in the name of God, to love someone she
does not know. . . . Leaving the temple she is thrown into the arms of a man
who calls himself her husband, he enjoys her without having won her,
without her consent: this is marriage such as it exists in our customs."[5]

Scarcely an eighteenth-century novel or comedy exists without the
specter of an ill-suited arranged marriage and its unfortunate consequences. The question of whether young people ought to be permitted to
follow their hearts or whether they needed to be guided by the practical
wisdom of their families was hotly debated across the century and was one
of the prime issues of emerging individualism in its battle with the priority

accorded to the family. Fr.-V. Toussaint examined the problem in *Les Moeurs,* arguing that while a person had the right to marry, "it is not an injustice to a minor, a prodigal son or a maniac to deprive them of the exercise of that right, which they will inevitably abuse." Not acting to protect a child from his own rash decisions, said Toussaint, would be a dereliction of parental responsibility, "it would be a crying inhumanity to abandon him to the foolhardiness and thoughtlessness of his age."[6] On the other hand, for the conservative Augustin Rouillé d'Orfeuil, because financial considerations took priority over love, "most marriages bear the seal of reprobation, it's hell . . . quarrels, continual disputes, chicanery, lawsuits, separations, often total ruin are the just punishments for the profanation of the wise laws and the overthrow of that admirable order God himself established."[7]

Choderlos de Laclos described the dilemma in *Les Liaisons dangereuses* (1782), in which a conflicted mother could not decide whether to let her daughter marry the poor tutor the girl loved or a more socially prestigious partner whom she had never seen. "These marriages made according to calculations rather than appropriateness, the ones they call suitable, where everything suits except tastes and characters, are they not the most fertile source of these scandalous uproars that are becoming more frequent every day?" she asks her friend, the diabolically devious marquise de Merteuil. The marquise responds with a prim defense of traditional arranged marriage, pointing out that love is the most ephemeral of sentiments and that one day her friend's daughter may well reproach her for failing to exercise proper parental prudence on her behalf. Someday she may ask her mother: "Was it up to me to choose a spouse when I knew nothing about the state of matrimony?"[8] This observation, from the lips of the libertine Merteuil, is of course quite ironic in Laclos's scandalous novel, itself both a depiction and an indictment of the deteriorated state of French marriage.

All observers agreed that marital arrangements of the period frequently resulted in adulterous liaisons; the most famous couples of the eighteenth century—Voltaire and Emilie du Châtelet, Diderot and Sophie Volland, Melchior Grimm and Louise d'Epinay, to say nothing of Louis XV and his celebrated mistresses—were not married to each other.

According to many writers, the crisis in French conjugal life resulted in not only adultery but also alienation and misery for all members of the family. To Jérome Pétion de Villeneuve, family love was heaven on earth, but he admitted: "I say with sadness, I repeat to the shame of our century: how rare these happy households are! There is no longer any union in families, that frank goodness, that true cordiality have disappeared; fathers and mothers, spouses, children live together like strangers and treat each other as such."[9] If marriage spawned misery, it could not produce the progeny it was allegedly instituted to insure. Unhappy couples, at least in the higher echelons of society, were perceived as avoiding having children. According to Madeleine d'Arsant de Puisieux (1720–98): "Families have never been less numerous than during these last several years: they are limited to one or two children. Would this be the effect of antipathy between married people? Only women from the provinces and the common women in Paris have many children and make them healthy and well-constituted. Among the titled nobility, scarcely do we see one offspring whose health can be counted on. Here is one of those disorders in the State meriting the attention of those who know what produces wealth and who have an interest in not letting it be impoverished."[10]

Often formed without the desire of the interested parties, maintained in an atmosphere of surly mistrust, and producing only the minimal heir necessary to continue the line, marriage was represented in eighteenth-century French literature as the source of endless grief. The only alternatives for unhappy couples were the rare *séparation des biens et des corps*, without possibility of remarriage, the civil death and virtual imprisonment of the wife accused of infidelity,[11] the exceptional ecclesiastical annulment for cause, or, as Roderick Phillips suggests without irony, spouse murder.[12]

Divorce for Fertility

While the personal sufferings of ill-matched spouses provided ample material for literary depiction and sporadic calls for reform, it was the threat of depopulation that provided the impetus for a focused new campaign to resolve the problem of unhappy marriages. With the *Lettres persanes'* accusation that indissolubility was a major barrier to national demographic success, a surefire formula was invented to appropriate the moral superiority of the Church, not by means of ponderous perorations but with lethal wit. As Montesquieu commented: "Society's fashionable tone largely consists of speaking about bagatelles as though they were serious matters and of serious matters as though they were bagatelles"[13]—nobody had mastered that tone better than he.

In the more circumspect *Esprit des lois*, Montesquieu returned to the two questions of divorce and of encouraging population. At this point he jettisoned the synthesis of the *Lettres persanes* and treated the issues separately.

He argued in favor of legalized divorce, defined as a mutual decision to end a marriage, as opposed to repudiation, by which a husband unilaterally dismisses his wife. In the century's complex discourse of male-female relations, repudiation harkened back to ancient patriarchal privilege, whereas the Catholic doctrine of indissolubility was seen as protecting women from arbitrary expulsion.[14] Divorce, in turn, carried a protomodern, egalitarian connotation. From the *Lettres persanes* and the *Esprit des lois* emerges a consistent position in favor of laws and institutions supporting female equality in Europe. Montesquieu's great principle, that the moral forms of family life and the political structures of government were inextricably linked, lead him to conclude that "since time immemorial in Asia, we have seen domestic servitude and despotic government walk hand in hand." Because he claimed that women in Europe, at least Northern Europe, had "naturally good morals" and passions that were "calm, indolent, simple," their relative liberty and equality were consistent with Western traditions of government (2:514).

In a chapter titled "Divorce and Repudiation," Montesquieu went beyond even egalitarian divorce to favor a right to repudiation held only by the wife: "In climates where women live under domestic slavery, it seems that the law ought to allow women to repudiate and men only to divorce" (2:519), a provocative stance indeed. As in the *Lettres persanes,* in the *Esprit des lois* Montesquieu seemed to envisage the breakup of marriage as a means of changing spouses in the interests of a new union, not as an end to domestic life. "The fundamental principle of divorce . . . does not suffer the dissolution of marriage except in the hope of another marriage" (2:760).[15]

While this "principle" would seem to link divorce to populationism, by and large in the *Esprit des lois* Montesquieu treated divorce and demographics as separate issues. A depopulated nation must encourage increase in its citizens' numbers not by tinkering with the laws governing marriage to produce more babies but by adopting agrarian reform to help poor families.

> The evil is almost incurable when depopulation is longstanding due to an interior vice and bad government. To repopulate a State depopulated in this way, there's no use waiting for the help of children yet unborn. It is too late; men, in their wilderness, have no courage, they have no industry. With sufficient land to nourish a people, there is scarcely enough to feed a family. The poor people, in these areas, do not even have access to the untilled

fields. The clergy, the Prince, the cities, the great, a few important citizens, have imperceptibly become the proprietors of the whole land; it is uncultivated. In this situation, what must be done in the entire country is what the Romans did in a part of theirs, distribute land to all the families who have nothing, procure for them the means to reclaim the fields and cultivate them. (2:712)

Montesquieu had been the first to elaborate the argument that divorce was desirable for populationist reasons in the *Lettres persanes,* and his final message in that work remained the same as the one expressed in the *Esprit des lois.* Marriage should be dissoluble for the benefit of individuals. As for governments interested in boosting population, Montesquieu, like Fénelon, Boisguilbert, and Vauban, held that they should improve the well-being of their citizenry by land reform.

Nevertheless, legalizing divorce to revitalize the birthrate was advocated with mounting enthusiasm in the decades following the *Lettres persanes.* Maréchal Herman-Maurice de Saxe (1696–1750), for example, proposed a serious plan for repopulating France for military purposes in his posthumous *Réflexions sur la propagation de l'espèce humaine.* Saxe, himself a notorious philanderer, blamed Christianity for demographic decline and called for drastic change in the concept of marriage in France. He described the "extraordinary diminution of the world since Jesus Christ. I am convinced that some day we will be obliged to change religion in that respect because if one considers how much the established usages are contrary to propagation one will not be surprised at this diminution. According to the Gospel, the first commandment God gave man was BE FRUITFUL AND MULTIPLY. Women must be paid for their babies. In the future no marriage should be valid for more than five years and there should be no renewal without children . . . because marriage was established only for population."[16] Saxe imagined divorce and marriage limited by reproductive success purely as a spur to population growth for military purposes or economic advantage, though he suggests a more conservative five-year limit to the "conjugal contract" compared to the one-year term mentioned by Montesquieu.

The German pastor Johann Peter Süssmilch took issue with the logic of approving a change of partners in the interests of procreation. "It's a pretext without foundation to invoke innumerable quantities of men who could be born from a woman who was passed from one hand to another, like a ball, so that each one could get the most out of her. This is really a crazy idea

that only an Usbek and not a first-class Christian intellectual could entertain." Süssmilch argued that the sterile partner would continue to be unable
to procreate in a new union and therefore divorce and remarriage would
only pass the problem on, not resolve it.[17]

Denis Turmeau de la Morandière, in his tract proposing to encourage
foreigners to settle in France, fulminated against the corruption of the
government, the depravity of the times, and the manpower drain of emigration. His harshest words, however, were reserved for indissolubility because of its devastating demographic effects, denying a second chance at reproduction to "husbands who married sterile women, or women, suitable
for fecundation, who married men who were impotent from birth."[18]

The philosophes did not take up the cause of divorce for natalist reasons
in any systematic way. Antoine-Gaspard Boucher d'Argis's passage on "Divorce" for the *Encyclopédie* handled the hot topic in the wily encyclopedic
style, bringing up embarrassing precedents from national and ecclesiastical
history without comment. "It is certain," he assured his readers, "that in the
time of Marcus Aurelius, a Christian woman publicly repudiated her husband, as St. Justin informs us, which proves that divorce took place among
the Christians." As for France itself, the "Kings of the first and second
races" routinely exercised the right to rid themselves of unwanted spouses,
including the most prestigious of such early sovereigns: "Charlemagne repudiated Théodore," he pointed out.[19]

Populationism did not emerge as the spearhead of a veritable strategic
attack against indissolubility until 1768. Two surges of prodivorce writings,
mainly the work of obscure publicists, appeared in France between 1768 and
1774 and again beginning in 1789. The first cluster of texts, like so much
eighteenth-century polemic, presents a tangle of titles, conflicting attributions, and elusive authors.

Texts of the Populationist Divorce Campaign, 1768–1774

The following chronology of texts and attributions involving "Cerfvol" is
necessary for understanding the subsequent argument:

1768

[with Philibert], *Cri d'un honnête homme*
*Mémoire sur la population dans lequel on indique le moyen de rétablir et de se
procurer un corps militaire toujours subsistant et peuplant*

1769

Législation du divorce précédée du cri d'un honnête homme qui se croit fondé en droit naturel et divin à répudier sa femme
*Le Divorce réclamé par Madame la Comtesse de * * ***

1770

*Parloir de l'abbaye de * ou entretiens sur le divorce, par M. De V***, suivi de son Utilité civile et politique*
Cri d'une honnête femme qui réclame le divorce conformément aux lois de la primitive église, à l'usage actuel du royaume catholique de Pologne, et à celui de tous les peuples de la terre qui existent ou ont existé, excepté nous

1771

L'Intérêt des femmes au rétablissement du divorce
Hubert de Matigny, Hilaire-Joseph. *Consultations sur le divorce, pour un mari [le sieur de Crosane] qui se trouve dans le même cas que Simon Sommer et qui demande si, d'après son mémoire à consulter, et la consultation de M. Linguet, il peut également requérir du St Père une dispense de se remarier* (also attributed to Cerfvol).

1774

Supplément aux Mémoires de M. Palissot, pour servir à l'histoire de notre littérature, ou Lettre à M. Palissot sur un article de ses Mémoires

1775

Le Radoteur

The well-known radical lawyer and journalist Simon-Nicolas-Henri Linguet seems to have contributed four pieces to this debate,[20] starting in 1761 with a *Recueil sur la question de savoir si un juif marié dans sa religion peut se remarier après son baptême lorsque sa femme juive refuse de le suivre et d'habiter avec lui,*[21] followed by a chapter in 1767 of his *Théorie des lois civiles ou Principes fondamentaux de la société,* and, in 1771, *La Légitimité du divorce,* a *Mémoire à consulter et consultation pour un mari dont la femme s'est remariée en pays protestant et qui demande s'il peut se remarier de même en France.*

Quérard also attributes this last work to Cerfvol, while François Ronsin claims it is plagiarized from Phil[i]bert.[22]

As this chronology demonstrates, Cerfvol alone is credited with nine books favoring divorce within a seven year period, and four other works on the same subject (those of Phil[i]bert, Linguet, Hubert de Matigny, and the pseudo-Palissot) are attributed to him as well. In addition, the catalog of the Bibliothèque Nationale lists the name Cerfvol in connection with five works from 1766 to 1772 treating subjects other than divorce: *L'Aveugle qui refuse de voir*, *Chimerande*, *Du Droit du souverain*, *La Gamologie*, and *L'Homme content de lui-même*. According to Quérard, however, "Cerfvol produced twenty volumes on subjects other than divorce."[23]

Cerfvol's career is of interest in the context of the divorce controversy because he appears to have led the astonishingly prolific populationist propaganda campaign in favor of divorce while publishing numerous other books. There is, however, reason to doubt that an individual named Cerfvol ever actually existed. There are two theories about the identity of this writer. One holds that Cerfvol was not a real person and that the impetus for the writings under his name was not concern about the birthrate but rather a political conspiracy involving madame Du Barry, the abbé Terray, and the duke d'Aguillon, with the cooperation of Linguet.

The evidence for this explanation of Cerfvol's oeuvre is circumstantial. A number of works about Louis XV and his relationship with madame Du Barry suggest that after the death of the queen, Marie Lesczinska, in 1768, an effort was undertaken to obtain a divorce for the favorite from her purely nominal husband in order for her to be able to marry the king.[24] Linguet's memoir, according to the Goncourt brothers, "was a means of testing public opinion, perhaps an attempt to bring about a general law from which madame Du Barry could profit." It contains references to the encouragement given to madame Du Barry "to play the role of mme de Maintenant . . . by arranging occasions to alarm the Monarch's conscience and to furnish him with the means to reconcile his love and his religion, as his grandfather had done," that is to say, by marrying his mistress.[25]

What is indisputable is that in 1770 Linguet defended the duke d'Aiguillon, the favorite's friend and protector, and was for another year or so in close contact with Du Barry's intimate circle. Linguet himself addresses the rumors in an introduction to the 1789 edition of the *Légitimité du divorce*. He comments on the various speculations going around Paris concerning his work and identity. "The most reasonable of these follies was that the duc d'Aiguillon and I, we were plotting to marry off the countess Du Barry to the King. As her husband was alive, we had to unmarry her; thus my memoir for the carpenter of Landau was a stepping stone toward lifting her to the throne, and my *paradoxes* in favor of unhappy spouses a manoeuvre to give France a queen" (ix).

It is not possible at this juncture to know whether Linguet was responsible for some or all of the works "testing public opinion" signed "Cerfvol"— and the word *cerfvolant*, to be sure, means "kite," a traditional way of trying out the winds[26]—or whether a real Cerfvol existed and wrote works incorrectly attributed to Linguet.[27] Cerfvol disappears in 1775, announcing his own death in the 1774 work signed Palissot but attributed to Cerfvol. Thus his whole career consists of the period from 1768 to 1774, the interval between the death of Marie Lecszinska and that of Louis XV, the period during which the legalization of divorce would have permitted the King to remarry.

On the other hand, according to the theory of Giacomo Francini, Cerfvol and Phil[i]bert were noms de plume for Charles Palissot de Montenoy, who used the pseudonymous publications to vent his frustration over his unhappy marriage, which, although it produced two children ("the consolation of my life"),[28] eventuated in the imprisonment of his wife. Francini notes numerous similarities between Palissot's style and that of Cerfvol, as well as parallels between Palissot's biography and the various personae assumed by the narrators of Cerfvol's works. According to Melchior Grimm, "after having [his wife] thrown out of the house for her disorderly and scandalous conduct,[Palissot] complained bitterly about having to stay single when his age, his health and nature's urging moved him to give citizens to the fatherland." Grimm comments that *Le Parloir de l'Abbaye de* ***, *ou Entretiens sur le divorce* was being falsely attributed to Voltaire.[29]

With the death of Louis XV, this murky, large-scale guerilla campaign against indissolubility abruptly halts; the last reference to Cerfvol is 27 April 1775, the date of a tacit permission to publish *Le Radoteur*. In the absence of conclusive documentation it is not possible to determine whether the mass of prodivorce materials published during this brief period was the result of a concerted public relations campaign involving the king's mistress, the duke d'Aiguillon, Linguet, Voltaire, perhaps Palissot, and possibly other unknown contributors to the Cerfvol corpus, although that seems to be the most likely hypothesis. What is indisputable, however, is that in these works populationism is presented as taking priority over all other values. In Cerfvol's words: "There is no Frenchman, observing the disastrous consequences of a depopulationist system, and being consulted on the choice of means appropriate to remedy the ill, who would not answer: 'All means are good if they are effective.'"[30]

The other arguments presented by Cerfvol for wishing to see divorce established were protean and sometimes paradoxical; the ultimate populationist goal, however, was unchanging. It is the juxtaposition of his fluid reasoning with his fixed purpose that deepens the impression of reading a collective public relations campaign rather than the work of an individual author. Whatever the real origins of the Cerfvol texts, and whatever reasons are evinced in favor of divorce, the unchanging argument permeating all these writings is based on the supposed crisis in France's reproductive capacities.

In the Cerfvol oeuvre of prodivorce works, every device known to eighteenth-century fiction was employed to persuade readers; it is a veritable encyclopedia of rhetorical strategies. Arguments against indissolubility were presented as epistolary exchange, dialogue, and confession; miniature exemplary narratives of marital misery were analyzed and commented upon by sympathetic personages. The authorial figure appeared in a variety of guises: Phil[i]bert, for example, claimed to be an "honnête homme," a blameless husband reduced to despair by a debauched wife. Although legally separated from her, he could never remarry and enjoy legitimate offspring. Cerfvol's authorial personage was presented in nine different works as a cast of characters including: a scientific demographer, interested only in repopulating France for military purposes; a happily married husband and father, "because he alone may discuss this question. He is a pilot on the shore who observes the tempest in cold blood and can faithfully describe it"; a Rousseauvian sort of legislator, superior to man's passions but committed to his welfare and reproductive success; a respectable woman caught in a miserable marriage, yearning to be free to resume life and become a mother; a pair of unhappily married aristocratic women discussing their situation with a priest; and a philosophical woman of the world, the reform-minded "comtesse de XXX." Where the authorial voice purports to speak directly, the prose often mimics the tone of the philosophes, by turns flippant and didactic. Several of Cerfvol's works were also attributed to Voltaire, and echoes, not always felicitous, of the patriarch's tone are found throughout.

The first work in this corpus, the *Mémoire sur la population*, begins with an anxiety-provoking tableau, developing several themes already seen in Montesquieu. Not only were there fewer French than there used to be, the author maintained, but the modern race lacked the size and vigor of their ancestors. Cerfvol was alluding to the perception that France was being gradually debilitated by the spread of syphilis, a subject that was to preoccupy a number of writers throughout the eighteenth and nineteenth centuries. The disease was seen as causing sterility in some cases and in others an even more calamitous result, a tainted race. "The man who conserves enough potency from his first debauchery to reproduce himself does more harm to Society that if the whole principle were extinguished in him," Cerfvol explained. "To his wife he communicates the seed of corruption residing in him, accelerating its destruction, and what is born of this commerce?—ephemeral beings, individuals similar to those plants cultivated for vanity's sake alone, that cost a great deal and produce nothing. The destruction of these creatures, who may be regarded as the last gasps of dying nature, is always imminent and if by chance they live to the age of virility, their posterity cannot be counted among the number of men." These unhealthy beings were a further menace to the provinces because they infected their wet-nurses, and if they survived to be inducted into the army they spread "the principles of insanity they received from their fathers and mothers" (9–10).

Thus, according to Cerfvol, it was "incontinence," a peculiarly French penchant, that lead to population decline. The inconstant French, restive under the conjugal yoke, contracted venereal disease or wasted their reproductive energies in sterile liaisons.[31] Cerfvol noted, "The wisest course to follow, in that case, is to make the best use of the national vice. Perhaps with a frivolous race it is only a matter of not admitting the irrevocability of acts where the contracting parties had perpetuity in mind without the strength to achieve it" (25). By prohibiting divorce, the government had produced a lethal contradiction to the French character, "the indissolubility of engagements contrasts so perfectly with the national shallowness and inconstancy that it would be amazing to see it subsisting in France if one were unaware of the popes' motives in introducing it" (26). Cerfvol repeats the accusation that by forbidding divorce the Vatican ensured itself a powerful and lucrative hold on annulments.

It was the prohibition of divorce alone, he claimed, that was responsible

for the nation's plummeting birthrate and for the derisible quality of its offspring. "Let us not look for the true cause of our depopulation elsewhere
than in the indissolubility of marriage. All the other causes are derived
from that one." (27). In opposition to critics of the tax system like Vauban,
Boisguilbert, and Montesquieu, Cerfvol took pains to exculpate the
government's fiscal policies in the matter of dwindling population. Taxes
were blamed by critics of the monarchy, he claimed: "that's the cause they
will always cling to because if you dare attack corruption you sound like a
boring preacher, because the most mediocre writer is sure to have readers in
denouncing the government. A minister . . . must not regulate his actions
on what [the public] approves, but on what they ought to approve" (11).
This shifting of blame away from the government would seem to lend support to the notion that Cerfvol was positioned close to the throne. Not an
oppressive economic system, as critics of the regime suggested, but moral
corruption and papal intransigence lie at the heart of France's demographic
decline. Make divorce legal, and new marriages, founded on desire, would
soon repopulate the kingdom.

Divorce, as Cerfvol explained, was not an innovation on French soil. On
the contrary, it had been well established in the past, even under Christianity. Marriage, Cerfvol claimed, echoing Linguet, was fundamentally a contract. "This contract, like all other acts of society, was subordinate to the
civil power and susceptible of dissolution in certain cases, well after the period when we adopted Christianity" (77).

According to Grimm's account in the *Correspondance littéraire,* Cerfvol's
book was brought to the attention of M. Séguier, attorney general (*avocat
général*), who was forced "to conclude that it should be burned." The executioner was ordered "to light the fire and to throw the *Mémoire sur la population* on it, in the presence of the court clerk." Grimm referred to Cerfvol
as "a poor devil of the class of speculative philosophers whose number has
increased so prodigiously in the last twenty years."[32] Grimm's dismissal of
Cerfvol, even with the latter's anticlerical bias, was typical of the *Correspondance littéraire*'s policy of denigrating authors outside the circle of philosophes and their friends.

Cerfvol's campaign coincided with the demographic works of Messance,
Moheau, and others in the 1760s and 1770s which contradicted the thesis of
France's depopulation. Cerfvol was not alone in being undeterred by their
revelations. Well into the period of the French Revolution, many writers

were still claiming a dangerous diminution of the French population, making it clear, in the words of James Riley, that "it was chiefly political and moral rather than demographic issues that were at stake."[33]

Of the flood of writings favoring divorce in the eighteenth century, few failed to invoke the favorable effect on national natality as a consideration of supreme importance. Beneath this apparent near unanimity regarding the desirability of divorce, however, lurked widely divergent agendas for social change. The campaign against the Church seems to have been paramount for most writers. For others, legalized divorce was associated with achieving equality and liberty for women, while for others yet it carried exactly the opposite significance. For another major group, divorce was just one element in a radical restructuring of sexual relations intended to maximize national fertility for military, commercial, or patriarchal purposes, at the cost of all other considerations.

Diderot went through a personally and intellectually tumultuous period in the early 1770s, attempting to grapple with his adulterous passion for Madame de Maux, the stultifying bourgeois marriage of his beloved daughter, Angélique, and his role as moral and political advisor to Catherine of Russia. In a collection of observations and opinions composed in Russia and addressed to the empress, he endorsed the legalization of divorce. For a man as normally lucid as Diderot, these remarks about divorce point to deep, unresolved conflicts. He begins by pointing out that "indissolubility is contrary to the inconstancy so natural to man" and that "in less than a year the flesh of a woman belonging to us is nearly as familiar as our own"—in this context apparently a negative attribute. Nevertheless, he explains to Catherine, legal divorce would not frequently be used, because "the freedom to separate makes it so that people rarely separate." This paradoxical notion was often expressed by advocates of divorce, apparently in an attempt to deflect accusations that they would contribute to destroying the family. Diderot is predictably in favor of removing marriage from ecclesiastical control. "Is it not strange," he asks the empress, "that the Church remains the depository of the three most important acts of life: birth, marriage and death?" Diderot denounced separations precluding remarriage as "detestable." They were "even more contrary to population than indissolubility."[34]

Diderot assures Catherine that the fate of children is not the "embarrassing point about divorce. They must belong to the Republic." Since Catherine's Russia was about as remote from a republic as a country could be, his advice seems, to say the least, theoretical. Children could not stay with their remarried fathers and mothers, he suggests, because they would be "regarded as strangers," and their very lives might be in danger. "Who knows what greed does not suggest?" He brings up the possibility of guardians, only to dismisses every type of guardianship for different reasons. Finally a Diderot uncharacteristically stumped by reality tells Catherine: "It's a very thorny question of legislation, one of those cases that really is suitable for your Imperial Majesty, whose keen intelligence likes to be exercised." He does not, however, give up altogether, suggesting that assets of divorcing couples be divided in such a way that a "man would scarcely be able to change wives twice nor a wife to change husbands twice." As if realizing that two changes would not go far in a world where one grows tired of a wife's flesh within a year, he finally exclaims: "How difficult this question is!" (204–5).

Ch.-Antoine Pilati de Tassulo suffered from no such ambivalence in his *Traité du mariage* (1776), in which he claimed that Nature and the "objective of marriage" demanded only that the union last "a long time," not that it be indissoluble. Pilati shared with other prodivorce writers a common persuasive strategy, which consisted of elevating the importance of demographics while denigrating the authority of Catholic doctrine. To undermine the Church's traditional opposition to divorce involved reversing figure and ground. For most people in eighteenth-century Catholic France, divorce still remained a scandalous aberration, unheard of, an unthinkable outcome of marriage. To counter the perceived universality of *le mariage indissoluble,* propagandists presented a world in which divorce was normal, not monstrous, and moral, not vicious—a world in which only a few, small, occidental, Catholic nations perversely resisted the overwhelming acceptance of marriage as a reversible and repeatable act. Elsewhere, they argued, in antiquity, in the Bible, and in Muslim and other civilizations of the earth, even in Catholic Poland, men and women married, parted, and were released from their vows to marry again. "The constant practice of all peoples of the universe confirms this impression," Pilati insisted, "there is only one small branch of Christians who are stubbornly attached to the opposite opinion, and this has been true only for a short while."[35]

While it seems that many of the philosophes remained concerned but ambivalent about both population and divorce, reluctant to commit the resources of the *Encyclopédie* and ancillary publications to an all-out campaign for these causes, there were those, like baron Paul-Henri d'Holbach

(1723–1789), who came out resolutely against indissolubility. In a variation on the striking image invoked by Charron and Montesquieu, comparing indissoluble marriage to a living man chained to a corpse, d'Holbach claims: "No social law can authorize such a flagrant abuse. Is it not the same thing as imposing the [tyrant's] dreadful punishment on a husband, to force him to hold in his arms an infected and corrupted adulteress, one who in his heart he must abhor?" Chained to a cadaver or locked in the embrace of a diseased and despised traitor, the hostage husband provided powerful images of the intolerably claustrophobic intimacy created for men by indissolubility. D'Holbach favored divorce less for demography than for the protection it would afford the family inheritance against "an impudent woman, a wicked step-mother, who gives usurpers as brothers to legitimate children!"[36]

Unlike the *Encyclopédie* of Diderot and d'Alembert, Fortunato-Bartolomeo de Felice's *Code de l'humanité* of 1778 was systematically prodivorce. Felice's arguments were closely reasoned and carefully organized, taking into sympathetic account the Church's position on indissolubility, recommending patience and Christian humility in bearing the stresses of conjugal life, and expressing concerns over possible abuses if divorce became legal. Nevertheless Felice labeled divorce "a necessary evil." Couples who are not capable, for whatever reason, of forming a true conjugal partnership, "do not procreate children, they don't raise children conjointly, they are useless to the conservation of the human race and condemned by an absurd legislation to a forced celibacy,"[37] he concluded.

In the decade following Felice's argument, fewer publications appeared championing divorce sentiment and the controversy appeared to be winding down.[38] All that was to change, of course, in 1789, when the nation itself took on the task of conceiving, drafting, and implementing its own legislation regarding marriage, in a context of liberty, equality, and fraternity, as well as demography. In the meantime, another reproductive issue was engaging the attentions of many French natalists: would a man not have more children if he had more than one wife?

CHAPTER FIVE

Polygamy

Fertility and the Lost
Right of Man

Certainement un homme aura plus d'enfants avec vingt femmes qu'avec une seule. ANDRÉ-PIERRE LE GUAY DE PRÉMONTVAL, *La Monogamie,* 1751

Christianity and Polygamy

While the movement for divorce appeared to be headed along the road to modernity, populationist arguments were used to advance other, more ambiguous causes. The same pseudopragmatism that pushed in favor of procreating abundantly by "freeing man's most basic instinct from the yoke of superstition and fanaticism" with legal divorce was also available to proponents of legalized concubinage, the sale of women, the decriminalization of incest and rape, and polygamy in a scale of practices sliding from the theoretically egalitarian to the straightforwardly misogynistic. Having dismissed church strictures against such practices as unnatural and oppressive, and having substituted the value of population for discredited religious virtues, there was, for many writers, nothing to stand in the way of the most radical reordering of sexual relations, always provided it was in the name of procreation.

In the grip of the depopulation delusion, the subject of polygamy took on new dimensions and heightened intensity in the eighteenth century. An abundant literature flourished urging multiple wives as both a lost right of the male sex and an infallible recipe for population growth.

The idea that polygamy was better suited to abundant procreation than monogamy was not new in eighteenth-century Europe. The religious wars of the sixteenth century had thrown into confusion the questions of what constituted marriage and under whose rules it was to be regulated. Martin Luther abjured his religious vows to marry a former nun, denouncing the evils of clerical celibacy in the name of the biblical injunction to "be fruitful and multiply," a major act of revolt against Catholic doctrine in matters of sexuality. The emphasis of Luther and his followers upon fertility rather than chastity coincided with their insistence on the respect due the patriarchs of the Bible, whose polygamy was nowhere condemned within the sacred texts. While polygamy never became central to Protestantism in Europe, it haunted the margins, emerging in such manifestations as the Anabaptist regime in Münster (1534) and the widely debated controversy over the efforts of Philip, Landgrave of Hesse, to have reform theologians approve his bigamous marriage to Margarete Von der Sale.[1] Pope Clement VII's negotiations with Henry VIII included considering the polygamous solution to the king's dilemma as well as the divorce option. For Catholic France it was *Tametsi*, the doctrine of the Council of Trent in 1563, that definitively anathematized polygamy.[2] Although France never officially accepted Trent as binding on French Catholics, Tridentine strictures on marriage were incorporated into the Edict of Blois of 1580 and effectively interdicted polygamy in France both in faith and in law.

The informal plurality of households and acceptance of bastards that had been permissible in pre-Tridentine France became increasingly problematic after the Reformation, and by the eighteenth century concubinage, even that of the king, was officially not tolerated by the Church.[3] The struggle to keep the reigning monarch to the discipline of monogamy took place over generations of French kings and was only successful with Louis XVI. In the *Esprit des lois*, Montesquieu, following Tacitus, explained that the Frankish kings and a few nobles had had more than one wife not out of lust but to demonstrate their superior social status: "These marriages were less a sign of incontinence than an attribute of dignity" (2:550). The expansive sexuality of the late Bourbon kings, save the last, suggested vestiges of the old royal polygamous privilege, motivated, however, perhaps less by dignity than by incontinence. Nevertheless, royal adultery was denounced as mortal sin, even more blameworthy than for other men because of the scandal it displayed to the faithful.[4] Louis XIV's efforts to ensure the continuation of the Bourbon line by placing his legitimized bastard sons, the dukes of Maine and Toulouse, in the line of succession to the throne after his legitimate heir, the duke of Anjou, demonstrates how imperfectly Louis XIV accepted the Church's limitations on his procreative prerogatives. The comte de Boulainvilliers argued in 1728 that tradition permitted such promotions to the royal line, listing many examples of royal bastards from the ninth-century Arnould, king of Eastern France and Germany, up through William the Conqueror who were not excluded from the throne. As Boulain-villiers pointed out, the line between monogamy and the quasipolygamous status of the king's concubines was not firmly drawn until Henri IV suppressed the claims to nobility of illegitimate offspring.[5]

Humanism and the Challenge to Monogamy

Alongside what Flandrin has called the Stoico-Christian doctrine of marriage prevailing in France after Trent, a certain tradition of Gallic humanism that found polygamy congenial continued to surface in freethinking authors of the seventeenth and eighteenth centuries as well as at Versailles. Pierre Charron, whose approval of celibacy and of divorce were examined earlier, pointed out the disadvantages of Catholic monogamy:

> According to the strictest Christianity, marriage is held in tight check. The only easy part is getting in. Other nations and other religions that tolerate and practice polygamy and repudiation [enjoy] the liberty to take women and leave them, in order to make marriage easier, freer and more fertile. [They] accuse Christianity of having . . . prejudiced friendship and multiplication, the principle aims of marriage, in as much as friendship is the enemy of all constraint & maintains itself better in honest liberty. One can see how much polygamy profits multiplication among the nations practicing it, the Jews, the Muhammadans and other barbarians piled up masses of four hundred thousand in battle.[6]

Population, however, was not central to Charron's thought, it was merely one more stone to throw at the institution of Christian marriage, in which the disabused Canon of the cathedral of Condom found so much to reproach. The point was taken, however, that the rigorous ideal of Christian monogamy was out of touch with reality in a way that mating customs in other religions were not. More realistic in their knowledge of men's needs, unhampered by the illusory symmetry of one husband, one wife, "barbarians" produced more men to be deployed in battle than did Christians, demonstrating their superior grasp of Realpolitik.[7]

Charron, like almost all commentators on marriage, Catholic, Protestant, and freethinking alike, specified a duality of "purposes" or "aims" of conjugal life. One finality was always procreation, while the other varied significantly from author to author. "Friendship" in Charron seemed to correspond to what John Milton, in his impassioned appeal for legalized di-

3. Daniel N. Chodowiecki, Frontispiece to Lady Mary
Montague, *Letters of the Right Honorable Lady
M . . . y M . . . e, written during her travels in
Europe, Asia and Africa* (Berlin, 1740).

vorce,[8] referred to as "companionship," a generally pleasant conjugal rapport. That "friendship" would improve if men could only "take women and leave them" at will would seem to indicate that the burden of friendliness fell mainly on women. The notion that demoting women from their status as permanent monogamous wives to that of transient members of a harem would improve their dispositions was elaborated by many writers across the century and into the next, gaining popularity as the Revolution approached.

Some authors expressed their awareness of a certain lack of rigor in masculine reasoning about relations between the sexes, no matter how philosophical the intent. The *Encyclopédie* listing for "Femme," by Desmahis, for example, begins with a frank description of the male writer surrendering reason to fantasy when his subject is woman: "Woman . . . this name alone touches the soul but it does not always elevate it, it engenders only agreeable ideas which a moment later become disturbing sensations or tender feelings and the philosopher who ought to be engaged in contemplation quickly becomes but a man in delirium or a dreamer in love" (13:931).

A vast eighteenth-century corpus of literature spawned by a combination of delirium and natalism, a melange of reproductive pragmatism and pornographic apologetics, argued for a "rational" *use* of women in a masculine world liberated from the tyranny of the Catholic Church and ruled by objective numerical data. Even in many relatively sober theoretical writings suggesting solutions to the problem of depopulation in eighteenth-century France, erotic subtexts and agendas of domination were not far from the surface. A few writers like Montesquieu, Guay de Prémontval, doctor Esprit-Michel Laugier of Marseille, whose treatise on marriage was based on the absolute value not of population but of equality between the sexes,[9] and Condorcet, whose dedication to the principle of human equality was without qualification,[10] expressed opposition to this powerful current of populationist "reform." Except for the small group who, on *philosophical* grounds, assigned an abstract human equality an ethical value *above* population growth, most of the natalist writers favored schemes as firmly male-oriented as Tridentine Catholicism.

Polygamia triumphatrix and Pierre Bayle.

Late in the seventeenth century the subject of polygamy was again brought to the public eye by a curious work that provoked considerable controversy in England and on the Continent: Johann Leyser's Latin treatise *Polygamia triumphatrix* of 1682, translated into English and German in 1737 and into French in 1739.[11] Leyser made the case that the words in Genesis, *be fruitful and multiply,* did not constitute a benediction, as Church fathers had traditionally held, but a commandment, an imperative equal in authority to the Decalogue. Since men were *obliged* by God's express words to reproduce and were so constituted as to be able to father several children in a year, whereas women could not, Leyser held that restricting the male sex to only one wife violated both divine and natural law. He cited numerous examples of the ubiquity of polygamy in ancient times and other cultures, providing a sort of encyclopedia of sexual pluralism.

Leyser was careful to specify, however, that *polyandry,* or the practice of several husbands for one wife, would be an abomination, contrary to the Ten Commandments and to natural law. Pierre Bayle (1647–1706), the great skeptical Protestant writer exiled in Rotterdam, treated *Polygamia Triumphatrix* to a long and detailed analysis in the April 1685 *Nouvelles de la République des Lettres.* He took a jocular tone in dealing with Leyser's pronouncements, affecting the kind of genial misogyny Charron brought to bear on marriage. "When we examine the thing," he commented, "it is clear that the law of God, so often directly opposed to man's temporal happiness, has accommodated it very well when it prohibited us from having a multiplicity of wives." He went on to point out that widowers, having experienced conjugal life, would never wish to take on several spouses. Bayle categorized Leyser's book among those paradoxical works that "praise fever or folly, either by playing an intellectual game or because of a bizarre obsession" (256). He discussed the author's exhortation to husbands to "recover the domination he claims nature has granted them over the [female] sex, which he deplores men having given up, to become only the vile slaves of those who ought to be theirs." Bayle deplored Leyser's lack of "gallantry" but summed up his reservations about the book in one objection to polygamy: "It only takes one single consideration to reverse the foundation of his system, which is that the number of men being equal to the number of women, one cannot establish Polygamy without exposing some men to the necessity of celibacy, and hence it follows that wherever Polygamy has been common, eunuchs have been common as well. Thus it is not a more certain means of fertility than ordinary marriage, but rather an occasion for a thousand disorders of all kinds" (259).

Bayle came back to Leyser later in the same issue, publishing a letter of M. Masius, minister of the Danish envoy to the Court of France, relating the curious career and demise of the apologist for polygamy. Masius describes Leyser as "built in such a way that it would be difficult to make a husband for one woman out of him, still less did he need several" (260). Forced to leave his country, he ended his days at Versailles, where he had attempted unsuccessfully to live on the bounty of his polygamous "patrons." He died on his way back to Paris, where, according to another *Nouvelles* entry (December 1685), a book was found among his papers "containing the names of all the polygamists of the century" (437). In that same *Nouvelles*, A M. Brunsmannus, a minister from Copenhagen, wrote a refutation of Leyser's work called *Monogamia victrix,* pointing out that the author had been banished from Denmark and that his book was burned by the executioner in Sweden. Polygamy and Leyser come up again in Bayle's long (365-page) critique of Maimbourg's *Histoire du Calvinisme,* in which the author amused himself by juxtaposing Catholic clerical celibacy with the "be fruitful and multiply" of Genesis, repeating Leyser's description: "considered as a Commandment no less binding than the Decalogue" (316). In 1685, however, the tocsin of depopulation had not yet sounded, and the M. Crisante whose letter Bayle was quoting could state that "even if these words at one time had an imperative significance, it would have ceased several centuries go, that is to say, when the world was repopulated. If that were not the case, each man's duty would be to work at the multiplication of individuals as much as he could . . . the more one planted children everywhere one went . . . the more one would fulfill one's duties as a good Christian and a citizen" (316).[12]

Bayle returns to the question of polygamy in the ironic entries "Lamech," "Sara," and "Mahomet" of his 1697 *Dictionnaire historique et critique.* Nothing delighted the erudite and impious Pierre Bayle more than episodes in the Bible in which a revered figure was described behaving in ways that blatantly defied accepted Catholic morality. Bayle used Lamech, direct descendant of Cain, credited with being the first polygamist, as a vehicle for his aspersions on biblical obscurities, Christian morality, and traditional rabbinical and scholastic commentary. Lamech's violation of what Bayle called the "monogamatic law established in the terrestrial paradise" (3:40) is associated with the corrupt seed of Cain. However, Bayle pointed out, Lamech's descendants showed no signs of suffering divine disapproval; on the contrary, they received all manner of temporal benedictions, thus apparently putting the seal of God's approbation on polygamy. In one of his numerous notes to the entry, Bayle commented again on Leyser:

He is a funny fellow, the author of *Polygamia triumphatrix,* who has spent
his fortune and his life working for the dogma of the plurality of wives, he
who had one too many wives with only one. He treats Lamech's resolution
to marry two as an heroic act . . . Lamech was the first who dared to take the
first step with heroic courage . . . he commented, not in words but in actions
on the text of the universal Law: *Be fruitful and multiply,* a Law that is a true
commandment and not a simple blessing. This is how the poor author became preoccupied with polygamy: it became his obsession. (3:40, n. a)

While condescending to Leyser and casting aspersions on both his virility and mental stability, Bayle took advantage of his thesis to disparage the
Church's intransigence in conjugal doctrine. "Sara" offered another irresistible occasion for demonstrating the immorality of the Old Testament, the
inanity of Catholic theology, and the irresistible wit of Pierre Bayle
(4:142–47). The entry is laid out in the author's typical eccentric style. Five
pages in folio contain only forty-five lines of large-face entry, embellished
by a few explanatory marginal references. All the rest is devoted to a
strange commentary consisting of double columns of expansive notes, some
as long as essays themselves, with tiny columns of secondary references in
either margin.[13] The main body of text briefly and somewhat incoherently
retells the story from *Genesis* of Abraham's long-sterile marriage to Sara,
whom Bayle referred to as the Patriarch's sister, her attempt to procure a
child of Abraham by her servant Hagar, and her supernaturally abundant
lactation after the birth of Isaac.

After insinuating that the patriarch was prostituting his wife / sister for
his own advancement, Bayle speculated at great and somewhat salacious
length about Sara's octogenarian beauty and sex life. It was the morality of
those theologians apologizing for Abraham's bigamy on the grounds that
he wanted to have children that called forth Bayle's most eloquent sarcasms: "Provided only that one proposes to leave successors," he asked, "a
woman may encourage her husband to possess their servant & a husband is
allowed to follow this fine advice?" Calvin, Bayle claims, "doesn't find any
excuse for them in the usage of polygamy already established among the
nations. He claims that it was not up to them to defy the Law that married
them one to one" (4:147).

Bayle was happy to put the Church in the awkward position of having
either to condone the patriarchs' plural marriages or to argue that they did
not really constitute polygamy and then describe the scholastics' convoluted

attempts to wriggle their way out of the difficulties. For Bayle, the purpose in describing biblical polygamy certainly had more to do with discrediting the Catholic faith than with urging a plurality of wives in the Europe of his day. Entirely different tactics to the same end were involved in the composition of his text for "Mahomet" (3:256–72). In the principal entry under that name, typically brief, in keeping with Bayle's peculiar style, lust and misogyny, not paternal enthusiasm, motivated the prophet. Bayle noted that Mohammed wished to "establish a code filled with harshness toward women. However he furiously loved possessing them and strange things are told of his vigor in that regard. His lubricity was undoubtedly the cause of his permitting polygamy within certain limits and concubinage without limit" (3:262).

On these few lines Bayle built a vast and complex structure of reference, innuendo, and scabrous detail, suitable for undermining confidence not only in Islam but also more pointedly in divine inspiration. He questioned the Mohammedan practice of permitting four wives from the perspective of a man's sexual energies, asking whether "the condition of these four wives is not deplorable, under a law that gives the husband the right to deprive them of their due and to give it to as many pretty slaves as he can buy? This diversion of matrimonial funds, does it not reduce [his wives] to indigence and extreme suffering?" The traditional answer, that the Mohammedan husband is obliged to sleep with each of his wives once a week, only occasioned further ribald hilarity on Bayle's part. If a woman has to enforce her marital rights through the magistrate, said Bayle, the conjugal act "must not be a very tasty dish" ("*ne doit pas être un grand ragoût*"). In semiserious terms he went on to denounce Islam's treatment of women, which allegedly denied them entrance to paradise but forced them to witness, in the afterlife, their husbands' pleasures with celestial *houris,* divine prostitutes said to provide eternal rewards for worthy Mohammedan males.[14]

Ascribing Mohammed's approval of polygamy to his lascivious temperament, Bayle recounted that the prophet, "in order to put a good face on the incontinence that had pushed him to marry several women, supposed that God had revealed to him that it was permitted and inserted that article in the Koran" (3:263). The founder of Islam went on to seduce his little servant Marina, not yet nubile, thus enraging his two wives, who spread news of his dereliction to the faithful. "To remedy this great scandal he pretended to hear a voice from heaven letting him know that he could do whatever he wanted with his servants. This is how this impostor began by committing a crime and finished by converting it into a general law. It had nothing to do with fanaticism. A good touchstone for measuring the good faith of those who claim to be inspired . . . is to examine whether their doctrine changes direction as the times change and whether their own interests are not the same throughout" (3:263).

In this passage Bayle stressed the connections he perceived between Mohammed's private life and the laws he promulgated, describing the practice of multiple wives as legalized lasciviousness, whereas in the Old Testament entries he demonstrated that polygamy might be held compatible with Scripture on populationist grounds. It is clear that in his manipulation of these rather sensationalistic texts it is not polygamy per se that interests him but its possibilities as an aggressive instrument in some unfinished Reformation quarrels.

In his various discussions of polygamy, including his analysis of the sex ratio, Bayle reminded his readers that castration lurked in the shadows of the harem fantasy. With which man was the male reader to identify, the one sexually privileged master of the seraglio or one of the numerous sexually deprived eunuchs? Bayle returned often to the scandalous, titillating, yet anxiety-provoking subject of polygamy in the *Dictionnaire* and the *Nouvelles de la République des Lettres* and in many other articles in following years. Bayle's ultimate refutation of polygamy, on the grounds of equal numbers of men and women, relied for its authority on nature rather than Scripture. The language nature speaks is mathematics. Defenders of religion in turn took up the challenge and found not a random outcome but God's Providential Will in the ratio of male to female births.

Oriental Practices: *Les Lettres persanes* and *Mahmoud le Gasnévide*

Thanks to Bayle and other writers, by 1720, when Montesquieu was composing the *Lettres persanes,* the notion that polygamy facilitated erotic pleasures more than monogamy was familiar to readers of skeptical or "libertine" writings.[15] Alarm over a perceived decrease in population brought a new urgency to the pleasant habit of denigrating Catholic sterility by comparing it to the allegedly fecund pagan and infidel practice of polygamy.

In the *Lettres persanes,* however, Montesquieu denounced not just Catholicism but Islam as well for antinatalist institutions. Not only did too many wives hamper the sultan's generative efforts, the very structure of the harem hindered childbearing. Besides depleting the energies of the master, the harem wasted the reproductive energies of women slaves, who were denied the right to procreate, and destroyed the virility of those male slaves guarding the wives. Between virgins and eunuchs, Usbek claimed, it was scandalous that "one man alone occupies so many subjects of one sex and the other, killing them as far as the State is concerned, and rendering them useless for the propagation of the species" (1:301).

Despite the entertaining striptease competition among Usbek's wives that Montesquieu evoked in letter 3,[16] and several other racy harem scenes, for the most part polygamy was depicted unfavorably in the *Lettres persanes,* both in the letters addressing population and in the tragic closure of the novel as a whole, constituted by the self-destruction of Usbek's harem and the suicide of his favorite wife, Roxane.[17] Montesquieu parted company with Bayle and still more with Charron in that he rarely adopted the good-natured, slightly contemptuous misogyny of the earlier writers. He even provided a complacent description of an inverted harem, a polyandrous household where one wife possessed a plurality of husbands. In letter 141, the fortunate Anaïs enjoys the favors of a whole male harem in paradise. The arguments for male-female equality expressed by Rica in letter 28 succinctly summarized Enlightenment feminist thinking,[18] and the rejection of polygamy in the novel repudiated the instrumental role assigned to women in other literature on the subject. Most significant, from the perspective of populationism, was the infertility of Usbek's harem. In his whole establishment, with its four wives and numerous slaves and concubines, according to Montesquieu, there was but one child.

Jean-François Melon, friend of Montesquieu, secretary of John Law and of the Regent, took a different approach to the plurality of wives in his 1730 oriental tale, *Mahmoud le Gasnévide.* Amidst many pages of serious financial and political arguments, since Melon too was concerned with political arithmetic, he included a lengthy defense of polygamy. Contradicting Montesquieu, Melon claimed the plurality of wives would result in a higher birth rate because the husband's labors would be lightened by the promise of numerous progeny. In a perennial trope, flippantly offered, he compared the husbanding of women to that of the earth: "The laborer who opens the earth with his plow stands up agreeably under the strain because he hopes for an abundant crop & lovers are always happy when they have the hope of love's sweet harvest."[19]

Unlike the dangerous rivals portrayed in the *Lettres persanes,* in Melon's fantasy the wives of Mahmoud were not jealous of one another. On the contrary, they were the dearest of friends, saving up their allowances to buy him more female slaves. "Enjoy all the objects in the universe," they implored their husband, "your spouses are destined only to share your glory & to give your subjects heros as great as yourself."[20]

In this masculine daydream, Melon argued, like Leyser, for polygamy as a lost natural right of the male sex, still preserved among peoples less corrupted by civilization: "These men we call savages enjoy the Natural Right that renders them the Husbands of all women. Various Legislators have deprived the civilized peoples of this liberty. Let us leave to the infidel nations the sad satisfaction of enjoying only one object and of being stuck with her as property for life" (91). The overall impression created by the discussion of conjugality in *Mahmoud le Gasnévide* is that Christianity's marital formula of one man, one wife (*mariage d'un avec une*) for life was both unbearably repressive for men and laughably parochial. The wider world, Melon suggested, tolerated a broader range of sexual arrangements.

Against Polygamy: The *Journal de Trévoux*

While Melon was toying with erotic Eastern fantasies to amuse his jaded Regency readers,[21] the Church was still wrestling with an adequate response to the perfidious insinuations of Pierre Bayle. The entry on Sara in his *Dictionnaire historique* elicited a large-scale refutation in 1736. A twenty-five-page "Dissertation sur la polygamie des Patriarches, où l'on réfute les calomnies que M. Bayle fait à ce sujet contre le Père Fenardent Cordelier, contre St. Augustin & les autres Saints Pères," by père [Charles] Merlin, Jésuite, appeared in the *Journal de Trévoux*.

Why did it take the Jesuits thirty-nine years to answer Bayle's passage on Sara? It may be that with the publication in French of *Polygamia triumphatrix,* the idea of polygamy was starting to become fashionable in ways that were discomfiting to the order. "The delicacy of the subject," said père Merlin, "obliges me to neglect several of my strong points and confine myself to what is absolutely necessary to shut the mouth of impiety" (403). Merlin set himself the considerable task of defending revered theologians in the logic and morality of their apologies for Abraham's problematic polygamy. As the Church fathers were not in agreement among themselves as to whether Abraham's relations with Hagar amounted to polygamy, or whether they constituted rather a "figure" of some arcane theological mystery, or whether God approved the concubinage because its intentions were directed to fertility, not lasciviousness, Merlin's argument was painfully convoluted. He made a great effort to refute the Manichean heresy which declared that any God who permitted the florid polygamy described in the Bible was "not the good Lord but the bad Lord." Such impertinences were hard enough to deal with, Merlin complained, but "God spoke thus to Abraham: *I shall make Ismael the father of a great people because he is your son.* The order for Hagar to return & these miraculous favors for her, for Abraham & for their son, do they not constitute an approbation of their commerce? Anyway, how can one prove the opposite to a Manichean?" (407).

The apparently divine association between polygamy and population increase, so impolitically demonstrated by God's endorsement of Abraham's as well as Jacob's polygamy, was more than Merlin, with the best will in the world, could explain away. He attempted to present Saint Augustine's reasoning, "which is also the unanimous doctrine of the Holy Fathers concerning Polygamy," but he was quickly bogged down in "obscurities." While some scholastics were of the opinion that the patriarchs were under a special dispensation from "natural law" to populate the earth by means of plural spouses, others, like Tertullien, for example, thought such an interpretation was fallacious. Merlin was adamant: "So many obvious and precise testimonies do not allow us to doubt that the constant and unanimous persuasion of the Fathers of the Church was that polygamy, such as they understood it, was simply and absolutely permitted by natural law; that it was never forbidden by any political law before Jesus Christ, that in the ancient times it could have been innocent and legitimate not only among God's people but among all peoples, in a word, the Patriarchs needed no dispensation to make use of it" (411). Thus, according to Augustine, polygamy was part of the old law, abrogated by the advent of Christ. Other authorities, unfortunately for Catholic orthodoxy, believed that was not the case, but, rather, a divine dispensation to marry several women was granted to certain patriarchs by means of "inspiration"; others believed only that it "was bestowed on Noah for all his descendants up to Jesus-Christ in virtue of the words *be fruitful and multiply and fill the earth,* which had a different meaning, not authorizing polygamy, when they were spoken to Adam. Others claim that Abraham alone received this special privilege . . . others limit this prerogative to God's chosen people," and so on. In any case, Merlin decided, theologians "preferred to assume there was a dispensation rather than admitting that God would honor men who were habitually adulterous and incestuous with his revelations and his most special favors, that is reasonable. But Monsieur Bayle, guided by Calvin, would rather believe God treats corrupt men as his friends than entertain a conjecture which is necessary if you suppose the sanctity of the Patriarchs and the opposition of polygamy to natural or divine law. I do not know what to call that, if it is not madness, it is impiety" (413).

Unable to reconcile various theological pronouncements on polygamy, Merlin elected instead to attack Bayle: "Does he want to have concubinage, adultery & incest regarded as minor sins that are not in the least incompatible with the love of God and in this way flatter the corruption of so many scoundrels attached to his writings by cynical impudence?" he asked. As tempting as this interpretation of Bayle's motivation was, Merlin realized he had other, yet more sinister ends in mind. "His impiety has even more pernicious views . . . he is working to destroy the authority and divinity of the two Testaments" (408). Père Merlin's intuition, of course, was correct. Although the philosophes, by and large, did not embrace polygamy as part of the project of Enlightenment, the subject was a philosophe's dream because of the opportunities it afforded for scandalizing the righteous and for reasoning about society in a radical way. It was not long before it blossomed into one of the century's most controversial topics.

L'Esprit des lois and the Sex Ratio

Montesquieu returned to polygamy in 1748 in the *Esprit des lois* (bk. 16, chap. 2). He began by differentiating between slavery, properly speaking, and the situation of the polygamous wife, which he called "domestic servitude," the distinction being based on the notion that "slaves are established for the family more than they are in the family," whereas wives, although in other ways enslaved, themselves constitute their husband's family. In this chapter Montesquieu explained his view of the natural source of polygamy: climate. In warm latitudes, he stated, girls become nubile at an early age but also lose their sexual charms at an early age. Since they have no sense during the years when they are attractive, and no attractions by the time they become sensible, Montesquieu concluded "it is therefore simple for a man to leave his wife and take another one, when his religion does not oppose it, and for polygamy to be introduced."[22]

Wishing to provide an objective, natural basis for human institutions, Montesquieu picked up Bayle's argument against polygamy: the sex ratio. Whereas Bayle claimed that equal numbers of male and female births would make polygamy unfair to some members of the male sex, Montesquieu held that the sex ratio actually varied according to climate, determining whether a plurality of wives was tolerable. The original title of his chapter had been "How the Law of Polygamy Is a Question of Calculation," but in response to strong criticism he had changed it to the more innocuous "Polygamy, Its Various Circumstances." According "to the calculations made in various parts of Europe," Montesquieu began, "more boys are born than girls; on the contrary, reports from Asia and Africa tell us that more girls are born there than boys. The law of only one wife in Europe and the one permitting several in Asia and Africa have thus a certain connection with the climate" (2:511).

The sex ratio is one of those demographic phenomena that fascinated Enlightenment thinkers from a variety of perspectives and was used to serve more than one agenda. Whether males and females were born in equal numbers and whether the ratio was everywhere the same were much debated questions at the end of the seventeenth and throughout the eighteenth century. Not only were the statistics disputed, but their significance was also subject to a century- long controversy. A comment from Vauban's "Description de l'élection de Vézelay" demonstrates the vagaries of the data in the framework of a naturalistic explanation. He claimed that the area "naturally produces more boys than girls. That is rarely found in other provinces of the kingdom where ordinarily more girls are born than boys: the coldness of the region could very well be the cause!"[23]

In England the forces of Christianity had been marshaling to combat the use of natural observation to undermine belief in God. The scholarly Robert Boyle endowed a lecture series intended to turn materialist thinking to the defense of revelation. The Reverend William Derham published thirteen of the Boyle lectures in a collection titled *Physico-Theology or a Demonstration of the Being and Attributes of God from His Works of Creation* (seven editions from 1713 to 1727), in which Derham used the nascent science of demography to demonstrate the existence of divine benevolence. At nearly the same moment appeared the physician and mathematician John Arbuthnot's 1712 "Argument for Divine Providence, Taken from the Constant Regularity of the Births of Both Sexes," a five-page essay presenting roughly equivalent numbers of male births and female births in London from 1629 to 1710. Alain Desrosières discusses how Arbuthnot (1667–1735), physician to the queen of England and translator of Huygens's treatise on probability, had interpreted newly established data showing that while more male babies were born in Europe, the gender imbalance was corrected by the higher childhood mortality of boys. Arbuthnot detected the hand of Divine Providence in these numbers, ensuring that "later some women would not find themselves condemned to the sad condition of celibacy."[24] While the birth differential had been remarked upon since at least the fourteenth century,[25] Arbuthnot added a new dimension to the discussion by analyzing the probabilities of such an occurrence, asserting that the chances of conceiving either sex were about equal. Arbuthnot concluded that among the innumerable signs of "Divine Providence to be found in the works of Nature" was the exact equilibrium between the numbers of men and women, universally observed. Thus, he argued, it is guaranteed that "each Male has his Female. This equality of Men and Women is not the effect of Chance but of Divine Providence."[26]

Throughout the eighteenth century, Arbuthnot's findings set off controversy concerning the nature of probability and the meaning of *chance*, involving such mathematical notables as Nicolas Bernoulli (1687–1759), W. s'Gravesande (1688–1742), B. Nieuwentijdt (1654–1718), and, above all, Pierre Laplace (1749–1827). While fluctuations in the sex ratio continue to the present day to raise fruitful questions concerning the biology of human reproduction as well as mathematical, statistical, and even social debates, since the eighteenth century demographers have generally accepted that under normal conditions approximately 105–106 male births occur for every 100 female births.

Montesquieu, however, rejected Arbuthnot's generalization of England's higher birthrate for males to the whole world, arguing that he was wrong to conclude "it was the same thing in all climates."[27] Reasoning back, like Vauban, from the phenomenon to a "climactic" cause, in line with the underlying theory of the *Esprit des lois*, Montesquieu held that polygamy must be based on an excess of female births over male. Consistently pursuing his mathematical thesis, he stated that polyandry, or a plurality of husbands, was also practiced in some areas of the world where the climate made such an arrangement desirable. "According to the calculations made in several parts of Europe, more boys are born than girls: on the contrary reports from Asia and Africa tell us that more girls are born than boys in those places. The law of only one wife in Europe and that permitting several in Asia and Africa thus have a certain connection to the climate. In the cold climates of Asia as in Europe, more boys are born than girls. According to the Lamas, that is the reason why, in their countries, a woman may have several husbands" (2:511). To follow Montesquieu's logic, one would be forced to conclude that Europe might also tolerate polyandry, in accordance with its climactic character.

This whole argument provoked an uproar of indignation. For the male readers fantasizing over the pros and cons of the harem, the idea of a reversed form of marriage in which the male was reduced to "domestic servitude" was intolerable. Echoing Leyser's view that polyandry was an "abomination," all but a few of the numerous writers commenting on polygamy in the latter half of the eighteenth century hastened to establish the principle that whatever other permissive sexual arrangements might be countenanced around the world, a plurality of *husbands* was clearly out of the question.

The *Journal de Trévoux* attacked *L'Esprit des lois* following its publication, targeting especially Montesquieu's argument about climate and his failure to condemn polyandry (April 1749). "The polygamy of a woman who has several husbands," complained père Guillaume-François Berthier, chief editor of the journal and energetic enemy of the philosophes, "is a monstrous disorder which has never been permitted in any case, which the author does not distinguish in any way from the polygamy of a man who has several wives."[28] Montesquieu's nonchalantly egalitarian suggestion about a hypothetical female right to multiple spouses symmetrical with that of the male seemed to constitute a threat that could not be decried too often.

Le Guay de Prémontval

A work coming to the defense of traditional marriage, *La Monogamie,* was published in 1751 by the well-known mathematician André-Pierre Le Guay de Prémontval (1716–1764) with a preface by his wife, also a mathematician, Madame Pigeon de Prémontval (1724–1767). *La Monogamie* began with an attack on the alarming popularity of *Polygamia triumphatrix:* "To succeed these days," the author charged, "it takes, in four words: frivolity, obscenity, impiety and malice, these are the characteristics of our century" (xxvi).

Despite his antipathy to Leyser, the author eloquently presents both the arguments for polygamy and those against it, but in the conclusion of this long work he refutes each apology for plural marriages. The defender of polygamy in the work, Ariste, repeats the rationale based on Scripture that had become standard across the century but goes on to emphasize the nationalist, populationist argument in great detail. Christianity stands condemned for "depopulating the universe," he claims, above all in the lands of the North. While in former times the burgeoning population of Scandinavia and the Germanic states came pouring down into Southern Europe in repeated waves, since the advent of Christianity and the suppression of polygamy, the numbers in those countries had thinned to a trickle.[29] Not only had

Christianity dried up the fecundity of the North, but it had also "by its un-reasonable interdiction shut itself out of the most populous nations of the world, including China among others, where polygamy is so sacred that it is the most insurmountable obstacle to the conversion of the inhabitants" (xxxvi). Ariste professed amazement at the prejudice against the institution of plural marriage among Christian sects, since "the thing is in itself ex-tremely useful and very appropriate to contribute to the propagation of the species" (6–7). While Ariste defended multiple marriages for the male sex, he was absolutely certain, on the other hand, about one thing. Taking more than one spouse was: "not for women because the plurality of husbands, ac-cording to natural scientists, placing an obstacle to the conception of the woman, while on the other hand employing the functions of several men in a useless way, is thus directly opposed to the objective and the essence of marriage which is nothing other than the multiplication of the species, whereas as everyone must admit a plurality of wives is the most appropriate imaginable means to fulfill this important objective" (76).

"Eudoxe," monogamy's defender, is puzzled at the beginning of his re-buttal, wondering how it is that "the Christian sects are in agreement in re-jecting polygamy yet most people are nonetheless convinced that it is ex-tremely useful for propagation and for this reason God tolerated it under the Old Law" (139). Eudoxe refutes each of Ariste's arguments in turn, in-cluding the populationist position. The main reason he opposes them, however, is once again based on the sex ratio. With an approximately equal number of males and females, polygamy would be unjust to other males, who would be "wounded in their most legitimate, not to say essential and most sacred rights." With the introduction of the language of *rights* into the dispute, the polygamy debate entered a new phase in which issues of property became explicit. Eudoxe offers an extended analogy between mar-riage and land ownership, comparing women to the earth in a context of laissez-faire capitalism. Since society permitted one man to possess twenty acres while another man had "not an inch," and since a "disproportion of fortunes . . . however great it may be, does not offend nature" why should one man not be allowed to possess twenty wives?

> Rather than distributing earth or vile metals, let us represent the society of
> men, ready to share among themselves far superior riches, in a word . . . that
> adorable sex, towards which a penchant inseparable from our nature pushes
> us with such sweet violence. Here the number of things to be possessed is

about equal to the number of possessors. The poor man calms the hunger pangs of his stomach as well and at less expense than the rich man. But what means are there for these nineteen men to satisfy the pressing instinct of nature? Let us conclude that every man has an essential right to claim marriage . . . and polygamy is injurious to that right. (227)

Having reached a conclusion based solely on the attribution of certain "natural rights" to the male sex, Euxode abruptly swerves into a different direction. "Unless one is of the impertinent and ridiculous opinion that women are a creation inferior to men, equitable laws concerning marriage must maintain an absolute equality between the sexes; nature having already established an equality of number and having compensated the one sex by more sweetness and attractions for the strength with which it endowed the other" (246).

Numbers then dictated equality between the sexes, according to the mathematician Prémontval. He replied with indignation to those who turned to Islam for a more "natural" model of relations between men and women, castigating the "arabesque maxims of the partisans of polygamy," according to whom there ought to be "satisfactions of all kinds for one sex and mortifications of every sort for the other. Such maxims can be received among half-savage people who know no laws but violence and who act only in cruel and tyrannical ways. But that among civilized nations there should be men . . . philosophes and even Christians who dare to justify the principle, this is in truth the greatest frenzy in human reasoning" (277). Prémontval, like Montesquieu, presented arguments both in favor of and in opposition to polygamy. By concluding with an impassioned appeal for symmetry in marriage, however, Prémontval was asserting the existence of an ethical and social value higher than reproductive success, the equality of human beings in a country that prided itself on being civilized. Of course Prémontval was defining civilization in terms of equality, a standard that would have been rejected by both the Christendom and the Islam of his day. This view placed him in the minority of writers on the subject, even in Enlightenment France.[30]

The *Encyclopédie*

The *Encyclopédie* by and large takes the Bayle-Montesquieu tack on the polygamy issue, using it to tweak the devout with the Old Testament's polygamous Prophets, the Gospels's silence on the subject, and the modern

Church's insistence on the indissolubility of sacramental marriage. In Diderot and d'Alembert's great publishing venture, controversial entries are often subjected to a sophisticated system of multiple formulations, by which certain attitudes, interpretations, and propositions are advanced in rhetorically unstable contexts, contradicted in other texts, and eventually consigned to a level of ambiguity that invites readings subversive of established authority. In the case of polygamy more than one kind of authority was so undermined. Three entries entitled "Polygamie" appear in the *Encyclopédie*, as do one "Polygame," one "Polygamistes," and one "Polyandrie." In addition, comments on the subject appear in other entries such as "Mariage," "Malabares," and "Femme."

The first polygamy entry, marked *Théologo & critique*, was written by the *Encyclopédie*'s most prolific contributor, the chevalier Louis de Jaucourt. The entire passage is devoted to parsing an enigmatic pronouncement of Lamech, the first polygamist mentioned in Genesis and, as we have seen, subject of Bayle's ruminations. It has no apparent bearing on the topic of plural marriages at all. The second entry, marked *Théolo*, is anonymous. It begins with a definition that is rather disquieting from the modern perspective: distinguishing between simultaneous polygamy, in which a man marries several women at once, and a successive kind, in which he marries them serially. As in the treatment of the words *divorce* and *bigamy*, to label second marriages, whether of the widowed or the divorced, as *polygamous* or *bigamous* is indicative of a wide conceptual gap between the way marriage was viewed under the ancien régime and its modern significance.

Jaucourt, however, used the category of *polygamous* to permit a much more disorienting critique of the whole institution of marriage. He established the obligatory distinction between a plurality of husbands—"something bad in itself, contrary to the principal objective of marriage, which is the generation of children"—and more than one wife, which was quite different and "not opposed to natural law or the first finality of marriage" (26:594). The rationale for the prohibition of polyandry could never, apparently, be repeated too often. It was reiterated at greater length in the passage under "Polyandrie." Here however, the anonymous author abruptly switched arguments to recount how among the "Malabares, women are authorized by the laws to have as many husbands as they please" (26:591), seemingly without any particular ill effect.

The text under "Marriage" goes further still. "In Arabia," according to Nicolas Lenglet du Fresnoy, five times imprisoned in the Bastille for writings offensive to the authorities, "several members of the same family have only one wife between them. In Lithuania noble women have a few concubines as well as their husbands. On the coast of Malabar, the nobleman's wives may have several husbands, although the latter may have only one wife" (21:76). The impression left by these entries is that while the *Encyclopédie* claimed to disapprove of it on demographic grounds, polyandry nevertheless had its place among the extant patterns of conjugality in the world. These casual references to marriages with multiple husbands were not buttressed by Montesquieu's assertions of climatic differences in the sex ratio and, in fact, would seem to make hash of that whole thesis, since the same climate could scarcely be attributed to both Lithuania and Malabar. The *Encyclopédie*'s penchant for piquant detail designed to undermine authority may have played a role in mentioning these examples of the dread practice.

The second, anonymous entry for "Polygamie" went over in detail the plurality of wives permitted by the law of Moses, noting that "the rabbis permitted the Israelites to marry as many as they could feed" (26:595), summarized *Polygamia triumphatrix* and its critics, and discussed Luther's tolerant view of the practice. The author concluded by returning to the Church's ambivalence toward second marriages in general, quoting St. Jerome's enigmatic commentary that "those who marry two, three, four, five and six times and even more are not condemned in the church, [and while] this repetition is not proscribed, it is not praised either" (26:596). The third treatment of "Polygamy" takes the reader on a world tour of polygamous peoples, pointing out the contradictions and inconsistencies of a great number of exotic matrimonial practices.

A different issue is raised, however, under the entry for "Femme," in which the author describes the negative effects of nonparity marriage on women: "The domestic servitude of *women* and polygamy result in a contempt for the fair sex in the Orient and finally render it contemptible. One may consult the excellent work on the *Esprit des Lois* on all these subjects" (13:927). The reader's conclusions after digesting this mixture of racy anecdote, religious injunction, demographic reasoning, and moral imperative are difficult to imagine. It would appear, however, that the certitudes of Catholic marital dogma have been cunningly trashed. The technique of juxtaposing multiple voices and conflicting opinions on a single topic, an elaboration of Bayle's system of notes and cross-references, creates an open-ended discourse, more likely to stimulate inquiry than to resolve issues. Whether the *Encyclopédie*'s collective view is that modernity ought to emphasize marital arrangements less constraining toward men or a greater equality between the sexes in marriage should emerge in post-Christian marriage is not obvious from these pages, since there is material to support either agenda.

Although Voltaire spoke up for polygamy in his essay "Sur l'Histoire générale," on the grounds that it must be beneficial to population, his remarks are probably best understood in the context of his lifelong Sinophilia, an infinitely advantageous position from which Catholic monarchical France could be bombarded with unflattering comparisons. After having extolled the Chinese for the Great Wall and their system of canals, he went on to praise their greatest achievement, an immense number of citizens, attributable to their prosperity and security. Contradicting Montesquieu, he claimed that not only China but all the countries of the East were both densely populated and polygamous. "Polygamy cannot be viewed as contrary to population," he insisted, "since India, China [and] Japan, where polygamy has always been accepted, are the most populous lands in the universe." To clinch his argument Voltaire turned to *Genesis,* that rich source of embarrassment to Christendom, maintaining that God permitted Jews to have more than one wife while promising them that "their race would be multiplied like grains of sand in the sea."[31]

To the fears of those foreseeing a shortage of women for some men under a polygamous system, Voltaire's reply began with an up-to-date reference to the surplus of males at birth. He pointed out, however, that war, "arduous professions, more murderous than war," and "debauchery," as well as "eunuchs and *bonzes*" (the clergy), probably ensured a surplus of women. Comparing European moral corruption to the rarity of adultery in the harems of the Orient, Voltaire ended his discussion of polygamy on a characteristic note of appreciation for the "tranquility" of the East as opposed to the exploitative aggression of colonialist Europe. Voltaire, the great antisystematic philosopher, predictably followed his own skeptical system, in which the plurality of wives in non-Christian societies could only be viewed sympathetically.

Voltaire's appreciation of conjugal diversity, as well as the kind of openended relativism practiced by Bayle, Montesquieu, and the encyclopdists, did not go uncensored by Catholic commentators. Jean-Baptiste-Louis Crevier, in his *Observations sur le livre de l'Esprit des Lois,* found Montesquieu's indifference to Christian morality, for example, reprehensible. If the

sex ratio were the only factor that determined the preference accorded polygamy in certain cultures, what about the certitudes of religion? Crevier
was unhappy that Montesquieu simply *reported* various marital usages
without registering appropriate moral sentiments. In a criticism applicable
to much of the philosophes' work, he declared that "it is not permissible to
speak of what is condemnable without condemning it. [Montesquieu] does
not justify polygamy but he suppresses the reasons that condemn it and he
presents those that can appear to certain minds to give it a tint of probability." What was even worse, according to Crevier: "If more boys are born
than girls, a woman will have several husbands! Never has anyone treated
this question so cavalierly. No legal scholar has ever spoken of a plurality of
husbands as a tolerable practice."[32] Catholic critics understood the effec-
tiveness of "philosophic" textual strategy: presenting subjects of moral controversy, like polygamy, without the usual framing discourse of denunciation permitted the unspeakable to speak for itself.

While they resented the advantages this technique of seemingly neutral
reportage afforded freethinkers, Church apologists were not above using
the same tactics themselves. The Jesuit père Jean-Jacques Dortous de Mairan, in a letter to a missionary in China, said that he thought the Church
should stay away from Providential explanations of demography. "These arguments that can cut both ways do more harm than good to religion," he
cautioned. Since the male/female ratio is about 50/50 in China, "we could
very well use that with the Chinese, to prove to them that the Christian religion, which forbids Polygamy, is in that respect closer to natural law and
justice than the [Chinese religion] that permits it."[33] On the other hand,
since, according to Mairan, China was overpopulated, it could be argued
that polygamy was providential, tending to limit undesirable demographic
increase, because a woman with only one-tenth of an interest in a husband
would have "far fewer children than ten women who each had their own"
(133). Thus Mairan felt the divine attitude toward population phenomena
was a subject best left alone.

Interest in polygamy increased in the 1760s and 1770s as more authors
addressed its supposed connections to population, although whether the
institution was viewed as natalist or denatalist depended on what other
agendas were being advanced. Certain commentators, like military theorist
Louis de Boussanelle, wished to reconcile Christianity with the lost privilege of the patriarchs by means of a newly phrased "purposes of marriage"
statement: "Since polygamy does not destroy the essence of marriage which

consists of the union of man and woman and it is not contrary to the principle objective of marriage which is the generation of children, God will always be free to dispense whomever he pleases from his laws as he has already allowed the Patriarchs, the prophets and the Saints of the Old Testament to take several wives." Besides, according to Boussanelle's largely respectful portrait of the female sex, polygamy had to be understood not so much carnally as a metaphor for divine truth. "All these Spouses devoted to David alone, according to Saint Augustine, symbolize the multitude of Nations formerly divided by the diversity of their cults and now reunited in Jesus Christ as their only husband."[34]

Both the theological implications and the mathematical underpinnings of the sex ratio were most carefully and thoroughly developed by the German theologian Johann Peter Süssmilch in *Die göttliche Ordnung*.[35] Süssmilch treated the problem at length, putting the debate into its European context and citing the numerous works that had appeared in German since Luther on polygamy and on related topics such as serial polygamy (or divorce) and concubinage.

Süssmilch was resolutely opposed to polygamy, claiming that the sex ratio is about equal and so a plurality of wives inevitably comes about at the price of a commerce in women tantamount to slavery; the other side of the coin would be castration for some males, an encouragement to "depravity" (homosexual practices) among men, and the possibility of polyandry. Süssmilch did not envisage polyandry in the kind of *folle marquise* mode of libertine fiction (as in Melon's *Mahmoud le Gasnévide* or Anaïs's harem in the *Lettres persanes*) but as the enslavement of one woman by a fratery of impoverished males who exploit her both domestically and sexually. Süssmilch was filled with admiration at the "Law established by the wisest of Creators" ensuring that "on the whole, the number of boys who are born is superior to the number of girls." Like Arbuthnot, he estimated the ratio at 105 to 100, reasoning that if there were more women than men it would lead to polygamy, which does not favor healthy procreation because "the men get worn out rapidly," echoing on a different note Montesquieu's impertinence in the *Lettres persanes*. Sodomy, castration, and sexual deprivation are visited on *some* men by the system of polygamy, and thus the wisdom of the Creator is demonstrated in providing the numerical basis of monogamy, which "avoids all these inconveniences."[36]

Süssmilch, after careful analysis of pages of statistics gathered from a variety of observers (Struyck, Nader, Graunt, A. Moivre) confessed he was

still puzzled by one question: Why were there more young women of mar-
riageable age than men? At last the Protestant pastor was able to discern
the Divine Plan in this numerical curiosity. The gender imbalance means
that not only is "every young man able to find a wife but a few young
women are left over for widowers who are still able to have children and see
to their upbringing" (2:507).

Polygamy, the Economic Opportunity: Comte Louis de Rantzau

With Louis de Rantzau's *Discussion si la polygamie est contre la loi naturelle
ou divine* in 1774,[37] a silent subtext of the populationist arguments for polygamy emerged into overt expression. Rantzau, a forthright apologist for
the aristocracy, was looking at the size of the indentured peasantry in countries like Russia and the state of Mecklenberg from the perspective of a
proprietor. As many other thinkers in France and elsewhere in Europe were
attempting to rationalize the practices of agriculture to increase returns on
investments, Rantzau was suggesting reforms in the marriage patterns of
serfs so that they might reproduce more profitably for their masters.

He argued for change in public policy, particularly in Russia and
Sweden, those countries of the North allegedly so depopulated owing to
the interdiction of polygamy. Although he dedicated his work to Catherine
II and Alexis d'Olechev, the empress's advisor, Rantzau's arguments, echoing Melon, Bayle, and those of Prémontval's "Ariste," went on to a systematic plea for plural wives in Western Europe as well as Russia. Rantzau did
not merely speculate on polygamy, as his contemporaries did; he actively
promoted its enactment into law, claiming its suppression was the effect of
Christian fanaticism: "I wish to examine Polygamy among these great im-
aginary sins," he said, "and see whether it is really against the law, natural or
divine, or whether that is not the invention of fanatics, who brought about
the suppression of Polygamy. It is not at all against the natural law, we can
assume it is as old as the world."[38]

Rantzau claimed that the main purpose of his work was to persuade the
"Princes of the North," notably Catherine and Frederick of Sweden, to legalize polygamy. Inverting the ancient maxim that measured the sovereign
by the number of his subjects, Rantzau claimed: "Nobody doubts that the
population of a State augments the felicity of the Prince," thus implying
that subjects in a monarchy existed for the sake of their sovereign's happiness rather than the other way around. Contradicting Montesquieu, he
stated that "as polygamy is the unique and surest way to populate a wilder-

ness, the Sovereign has a duty not to oppose it" (54–55). Rantzau dismissed female distress at this proposal in a few lines: "They'll get used to the new rules right away because few girls would prefer to remain virgins all their lives just because they don't want their husband to have the liberty of associating them with a few companions" (60). Rantzau envisaged a whole system of plural marriages organized along strict rules, among which he proposed that while gentlemen could take more than one wife, only serfs would be *forced* to do so, and nobles whose serfs reproduced well could rent or sell their excess offspring for profit.

Louis de Rantzau's work is instructive in the glimpse it affords of conflicting strands of population thought within the Enlightenment. He was not some Norman *hobereau* nostalgically clinging to the relics of an ancient nobiliary prestige in the face of poverty but rather a feudal physiocrat wishing to modernize the property base of the land-owning aristocracy by promulgating the most up-to-date retrogressive thinking. For if Rantzau labeled polygamy a time-honored male privilege, lost, like so much else of value, to the artificialities of contemporary civilized life, he also defined it as an economic reform to provide benefits for the future. The benefits, however, were not imagined as accruing to the *people* but to their masters, who would make vast fortunes by renting or selling the excessive peasantry off their estates.

Rantzau reminds us that the eighteenth century was a period during which slavery and serfdom were status quo in the Western world and were seriously defended, although the weight of public opinion was starting to shift against them. The *Encyclopédie* itself reveals the complexities of pre-Revolutionary thinking regarding institutions of involuntary servitude. In the entries for "Esclavage" and "Esclave," Lenglet du Fresnoy and the chevalier de Jaucourt, respectively, took a strong line of moral disapproval against the institution, relying on Montesquieu.[39] After tracing the history of slavery in various countries, Jaucourt declared categorically that he would show that "it is injurious to man's liberty . . . it is contrary to natural and civil law . . . it contradicts the forms of the best governments, and . . . it is in itself useless" (12:964). In this long disapproving discussion of slavery, Jaucourt referred to it at times as *servitude*. However, neither under the heading "servitude" nor under "serf" are there negative remarks in reference to natural or civil law. Lenglet pointed out without comment that forms of serfdom were still in existence in the Auvergne, in Burgundy, the Bourbonnais, the Nivernais, Berry, Vitri, and the Marche.

Polygamy, according to Montesquieu in the *Esprit des lois*, was not slavery, properly speaking, because slaves were instituted *for* the family, while wives were *in* the family. The condition of the wife in a harem, therefore, in his view, should be termed "domestic servitude." In the passage under "Polygamie," however, Lenglet du Fresnoy argued that while a plurality of husbands was "something bad in and of itself," that was not the case with a polygamy of wives, "which is in no way opposed to natural law" (26:594). Separating one form of involuntary servitude, specific to women, from general considerations applied to slavery, Lenglet exemplifies the ambivalence of the encyclopedists as they attempted to sort out the respective importance of universal principles versus specific privileges associated with masculinity and property.

Rantzau made no pretense of treating women or serfs fairly, no categorical imperative inhabits these pages. His program, based on his vision of natural law, while liberating male sexuality from the yoke of Church doctrine, would have subjected all individuals except property-owning males to a natalist regime of obligatory polygamy. While his program violates the moral values traditionally associated with the higher Enlightenment, it is rational, utilitarian in its way, and certainly devoid of the "superstition and fanaticism" attributed to the Catholic Church. Enlightenment mentality without Enlightenment morality pointed to a world of alleged reproductive efficiency justified by the profits of the propertied classes.

Another consideration was raised in Rantzau's essay, one that would become intensely popular among writers later in the century: to render marriage more fruitful it was advisable to suppress dowries. "There must be a law forbidding parents who have daughters and sons from impoverishing the sons by dowering the daughters," Rantzau demanded. "This way marriages will be founded on love and each man will try to unite with companions whose temperament & appearance suit him. For the interest of the State it's more important for men to be well off than for the fair sex to be rich." A class consideration overrode even Rantzau's gender priorities to some degree, however, since he would permit "a rich girl without a brother to make the fortune of some poor gentleman, known for his personal qualities, by according him her hand, and she may demand a legal promise in return that he will not bring in another woman during her lifetime" (67). Thus Rantzau recognized that polygamy degraded women, and he was prepared to permit the daughter of the gentry to be excused from sharing her husband, provided, of course, that she have no brother.

In conclusion, Rantzau remarks that while he was composing his book, a European sovereign was actually proposing legislation to legalize a plurality of wives: "The King of Sweden, Frederick, of the house of Hesse-Cassel, proposed to the Estates of his Kingdom to reestablish polygamy, and the two lower houses had really consented to it but the two higher orders were opposed to it for reasons I do not know, perhaps because the innocence of polygamy had not been sufficiently proven." (70–71). Even if Frederick's motives in bringing the possibility of legalizing polygamy to the attention of the estates had to do with dynastic considerations and the status of his bastard son, it is nevertheless significant that such a proposal could be made at all in a Christian country.

Cerfvol and Linguet

The indefatigable champion of divorce took issue with Rantzau in his *Article sur la polygamie, adressé à M. Le comte Louis de Rantzow à Woldoga*, four letters included in the *Radoteur* (1774). Cerfvol, whose works on divorce are discussed in chapter four, rejected Rantzau's argument that the "law of nature," signifying the observed (or imagined) behavior of animals, was the appropriate moral guide to human action. "There are those who believe they have done everything when they offer men rules of conduct derived from those of the animals [but] that is confusing the species and the faculties appropriate to them."[40] Cerfvol continued to favor divorce (serial polygamy, in the language of the *Encyclopédie*) while opposing the plurality of wives, or simultaneous polygamy. "Polygamy and divorce cannot coexist," he claimed, "it would open the door to the most shameful abuses and surrender one sex to the caprice of the other. What would become of the husband of three wives who hated him and whom he detested?" (74).

Cerfvol's sympathy was with the polygamous husband, who might find himself a detested minority of one in his own home. The authority usually conferred on the one male in relation to his several wives was reversed by Cerfvol to be labeled a disadvantage, thus revealing a kind of paradox in polygamous thinking. If the marriage of one man with one wife implied some level of parity between partners, a proliferation of wives showed evidence of their ontological demotion. On the other hand, a multitude of disaffected women within the household would leave the patriarch alone in the throng, and the more women he had married the more dangerously outnumbered he could become. The social and emotional meanings of numbers were central to the polygamy controversy, and Cerfvol invoked them again to provide his most important argument against a plurality of wives: "On the one hand the inertia and the vanity of a small group of men will keep thousands of women in sterility while on the other hand the reproduction of the people will be halted by the rarity of the feminine species" (77). Another facet of the arithmetic dissymmetry of polygamy conjured up the decisive argument against it: "if several women were given to one man, soon we would be reduced to giving several husbands to a single woman" (78).

The same year that Cerfvol contradicted Rantzau's claims for a plurality of wives, Linguet weighed in on the other side. The seraglio of Asia, so often decried since Montesquieu for its inhumane cruelty, was, in Linguet's view, much to be preferred to the convents of the West. If excessive women had to be locked up someplace, they were better off in the harem than in the "sterile colonies" of Catholicism. "At least they have one man to share among themselves, and a little something is better than nothing."[41]

Linguet's main point, however, was that despite the "inflated nonsense" of poets who insisted on referring to women as queens, the reality for women of the lower classes was a life of bleak poverty and back-breaking physical labor while upper-class women were either virtual slaves of their husbands or imprisoned in convents. "In Asia, at least, they care for and nourish the slave who was once loved in the seraglio" (70). While Linguet's paradoxical refutation of Montesquieu's thesis about Oriental despotism seems intended more to dazzle than to enlighten, he does bring to the question a sobering vision of women's lives in the West. Despite the Oriental despotism–Occidental liberty antithesis that Montesquieu had made so popular, according to Linguet, neither the daughters of the elite nor those of the poor were "free" in many meaningful ways.

The eccentric, self-educated, and prolific Rétif de la Bretonne (1734–1806) shared Linguet's view of women's oppression, but he found their universal lack of freedom more to be lauded than blamed. He was endlessly opinionated on the "reform" of sexual relations, ostensibly to bolster population. In his 1777 opus, *Les Gynographes,* he offered his version of the panorama of conjugal arrangements around the world, one worse than the next from the woman's perspective. This device, in which picturesque descriptions of female subjection and humiliation are piled up to form a mountainous mass of misogyny, was used by many writers as a prelude to arguments for polygamy in the West. Rétif's examples were especially sadistic:

The Angolese marry several women of whom the first enjoys great superiority over the others, to the point where she can sell them. Rarely do the men of Loangoa [sic] marry more than two or three women, who are less their wives than their slaves and who are loaded down with the entire weight of keeping the household. The Coresienne woman can scarcely regard herself as more than a slave since her husband, after having several children by her, can send her away with them without having to take care of her or them. Polygamy is permitted among the [Formosans]. They leave their wives when they feel like it. The Japanese have as many concubines as they wish . . . the least crime against modesty is punished by death by the offended husband.[42]

Rétif concluded his instructive travelogue by pointing out that the notion of *equality* in marriage was a symptom of civilized decadence. Like so many writers in the second half of the century, he claimed to be looking for the law of nature and finding it among the least developed populations. "The submission of the second sex to the first is principally established among the savage nations that are the least removed from nature: in this way it seems to us natural" (376). Particularly since Rousseau's first *Discours,* it had become fashionable to denounce civilization rather than congratulate it for having rejected the primitive. This argument, equating moral value with the archaic, was particularly congenial to populationist polygamy. Although all the philosophes resorted to extolling tribal wisdom and animal sanity at one time or another, ultimately the superiority of modern civilization over ancient tradition was not to be relinquished easily by the acknowledged proponents of Enlightenment. The baron d'Holbach objected to this kind of thinking: "They claim *it is necessary to return to primitive sources,* they do not see that it's returning to shadows, stupidity, troubles and violence."[43]

Moheau and Messance and Objective Analysis

In his *Recherches et considérations sur la population de la France* (1777), which J. Dupâquier termed "the first treatise on demography worthy of the name, with the exception of Süssmilch's *Göttlichte Ordnung,"*[44] Moheau is not certain about the exact numbers of men compared to women, but he disputes attributing any disparity to Providence. "We have seen that almost everywhere that census are taken there are more women than men," he observed, but "if Nature were following the interests of propagating the human race,

She would have made more women be born than men. But the order of production is the opposite and the masculine sex would predominate [if male mortality rates were not higher]." He estimates sixteen male births for fifteen female births but is uncertain about whether the climate has an influence on the natality differential.[45]

In 1766 and again in 1788, M. Messance undertook a systematic analysis of the data regarding the sex ratio in the parishes of a number of elections in France, including Lyon, the Auvergne, and Rouen. He found a ratio of 94.6 males to 100 females in France as a whole, with the proportion of males decreasing across the lifespan, conclusions from which Messance, like Moheau, was not interested in deriving evidence of God's intentions or the nature of polygamy.[46]

Carlo Pilati de Tassulo, in his *Traité du mariage* (1776), after pointing out the dangerous depopulationary tendency inherent in Catholicism, offered a strong defense of polygamy among the Jews of the Bible.[47] He was especially impressed with the wisdom of the rule Moses had established, permitting a *père de famille* to give his son a slave while waiting to make a suitable marriage for him. However, Pilati was pleased to note, when the son did marry, the concubine retained her rights to food and clothing. "This law was admirable," said Pilati, invoking a suddenly fashionable alarm, "because it prevented masturbation, so harmful to young people, without causing any disorder in marriage" (23). The legitimate wife maintained social superiority over the concubine, and, in Pilati's view, "such a law would be good for all countries" (24). The specter of a woman with a harem full of husbands continued to shake her Medusa's locks, as male writers never tired of voicing their indignation at the very idea. Pilati yet again refuted the dread polyandry thesis, threatening offenders with ostracism: "A proof that men will never permit a woman to have several husbands at once is that they do not even want their [widows] to remarry. Almost all Nations, ancient and modern, agree to regard with contempt, even aversion, second marriages for women" (25).

Pilati introduced a new objective into the list of marriage's finalities. "The objects of marriage," he announced, "are pleasure, generation, and the raising of children" (26). Putting pleasure ahead of procreation represents a real departure from the expressed priorities of the past, whether because by 1776 a new emphasis on individual happiness was making progress or because Pilati felt less constrained by reproductive ideology than his predecessors. He elaborated at great and somewhat incoherent length on Montesquieu's notions concerning the political dimension of patterns of matrimony, claiming that while "voluptuous" polygamy was allied with despotism, "austere" polygamy, involving the strict sequestration of women, inclined a society toward democracy. "Liberty for women," he warned, "would soon bring about a revolution in the government" (82).

The slippery issues of marriage, divorce, remarriage, multiple partners, and children's welfare are resolved in the most famous eighteenth-century natalist text besides the *Lettres persanes,* Diderot's stunning and strange *Supplément au voyage de Bougainville,* written in 1772 but not published until 1796, in which he went far beyond the century's arguments about reproduction, divorce, and polygamy to invent a new Utopian synthesis of morality, desire, and fruitful procreation. In this dialogue Diderot artfully blurred the distinction between divorce and remarriage, or serial polygamy, on the one hand, and simultaneous polygamy, on the other. The dialogue presented an island in constant need of repopulation because of a tribute owed to a neighboring island. In this fantasy, taking off from L.-A. de Bougainville's account in his *Voyage autour du monde* (1771), Tahiti had a moral system that permitted maximal libidinal freedom, provided that each sexual act was likely to lead to conception. Diderot had the ingenious idea of a country whose children were its only fortune. Rather than imposing a financial burden upon their parents, as they did in Europe, in Tahiti children were the only wealth. Since a sixth of the national product was earmarked for the children, parents with the most numerous progeny were the richest, and copulation had been promoted to an act of individual investment and collective patriotism. Sexuality was envisaged in a new framework here, one in a way appropriate to the mentalities of the dawning era of capitalist nationalisms. Diderot imagined a serial polygamy with a rather high turnover, a type of conjugality in which wives succeeded one another in more or less rapid succession, but one preserving, at least theoretically, the Christian parity of one husband, one wife (at a time) while affording stimulating erotic variety. Diderot's idea here was consistent with Montesquieu's suggestion that changing wives every year would have excellent results for population and the notions of Maurice de Saxe, who seriously suggested a five-year limitation on marriages. Diderot's Tahitians would never get bored with their wives' flesh because they could change partners as often as once a month. Divorce was accomplished with a simple farewell as couples were free to move on to other partners after the minimum cohabitation of one moon.

Diderot attempted to visualize the application of his Tahitian daydreams to the reality of Europe and concluded that sexual morals were good or bad depending *exclusively* on the demographic circumstances of a people, thus subscribing to Montesquieu's rule that "polygamy is a question of calculation." Where a sexual morality contradicted the overarching exigencies of population, it was harmful. For this reason, according to Diderot, the inhabitants of the crowded island of Formosa forbade women to give birth before the age of thirty-five and practiced crude abortion measures. It was not the desperate proto-Malthusian plight of the Formosans that fired Diderot's imagination, however; it was the exciting situation of the underpopulated Tahitians.

Unlike so many of his natalist compatriots, whose interest in the birthrate did not extend to the postpartum period, Diderot was emphatically intent on meeting the needs of children. As he had told Catherine that children should be raised by "the Republic," in the *Supplément* he stipulated that the entire island was devoted to taking care of all its offspring. Diderot thus reconciled the role of responsible adult fatherhood with maximal sexual liberation, or, to use a favored trope, he "combined the pleasures of vice with the honors of virtue," an impossible feat in Catholic Europe. As many modern commentators have noted, however, the price of his precarious synthesis of parental duty and libidinal fluidity was a Draconian punishment of infertile sex. By stigmatizing and exiling the sexually active infertile (especially female) members of society, Diderot's populationism compromised the great Enlightenment work of rehabilitating the passions and liberating the individual.

In this compelling little work, Diderot attempted to use populationism to reconcile some of the great polarities of his thought: the imperious need to press for the good of society as a whole and the equally urgent necessity of releasing individual human desire from its theological bonds. After the *Supplément,* Diderot would retreat from the attempt to synthesize libido and fertility into one coherent public policy, turning inward toward the troubled interrogations about human sexual needs in his later "secret" works, *Le Rêve de d'Alembert, Le Neveu de Rameau,* and the *contes.*

Bernardin de Saint-Pierre and Providence

In 1784 the great Christian apologist, abbé Jacques-Henri Bernardin de Saint-Pierre, mulling over polygamy, put the sex ratio to work proving the truth of the Christian religion. The very fact that the percentage of males in the population had only recently and uncertainly been identified demonstrated the superiority of Christianity over its rivals: "All [other] religions grant men a plurality of women in marriage whereas ours has permitted only one, well in advance of the discovery that the two sexes are born in equal numbers."[48] Bernardin de Saint-Pierre measured the length of animal gestations in various climates, concluding that the hotter the climate, the shorter the pregnancy, except in humans. "White women and negresses all carry their babies nine months, just as in France . . . This observation is very important because it proves that man's body is not subject to the same laws as the rest of the animals. It demonstrates a moral intention in Nature" (295). The abbé thus rejects Montesquieu's categorization of man as an animal whose moral character is in fact determined by natural phenomena. For Bernardin de Saint-Pierre, nature, under God's direction, provides for the moral improvement of men to the extent that they read her wisely. He sees a most original divine purpose behind the sex ratio, perhaps in support of empire: "This moral intention is apparent in the nearly equal proportion of births of the two sexes, and even the small difference because the North compensates for the South. There are a few more women in the South and a few more men in the North, as if Nature wished to invite the most disparate people to come together through marriage" (295). It was fortunate for the peace of mind of European men that the North-South differential wasn't the other way around. In any case, he argues, "it is not climate but education and opinion that form morality" (299).

In 1785, the *Mémoire sur la population de la France* of P.-A. Laplace (1707–1793) more or less definitively established the statistical evidence of the sex ratio in France. Interestingly enough, Montesquieu was wrong about the numbers of male versus female births, just as he was mistaken in his whole argument concerning the depopulation of the modern world.[49] From faulty data, his "fertile error," as Jean-Claude Perrot named it, he put together a devastating critique of Christianity on supposedly objective grounds and, incidentally, if not an apology, at least an ambiguous explanation of both polygamy and polyandry, one which seemed to stimulate the hopes, fantasies, fears, and reflections of generations of male writers.

Statistics and Political Argument

The incorporation of statistical methods and findings into the workings of an increasingly reform-minded government marked the decades preceding the Revolution. Eric Brian has traced the evolutionary process that led

France from being an absolute monarchy whose demographics were, in principle, the king's secret, to a modern state, dependent on the independent scientific integrity of its census and the data derived from it.

The administrations of Louis XV and Louis XVI engaged in decades of efforts to acquire the knowledge of population that Vauban, Fénelon, and Boisguilbert had so ardently pled for. Statistical theory and techniques evolved from quaint primitivity to moderate sophistication in the decades separating the *Lettres persanes* from the end of the ancien régime, as census projects were attempted by nearly every head of the treasury (*contrôleur général*). From Treasurer Dayton's publication of data about those paying the "gabelle," or salt tax (1726) to Orry's directives asking provincial administrators (*intendants*) for information in 1730 and 1744 to Bertin's project in 1762 and L'Averdy's in 1764, the administration demonstrated an ongoing effort to lay its hands on solid demographic data. Had the admonitions of Vauban and Montesquieu and all the rest played any role in spurring the government to go after demographic data? A comment from L'Averdy, the *contrôleur général* in 1762, would seem to indicate that the upper echelons of the royal administration wished to refute the depopulationist charge. According to L'Averdy, a certain provincial administrator, "prompted by assertions published in a number of writings about the decline in population and the increase in taxes and having had the zeal and the good sense to verify if these declarations were founded in regard to his district, recognized that they were pipe-dreams."[50]

Assembling reliable data was far from easy. Provincial administrators encountered suspicion and defiance on the part of the peasantry whose numbers they were charged with reporting. The *intendants* La Michodière (L'Auvergne) and Montyon, with their respective secretaries Messance and Moheau, experimented with a "universal multiplier" of births, obviating the need for a door-to-door headcount of population. The abbé Expilly continued efforts to get all the parishes in the country to provide reliable data on births, marriages, and deaths, but he was never able to publish the seventh volume of his *Dictionnaire* with all the appropriate statistics demonstrating a net rise in the nation's numbers. E. Esmonin suggested that the reason may have been "the hostility of the philosophic party which could not tolerate an intellectual daring to demonstrate that France was not depopulating, however badly governed it was said to be."[51]

Royal efforts to count the King's subjects continued through the end of Louis XVI's reign, under Terray and Turgot, yielding results for all of

France from 1770 to 1784 and partial data for 1770–89. The conclusion among experts and critics of the regime was that the government's statistics were flawed. J. Necker's attempt at an estimate relied on a faulty universal multiplier. Laplace, specialist in the calculus of probabilities, proposed that the Academy of Sciences do a census on a million people to get a true universal multiplier. As usual, the people themselves were hostile to outsiders asking questions and resisted the census. Although not fully realized, by the end of the ancien regime, Vauban's wish that the king know the number of his subjects had been included in the objectives of the state's administration.[52]

Notwithstanding this resistance to being counted, the French continued to argue more and more subjects on demographic grounds. One of the few in the eighteenth century to express dubiety about the application of statistics to moral issues was the great mathematician Condorcet: "On would think at first glance that a science which proceeds by numbers and rules of calculation is exempt from all charlatanism,—not in the least," he cautioned. "Clever men rightly count on the ignorance of people, they understand the infallible effect produced by a group of seven figures, an effect that can be greatly augmented by spelling out the word 'million'. I see . . . sensible people, who as soon as they come upon numbers in a book of political philosophy, feel all ready to believe as if by a kind of magic."[53]

Condorcet's skepticism was not shared by the public in general at the end of the eighteenth century. As the certitudes of religion lost their absolute authority, the rule of numbers laid claim to the prestige once enjoyed by revelation.

CHAPTER SIX

Rousseau and the Paradoxes
of Reproduction

Damned by the standard of fruitfulness and multiplication, threatened with invasion by the burgeoning Protestant states, and called unequal to his biological duties, the eighteenth-century Frenchman saw his masculinity treated with contempt by numerous authors in his own nation.[1] It is difficult to imagine a narrative containing a more unnerving message than the repeated story of demographic disaster caused by the Frenchman's poor performance as a man. To the extent that the relentless language of impotence, castration, effeminacy, disease, immorality, and failure was internalized, it nourished the guilty apprehension of an age. Depopulation anxiety called forth not only political solutions but eventually a personal redeemer as well.

From the great philosophes like Montesquieu, Diderot, and Voltaire to the least scribblers of ephemera, vast numbers of ambitious writers until the end of the eighteenth century seemed impelled to propose cures for France's alleged reproductive crisis, whether actually subscribing to its reality or not. But within this throng of prescribers to the infertile body politic was the one name most famously associated with children and family in pre-Revolutionary France. Jean-Jacques Rousseau's responses to the issues differed radically from those of his peers, though less in the messages conveyed than in the jarring personal intensity he brought to bear on issues of human reproduction and national interest. Whether too few people lived in France, whether conventional Catholic marriage was suffocating national libido, whether French men were too selfish, or too corrupt, or too effete to father families—these were for Rousseau not just philosophical issues and useful arms in the political battles of the day but deeply felt accusations, calling forth impassioned responses.

The textual postures assumed by Rousseau in his efforts to encompass human reproduction within his world-view are represented throughout his writings, from the *Second Discours* to the *Rêveries d'un promeneur solitaire*.[2]

A coherent whole can be perceived only by looking past what appear to be rational contradictions to an underlying, intermittently conscious unity. His writings about population, sexuality, and family are related less by logical postulates than by their common function of placing the author on the highest moral ground, from which criticism of Rousseau's procreative delinquency could be deflected onto some other body. His writings turn the attack away from himself, pointing the finger toward faulty governments, corrupt society, disruptive religion, and inadequately controlled women; his list of indictments included most of the usual eighteenth-century demographic culprits. The galvanizing emotional fervor of his writings, however, elicited new responses in his readers, ranging from instant partisanship to dismay.[3] His numerous self-contradictions disturbed many of his contemporaries, while others insisted on the ultimate integrity of the Rousseauvian vision.[4] Jean Starobinski points to an underlying coherence in the Rousseau oeuvre, a kind not usually associated with conscious thought, all the more powerful for being inaccessible to reason.[5]

The questions I address in this chapter are, What counsel, conscious or otherwise, did Rousseau's readers find in his references to population, marriage, and parenthood? and What did they make of his pronouncements? His rational lapses, so often debated from the eighteenth century to the present, did not seem to render Rousseau's preachings any less influential to great numbers of his contemporaries, as various constituencies among his disciples adhered to one or another of his positions, seemingly unmindful of his own self-refutations elsewhere in his work.

Autobiographical Allusions and Silent Mandates

Rousseau's population positions intimately involve the preoccupations with reproduction revealed in his autobiographical writings. As he so movingly recounts in the *Confessions,* he lost his mother at birth and at age ten was abandoned by his father. As an adult, he left the five children born to him and Thérèse, his illiterate servant-mistress, between 1745 and 1755, at the foundling home.[6] Throughout the corpus of his political and fictional writings, the questions of children, parents, responsibility, and population increase emerged as hot zones of personal uneasiness and conflicting energies. A curious dual structure contains the fraught topics, marked by a series of unequivocal public imperatives, which are in turn punctuated by certain absolute but unspoken dictates. These "silent" directives, which remain immutable although implicit, warn that population growth is dangerous to the human race and the family should not form, or, if it does form, it must not endure. On the other hand, the manifest messages of his works after the *Second Discours* consistently endorse the opposite points of view.

Faithful to the unstated dictates, Rousseau's fictional families are doomed: in his novel purportedly in praise of domestic life, *La Nouvelle Héloïse*, Julie loses St. Preux's child to miscarriage and eventually dies herself, leaving motherless the children she bore the husband she was so reluctant to marry in the first place, the baron de Wolmar. Her friend Claire is a widow who refuses to remarry. St. Preux's friend, milord Bomston, cannot decide between two women and so remains a bachelor on the advice of St. Preux, who himself, of course, never marries. Mary Trouille comments: "despite all Rousseau's arguments against celibacy as unnatural and anti-social, and despite his fine speeches celebrating family life as the foundation for the moral regeneration of society, not a main character is married when the novel ends."[7]

As for the protagonist of *Emile,* his educational fiction: "Emile is an orphan. It doesn't matter whether or not he has his father and mother" (4: 267). His upbringing is left to his tutor. When Emile himself becomes a father, he decides that "considering only the interest of my son I saw that I had to leave him to his mother" (4:910). Sophie, the mother, then dies, as does the son. Rousseau's ambivalence is epitomized in two successive letters between milord Edouard Bomston (St. Preux's friend) and Wolmar (Julie's husband). The British peer relates how he used to believe that all men had a procreative debt to the species and to the nation, but he had changed his mind. "The obligation to marry is not common to all men," he writes, it depends on the place one occupies in life. "It is for the people, for the artisan, for the villager that celibacy is illicit: for the orders that dominate the others . . . and who are always only too well filled, it is permitted and even appropriate" (2:654). Bomston's cynicism, perhaps intended only to hide a broken heart, is answered by Wolmar with the comment that "life is a gift that one only receives on the condition of passing it on, a kind of entailment that must pass from race to race, and whoever had a father is obliged to become one." (2:656). Julie sees family less in terms of duty than of nature: "Man is not made to be celibate and it is unlikely that a state so contrary to nature does not incur some public or private disorder" (2:668). Aside from milord Bomston's misanthropic pronouncement, opinion as well as sentiment are for the most fervently profamily in Rousseau's novel—but the plot refuses to go along with the program.

A similar disconnect occurs between Rousseau's praise of family life in his writings and his abrupt coldness when one of his followers attempted to obey his injunctions in reality. When the prince of Wurtemberg and his wife tried to apply Rousseau's system to the letter in raising their little Sophie themselves, they were amazed to find their project treated rather contemptuously by the master, who recommended they turn the child over to a governess instead. Emma Nardi comments: "Instead of rejoicing that a well-off aristocrat should manifest a strong enthusiasm for his theses, he barely disguises . . . his obvious malaise."[8]

Each of the political works shows the signs of the same split in its own way. In Rousseau's *Second Discours,* in answer to the question, "What is the origin of inequality among men?" (1755), Rousseau directly challenged the philosophes' assumptions about the value of population increase and the intrinsic primacy of the family. His contrarian posture permitted him to scold the philosophes for moral obduracy much as they castigated the Church. This is the last of his works to assume an overt antinatalist position.

In general, the great precursors and founders of the Enlightenment had sought to undermine the authority of Catholicism by placing themselves above, not below, the standards of morality the Church attempted to impose. Locke, Bayle, and Montesquieu, among others, demonstrated how to undercut theological authority by laying claim to moral superiority over Christians, not by questioning the validity of the very concept of moral value.

Thus the individual liberty in society championed by Locke did not include libertine sexual behavior. In his two *Treatises on Government,* which exercised such an influence on the French philosophes, Locke postulated an original monogamous family founded on responsible parenthood. To buttress his arguments, he reached for the authority not of Scripture but of nature. Specifically, the mating patterns of animals showed how human beings were meant to behave. Locke pictured animal sexuality as an orderly submission to biological destiny, equally imposed on the human race, which was considered as a carnivorous species. In instinctive obedience to natural necessity, rather than in conscious acquiescence to divine command, men as meat-eaters coupled monogamously, protecting their mates and dependent progeny. Caring for one's child is not behavior to be decided upon rationally, Locke cautioned, asking: "What Father of a Thousand, when he begets a Child, thinks farther than the satisfying his present Appetite?"[9]

Tending the family is *instinctual* behavior, but one that has been wisely implanted in our beings by a benevolent Creator. For the "end of *conjunction between Male and Female*," said Locke, "being not barely Procreation, but the continuation of the Species, this Conjunction betwixt Male and Female ought to last, even after Procreation, so long as is necessary to the nourishment and support of the young Ones, who are to be sustained by those who got them, till they are able to shift and provide for themselves. This Rule, which the infinite wise Maker hath set to the Works of his hands, we find the inferior Creatures steadily obey." Our duties are determined by our physiology, not our desires, according to Locke. It seems that

> in those viviparous Animals which feed on Grass, the *conjunction between male and female* lasts no longer than the very Act of Copulation: because the Teat of the Dam being sufficient to nourish the young, till it be able to feed on Grass, the Male only begets but conserns not himself for the Female or the Young to whose sustenance he can contribute nothing. But in beasts of Prey the *conjunction* lasts longer . . . the Assistance of the Male is necessary to the Maintenance of their common Family, which cannot subsist till they are able to prey for themselves but by the joynt Care of Male and Female. (321)

Men and women were obliged to stay together longer than the other animals for the good of the young, whose "uncertain mixture, or easie and frequent Solutions of Conjugal Society would mightily disturb" (321).

Montesquieu was in agreement with Locke. Along with the frequently risqué observations enlivening the *Lettres persanes* and even the *Esprit des lois,* he presented the burdens of parenthood as man's duty, one inscribed into his reproductive role and essential to the well-being of his offspring and of society. The good of the State was inseparable from right sexual conduct: "One may regard public incontinence in a State as the worst of misfortunes and the *certain sign of a change in the Constitution*," he warned in the *Esprit des lois* (bk. 7, ch. 9).[10]

In this way, the new liberty of thought encouraged by the early philosophes won its rights to the city by demanding an exemplary sexual morality for the benefit of society, one in its own way as exigent as that of the Church for the grace of God. Philosophy could openly flirt with taboo subjects like divorce and polygamy, but only in the implicit context of responsibly exercised paternity. Philosophy, in its official representations (if not in its more intimate speculations or private penchants), was scarcely less rigid in its condemnation of erotic indulgence than was religion; all that had changed was the rationale behind the repression.

So from the point of view of untrammeled sexual liberty, man, or the masculine subject, did not gain all that much in trading religion for high Enlightenment moralism. Even where divorce or polygamy were recommended for the sake of pleasure, the pleasure itself was teleologically grounded in reproduction. Pleasure and duty were inevitably linked in public discourse, no longer because of Scripture but because they were so inscribed in our animal nature, programmed for maximal reproduction and ensuring that the fleeting contact became the enduring commitment.

Rousseau's efforts to depict his own intrinsic innocence and explain away his own behavior came like rain in a drought, bringing relief to those alienated by the intransigence of the two great competing systems of thought and moral value, both so tiresomely insistent on linking sex and enjoyment to reproduction and obligation. In the ensemble of his political works, beginning with the *Discours sur les Origines de l'inégalité (Second Discours)* and continuing with the *Essai sur l'Origine des langues,* the *Essai sur l'Economie politique,* the *Contrat social, l'Emile,* and others, Rousseau brought forth a series of argumentative postures that operated to uncouple masculine libido from paternal duties while at the same time preserving a sense of moral superiority. Rousseau's work was not suggestive—he did not offer the reader a shared transgressive experience for the sake of libidinal stimulation; he promised more than that. Read correctly, Rousseau allowed the male reader to disassociate himself as far as possible from the consequences of his sexuality and his connection to wife and child while still feeling "virtuous." Rousseau's arguments concerning sexuality and procreation passed through three distinct phases.

The *Second Discours* labeled the family itself unnatural. In a heartfelt paean to solitude, solipsism, and the single life, Rousseau refuted Locke's thesis that impregnating a woman somehow entailed looking after children. Like Locke, he returned to the animal state of our earliest ancestors, but, rather than attempting to ascertain the experiences of a primal progenitor, he imagined himself to *be* early man and described his own subjective reality with astonishingly moving eloquence. Looking directly into "nature," without permitting himself to be led astray by "facts" or "mendacious books," he found that the family was not a natural but a cultural phenomenon.[11] To Locke's claim that the first society was composed of the man, the woman, and the child, Rousseau opposed another narrative: man, attuned only to his own needs, had no rule other than the maintenance of his psychic equilibrium. Separating sexual pleasure from its reproductive consequences and sentimental entanglements, Rousseau announced self-absorption as the original human condition. Not only were love and the family artificial human inventions having no place in the pristine heart of the uncorrupted primitive, but the mere recognition of another human being was an ominous aberration. Instead of courting the woman who struck his fancy, man as unspoiled natural creature waited passively until aroused by a passing female: "He listens only to the temperament he has received from Nature . . . and for him one woman is as good as another" (3:158). Sexual desire, in Rousseau's scheme of things, not only did not have paternity as its aim, it was not even natural to men. It was instead extrinsic to his psyche, imposed on him by a woman.

Even so, what about the consequences of sex? Did not intercourse naturally lead to pregnancy? Had the father no stake in his children? Not according to Jean-Jacques, whose primitive man was unaware of any such association. While sex does lead to pregnancy, in a state of ignorance, the *idea* of sex does not lead to the *idea* of pregnancy, and without mental representation there is no obligation. Since arousal is only a "blind impulse, without any sentimental feelings," it "produces only an animal act." Once the need is satisfied, the two sexes no longer recognize each other, and even the child is nothing more to his mother as soon as he is able to fend for himself. Women were as antisocial as men in Rousseau's depiction. "There is no reason for a man to look for the same woman nor for the woman to look for the same man" (3:218), Rousseau maintained, in a note contradicting Locke's argument for a natural couple (147n).

Females mated impersonally, raised the resultant progeny with casual indifference, and got rid of them at the first opportunity. Rousseau attributed a mother's willingness to nurse at all to the physical pleasure of being suckled, assuring the reader that primitive children were able to move seamlessly from the breast to self-sufficiency because man was not naturally a meat-eater but a grazer. Much of Rousseau's argument hung upon this distinction. If the human being was assumed to be naturally carnivorous, one would have to imagine a child making the transition directly from feeding at the breast to hunting the beast. For anyone familiar with small children, the toddler capable of surviving alone in the wild on leaves and fruits is already a stretch. How much less conceivable is the notion of a just-weaned child tracking down an animal, killing it, and eating it? While Rousseau points out that man is capable of varying his diet according to circumstances (3:135), in a long note he explains how physiological evidence reveals that "having the teeth and the intestines of fructivores, man should naturally be placed in this class" (3:199n). [12]

If the child was but an undifferentiated extension of her own body until it climbed down and went off to gather nuts and berries for itself, the mother knew no affective bond either; still less did either one ever make it into the consciousness of our guiltless male ancestor.[13] While in the modern world, corrupted by the forces of civilization, the "moral aspect of love is an artificial sentiment, cleverly celebrated by women," in nature, or the authentic world, "the savage obeys only the physical side, he has no more moral attachment for one object than for another. Each one calmly awaits the impulse of Nature, yields to it without preference, more with pleasure than with rage, and, the desire once satisfied, all desire is extinguished" (3:199).

To Locke's claims that all male animals fight over the possession of their females, a postulate which would account for at least some kind of male attachment to his mate, Rousseau invoked the sex ratio, pointing out that in the absence of a limited season of rut in human females, this rule "is not applicable to the human species where the number of females generally surpasses that of males" (3:159). Thus it was malign society, not innocent nature, which insisted on the family, an artificial corrosive bond that introduced grief into man's simple, spontaneous, anonymous sexuality: "the duty of eternal fidelity serves only to create adulterers and . . . the Laws of continence and honor themselves necessarily extend debauchery and multiply abortions" (3:159) in Rousseau's view. He saw that crimes and sins were the acts not of men but of laws and rules. Where nothing was forbidden, transgression did not exist and man was free to enjoy himself without remorse.

Without any mental representations, "mother, father, child, home" were empty signs for undreamt-of relations; they did not exist as intrusive realities, and therefore men were happy. "I'd like someone to explain to me what kind of unhappiness could be experienced by a free being whose heart is at peace and whose body is in good health," said Rousseau (3:152).

Catastrophic Population Increase

With the notion of man as happy-go-lucky lone wolf came an almost visceral dislike of groups. As Marcel Hénaff comments, "Rousseau seems to have a veritable phobia about crowds."[14] His revulsion to close proximity with his fellow men, expressed from the *Second Discours*, at the beginning of his career, to the *Rêveries d'un promeneur solitaire*, at its end, was supported by a kind of demographic theodicy. Man's initial paradise came to an end in the *Second Discours* not because he disobeyed God's will but rather because he obeyed it. Being fruitful and multiplying led to reproductive excess: "As the human race extended itself, woes multiplied along with men" (3:165). Since men proliferate rapidly in a state of nature, said Rousseau, their pullulation soon brought primitive contentment to a close. The first disaster was a population explosion, turning the carefree hunter-gatherer into an anxious farmer. Freely expressed sexuality brought about overpopulation and the entrapment of the human race as space became scarce, since, as he states in *Emile*, "man is, of all the animals, the least able to live in a herd. Men crowded together like sheep would all perish in a very short time" (4:276–77).

At this point Rousseau was directly challenging the Enlightenment's axiom regarding the value accorded to population. While Voltaire and others offered apologies for sexual pleasure, supposedly as a biological inducement to man's supreme duty—procreation—Rousseau took the opposite tack, labeling fruitfulness and multiplication not blessings but curses on innocent primitive men. "If you think about the excessive population that results from a State of Nature, you'll realize that the earth in that state would have quickly been covered with men thus forced to be together" (3:222).[15] The family, born of the population explosion, accompanied man's fall from primitive innocence into civilized hell. While this narrative seems to have been deeply satisfying to many readers and profoundly offensive to the Church, it had the disadvantage of pitting Rousseau against natalism, an all but untenable position in mid-eighteenth-century France, especially for a man who was becoming known for having abandoned his children.

After the *Second Discours*, the antifamily arguments cease to appear overtly in Rousseau's works, although antagonism toward crowds continues to surface. In the *Emile* (1762), Rousseau announces that the family is natural after all, because "children are so weak and helpless that they and their mother would find it difficult to get along without the attachment of the father and the care that results from it" (4:797). According to Victor Goldschmidt, "It is useless to accuse Rousseau of contradiction" on this score, because Rousseau somehow proves that in the original state of nature women would not give birth to a second child until the first was self-sufficient, although why this should be is not really explained.[16] At any rate, the next phase of human existence resulted from the proliferation of mankind, the crowding together of masses now forced to use their wits in order to survive, "a new situation that brought the husbands and wives, the fathers and the children together into one habitation. Each family became a little society" (3:168), perpetuating itself endogamously.

Incest: The Uncertain Taboo

As incest could not have been forbidden in a "state of nature," according to Rousseau, neither was it interdicted during the presocietal period: "It was quite necessary that the first men married their sisters. In the simplicity of their ways, this usage continued without inconvenience as long as families remained isolated and even after the most ancient peoples came together."[17]

This silver era of isolated family units, scattered across the earth, perpetuated by incestuous reproduction, also came to an end because of increased population. As people pressed in on one another, as they started to compare themselves to others and engage in competition, they finally came to look outside the circle of their immediate kin for mates. Now began the third phase of collective life, as young people from different families gathered around the spring or the well, partaking in festivities and engaging in courtship, a development that culminated eventually in exogamy and the interdiction of incest,[18] for Derrida the moment of "rupture between nature and culture." Derrida further comments that Rousseau's idea of incest "makes no mention of the mother, only the sister."[19] Neither Derrida nor Rousseau even mention the most likely scenario, involving the father.

Rousseau stated in a famously hermetic passage that the law against incest "is no less sacred for being of human institution. . . . Without the taboo the most atrocious morals would soon bring about the destruction of the human race" (5:406). In that case the question arises of how the human race managed to multiply so abundantly during its supposed incestuous phase. Once again Rousseau seems to espouse diametrically opposed positions on a key problem. A great number of his followers, however, understood Rousseau to be teaching that "incest" was the prehistoric default mechanism for sexual congress and its suppression one more unnatural cross civilized man has had to shoulder.

Rousseau did not bring up the incest taboo in a vacuum. The eighteenth century was haunted by its implications: how it related to population growth, whether it was local and socially determined or rather universal

and hence "natural," whether the philosophes were in favor of it or opposed.[20] Montesquieu had presented a provocative tale of sibling love in the
Lettres persanes, which would seem to suggest that the taboo was strictly a
tribal variable. In the *Esprit des Lois*, however, he attributed the interdiction
to a "law of nature" prohibiting sexuality other than that of the parents
within the household. Yet he then qualified the observation, admitting the
existence of many exceptions and pointing out that "religious ideas often
push men into such errors," citing the Assyriens and the Persians, who
"married their mothers," and the Egyptians, who "married their sisters . . . a
delirium particular to the Egyptian religion."[21]

In the eighteenth century, however, the word *incest* evoked more than an
ethnological variable or an unconscious wish. Within the context of the
struggle against the hegemony of the Catholic Church over sexuality, incest
played an important role. The history of what marriages would be considered incestuous is a long and in some ways mysterious one. To the primary
taboo against mating within the immediate consanguineous family, the
Church gradually expanded the category of diriment impediments, defined
as those calling for the nullification of an existing marriage once discov-
ered, to wider and wider circles of "affinities," by the eleventh century going
so far as the seventh canonical degree of kinship. In addition to "natural relationships," the Church prohibited the wedding of relatives by "legitimate
affinities" (marriage) or by "illegitimate affinity" (that resulting from illicit
couplings) or by "spiritual affinity" (relatives of one's godparents or confessor or cathechizer, as well as a variety of other truly obscure categories of
persons and their kin), thus producing, in Jack Goody's words, "a vast range
of people, often resident in the same locality, that were forbidden to
marry."[22] The *Encyclopédie* passage for "Empêchements" listed eighteen
theoretical types of prohibited unions and referred to the existence of
another half dozen (12:236–39). Strict obedience of these rules made it ex-
tremely difficult for many people in isolated rural areas ever to find someone they could rightfully marry.

In the *Encyclopédie* under "Dispense" (Dispensation), however, listed
without comment were the enormous number of dispensations from the
interdiction, granted by the Vatican to the upper classes and by the Bishop
to the masses. The process of being accorded a dispensation was cumbersome, expensive, and resented. According to Voltaire, "A man can marry his
niece by permission of the Pope for a fee which I believe is normally forty
thousand écus, including small change. I have always heard that it only cost

monsieur de Montmartel 80,000 francs. I know those who have gone to bed with their nieces much more cheaply than that."[23]

The utility to the Church of an expanded definition of "incest"—from brother-sister marriage to that between a man and the cousin of his god-mother's husband's brother-in-law, was not limited to according pricey dispensations. In a world without legalized divorce, it was sometimes possible to obtain an annulment, permitting remarriage, if it could be demonstrated before the appropriate ecclesiastical authorities that the couple had unwittingly committed "incest," even the most attenuated kind. Flandrin explains how annulments for technical defects (*vices de forme*) proliferated in the Middle Ages, leading to "an extreme instability in marriages: either the 'incestuous' spouses were denounced by a rival, or one of them, tired of his partner, demanded the annulment of their union."[24] For these reasons the Fourth Lateran Counsel (1215) reduced diriment impediments to the fourth degree. Annulments for a *vice de forme*, however, continued to be possible, if very expensive, through the eighteenth century.[25]

Thus while the "incest" taboo may evoke an Oedipal prohibition and a problem in the prehistory of mankind, it also carried totally different practical significance under the ancien régime. At once, preposterous barriers to otherwise desirable unions, or de facto ecclesiastical divorces, both controlled by the Catholic Church, could be negotiated at a price. Among the philosophes, Catholic definitions of incest were increasingly being questioned by midcentury. Toussaint announced that morally incest was "nothing in comparison" with adultery and that, moreover, genuine incest was rare. "To offend the modesty of a sister of a mother, or of a daughter; or to lend oneself to the lascivious advances of a son, father or brother: these are the only true incests, nature knows no others & the carnal commerce between distant relatives is only incestuous in name. These artificial crimes owe their origins to arbitrary regulations, & formal contraventions of the pure law of nature."[26]

In this context Rousseau's specific identification of the incest taboo as signaling the end of natural, free sexuality and the beginning of a burdensome regime of complicated, artificial, intrusive interference with human libido rang many bells, providing a theoretical structure for the resentment many people experienced and another vehicle for anti-Catholic sentiment. Rousseau had elaborated a genealogy of human misery going from man's pristine sexual solipsism to the incestuous family, rendered somehow necessary by excessive population, to eventual exogamy, accompanied by property, labor, slavery, and universal grief. He had, however ambiguously, placed incest under the sign of nature rather than sin, a taxonomic innovation appreciated by many of his followers.

Violence

Relinquishing incest, however, was not the only price men had paid for their fall into civilization, as Rousseau demonstrated in *Emile*. Sexuality in a "pure state of nature," it seems, came with its own set of rules, which could not be ignored with impunity. Not only could men find partners without regard to blood relationships or still less to spiritual ones, but "nature" also dictated that men be aggressive and women be passive in those crucial but delicate moments when sexual congress is negotiated. "In the union of the sexes each one contributes equally to the common goal [conception], but not in the same way," Rousseau cautioned. "From this diversity arises the first assignable difference in the moral relations between them. One [sex] must be active and strong, the other passive and weak; it is necessary that one desires and is able; it suffices that the other not resist too much" (4:693).

What does it mean for a woman not to "resist too much"? In a note Rousseau explains that "phoney, enticing refusals are common to almost all females, even among the animals, and even when they are most disposed to give themselves. You would have to have never observed their strategy to disagree with that" (4:694). Here Rousseau does not seems to be "putting away all the facts" but,[27] on the contrary, claiming authority based on his observations of animal sexual behavior. He announces finding ubiquitous male violence and female pretense of resistance, applying this paradigm to human behavior. Nor is this a passing thought; Rousseau develops a whole mini-essay, devoting considerable space to detailing the duplicity of women, who pretend to repel men's advances while actually conjuring them. "How much skill does she not need to make him take what she's burning to give?" he asks (4:695). This great divide between men and women is not a matter of culture but of nature: "The attack and the defense, the audacity of men, the modesty of women, these are not conventions, as the philosophes think, but natural institutions which it is easy to approve and from which all other moral distinctions are easily deduced" (4:696n).

It should not be inferred, however, that Rousseau actually was offering an apology for rape, because, in point of fact, rape in his scheme of things probably did not exist. "The freest and sweetest of acts does not allow real violence, nature and reason are opposed to it," Rousseau reassured his readers, "nature having endowed the woman with as much strength as necessary to resist when she wishes; reason because violence is brutal and a child would have no father if all men could usurp his rights" (4:695). "Anyway," says Rousseau, continuing his learned update of an ancient alibi, "nobody is talking anymore about violence now that it is so unnecessary and that men no longer believe in it" (4:696).[28] The same point is made in the *Nouvelle Héloïse:* "The attack is in general livelier than the defense, that is the intention of the Conserver of nature." (2:453). With the Conserver of nature on the side of the aggressive male, Rousseau as disabused man among men demonstrated that rape was at once justifiable and impossible.

Rousseau's implicit antifamily agenda underwent a series of transformations during the most productive phase of his career. In the *Contrat Social,* he announced that "the oldest and only natural society is the family," which would appear to reverse the position of the *Second Discours.* However, he also pointed out that in nature "the children remain attached to the father only so long as they need him to survive. As soon as this need ceases, the bond is broken. The children, exempt from the obedience they owe the father, the father exempt from the care he owes the children, all equally regain their independence" (3:352). In this scheme of things, man went from being a law unto himself, without obligation to his offspring, to surrendering himself to the State, which would assume responsibility for the children. The male citizen of the ideal State would in a sense be freed from the yoke of paternity almost like the primitive loner in the woods, because the State would take over the function of the fathers: "the education of children ought all the less be left to the lights and prejudices of their fathers since it is more important to the State than to the fathers . . . the State remains and the family dissolves," he claims in the *Economie politique* (3:260). Rousseau systematically coopted the language of family for that of nation, claiming that if children of the State "are surrounded by examples and objects which speak to them ceaselessly of the tender mother who nourishes them, of the love she has for them, of the inestimable benefits they receive from her, and of the return they owe her, let us not doubt that they will learn to love one another like brothers, never to want anything but what the society wants . . . to become one day the defenders and fathers of the nation whose children they for so long were" (3:261). *Mothers, brothers, fathers, children,*—these words are repossessed by Rousseau and deployed in a nationalistic context to lend weight to an ideology freeing the individual from familial responsibility and turning it over to the providential State.

For Rousseau, the idea of individual responsibility itself was deeply distasteful. As he recounts in the *Rêveries d'un promeneur solitaire*, "I saw that to do good with pleasure, I had to act freely, without constraint, and doing good lost it sweetness as soon as it became a duty for me" (1:1053). From the lap of mother nature to the embrace of the fatherland, Rousseau's male subject would know liberation from the annoying parental obligations and restrictions imposed by both the Church and the philosophes.

Just as Rousseau first declared the family artificial, then called it the only natural society, and finally imagined it superseded by the State, he also executed a double volte-face on the population issue. Having blamed man's fall into society on the multiplication of the human race, he goes on to proclaim in *Emile* that "there are two easy and simple rules for judging the relative merits of governments. One is population. In all countries that depopulate the State is tending toward its ruin, and the country which populates the most, even if it is the poorest, is infallibly the best governed" (4:851).[29] Here Rousseau parts company with Montesquieu, Voltaire, and other skeptics who asked whether the essential charge of the government was the happiness, rather than merely the number, of its citizens, joining the ranks of hard-core populationists like Mirabeau.

In the *Contrat social* Rousseau postulated a more nuanced relationship between population and the well-being of man, this one based on the institution of the State. Multiplication in this work has moved under a new sign; it no longer necessarily brings woe; it is beneficial or harmful to a nation according to the amount of land available for agriculture. In a kind of pre-Malthusian formulation, Rousseau prescribes the optimal relationship between resources and population: "Men make the State and the land nourishes men; thus the relation is that the earth should suffice to support the inhabitants and that there should be as many inhabitants as the land can nourish" (3:389). Here Rousseau is in step with Mirabeau's program to see every last acre in France under cultivation. The reasons are to be found in geopolitical reality: "If there is too much land . . . that is the cause of defensive wars; if there is not enough, that is the cause of offensive wars, the State finds itself at the discretion of its enemies [for subsistence]."[30] Thus the State, in addition to taking responsibility for the children, ought to control the reproduction of its citizenry to be sure they are neither too numerous nor too few.

Yet Rousseau insists on the meaning of absolute, not relative, quantity in the *Contrat social*, claiming that "the surest sign of the [people's] conservation and prosperity . . . is their number and their population. Don't go looking any where else for this much disputed sign. All things being equal, the Government under which, without extraneous means, without naturalizations, without colonies, the Citizens multiply the most, is infallibly the best" (3:420). He will make the same point in his advice to the Poles: "The infallible natural effect of a free and just government is population. The more you perfect your government the more you will multiply your people without even thinking about it" (3:1005–9).[31]

Following Rousseau from his *Second Discours* through his last writings, we see that he has done two things: first deploring population growth then rehabilitating it, he transforms it from natural disaster into the hallmark of good government, falling into step with the most aggressive natalists among his contemporaries.

Marcel Hénaff, among the commentators looking for a logical coherence to Rousseau's demographic thought, has explained the abrupt reversal on the subject of population by claiming that it is only the excess of people *in the city* that Rousseau had originally denounced, not the increase in rural areas. While Hénaff's observation is valid up to a point, even this compromise was subject to hedging. For example, in his *Projet pour une constitution pour la Corse* (1765–66), Rousseau prescribed a "rustic system" of insular self-sufficiency (3:907), eliminating trade, minimizing cities, and proscribing the arts, one that would preserve Corsica in its "natural, healthy state," remote from the "false luster" of neighboring countries (3:950). However the same problem emerges here. If Corsica accepted Rousseau's "rustic system," the inevitable result of such good government, according to his "great first principle . . . to extend and multiply the population" (3:928) would be a demographic surge. The problem would then be how to reconcile the virtuous proliferation of a scattered rural people, preserved from the moral degradation sweeping the rest of Europe owing to the sinister results of burgeoning population. Rousseau was sure that his system would cause Corsicans to multiply to such an extent that the amount of arable land would soon prove insufficient. At that point, he declared, "the country will be forced to establish colonies or change its government" (3:907). Once saturated with population, the sign of good government, Corsica would be obliged to introduce "industry, commerce and the Arts," to occupy the excessive population. Rousseau's system would lead to the adoption of the very aspects of European society he so furiously had denounced in his earlier writings.

In the period between 1756 and 1771, Rousseau labeled demographic expansion a negative omen, then a positive sign, and finally both simultaneously, while he escorted the family from its unnatural beginnings through its unsatisfactory apogee to its eventual usurpation by the State.

Rousseau's Regeneration of Family

The tale of shifting values does not stop here. At nearly the same time he was first damning and then praising population growth, Rousseau was creating a vast prescriptive glorification of domestic happiness, reinventing it and endowing it with new procreative vigor, even as he antithetically dismantled families. La Nouvelle Héloïse and Emile, in which marriage proves so elusive and fleeting, nonetheless offer detailed blueprints for a new vision of family life, a sort of naturally artificial construct that would demonstrate to the world at once the value of his "land of dreams" (2:693) and prove that, he, Rousseau, "was not an unnatural father" (1:1086).[32]

His description of the new, idealized, prolific family, in which women were strictly defined by their roles as wives and mothers, had not only a personal significance but a crucial political message as well. Sporadic disapproval of women's extramural existence had peppered the populationist controversy ever since the Lettres persanes. It took Rousseau, however, to capitalize on the opportunity afforded by demographic discontent to put women "in their place" in a way that offered a new, proto-Republican vision of masculinity. As Madelyn Gutwirth has demonstrated, the political and cultural elite of the ancien régime came strangely draped in the trappings of rococo femininity: "Insofar as its forms and uses expressed the gentle, civil, masculine tastes of a society whose official fable was its obsessions with pleasing women it came to be identified with them."[33] Pre-Revolutionary France was saturated with aesthetic homage to female beauty, its political life was inextricably allied with the influence royal mistresses exerted over Louis XIV and his grandson, and the aristocratic male, in lace and velvet, was himself fitted out in ways more suitable to a great courtesan than to the member of a warrior caste.

Rousseau's brilliant solution to the failure of national fertility was to attack the power elite through its women. The trouble with French population was, above all, French marriage, Rousseau argued, which had been ruined by the unnatural, spoiled, selfish behavior of women, who spent their time at the opera, showing off their figures, holding forth at salons, and flirting with other men, rather than staying home, obeying their husbands, and breast-feeding their children. Although the campaign had long been waged to encourage mothers to nurse their infants and avoid sending them out to wet-nurses, it was Rousseau who formulated the plea in such heart-wrenching, guilt-inducing terms that women from all levels of society took up the cause and helped make breast-feeding widely, if fleetingly, fashionable in France.[34] If only women were reformed, Rousseau admonished, all else would fall into place, putting an end to France's birth deficit. Of course Rousseau's fulminations could have only applied to a tiny upper class of privileged women, since the overwhelming majority of the poor led lives remote from the froufrou and indulgences of Paris or Versailles. In Rousseau's indictment, nonetheless, it was the French woman in general who had undermined the family and driven men away from their "natural" paternal role, and it was up to her to correct that sad state of affairs.[35] The reform of the frivolous sex, he claimed, would lead to the establishment of a proper family hierarchy, one naturally dominated by the central figure, the source of authority and the deity before whom the household knelt, the father. He described the way the patriarch ought to be treated: "The father of a family who finds happiness in his home is paid back for his on-going efforts by the continual enjoyment of the finest feelings known to nature. Alone among mortal beings, he is master of his own happiness because he is happy like God Himself, without wishing for more than he possesses" (*La Nouvelle Héloïse*, 2:467).

His wife, charged with maintaining this paradise on earth, should be dependent on the paterfamilias to the point of seldom leaving the house. "The real mother of a family, far from being a woman of the world, is scarcely less reclusive at home than a nun in her cloister" (4:737), Rousseau announced. While previous authors, particularly Catholic moralists like Fénelon, had urged modesty, sequestration, and obedience for women, Rousseau repackaged the vision as a reform at once patriarchal and natalist. His vision is not that of the Church—in fact he blames Christianity for discouraging marriage because its conjugal code is so severe that women have become intolerably ill-tempered.[36] "They banished everything from marriage that could make it attractive to men" (4:716).

Rousseau repeatedly expands upon his ideal gendered dichotomy, insisting that the world itself is naturally divided into two spaces: the house for her, where she may reign in the gladness of her heart, all the rest for him. "As soon as [young Greek girls] were married, they were no longer seen in public, shut up in their houses, they limited their activities to the household and the family. This is the way of life that nature and reason prescribe to the sex; from mothers like this are born the healthiest, the most robust, the most well-built men on earth" (4:705).[37] The sons should be sturdy, but for their mothers things were a bit more complicated: "Women should not be robust like [men] but for men, so that the men born of them would be robust too" (4:704). Only relatively robust and not too mentally acute either; Rousseau disapproved of women reading and writing. His Sophie had gotten through only two books in her life at the time of her marriage. Woman's eternal mission is not the life of the mind but the production of bodies, at least four per woman, says Rousseau, to keep the "species from perishing."[38]

Conjugal Debt Canceled

This scenario did not seem to enrage women readers, as one might assume, but, on the contrary, engaged the admiration of many. Mary Trouille points out that "Rousseau's eighteenth-century women readers often reacted with tremendous enthusiasm to his writings—and particularly to the ideals of domesticity and sensibility set forth in *Julie* and *Emile*."[39] But in addition to a flattering, sentimental portrait of the beloved mother reigning within her home and exercising "empire" over her devoted quasidivine husband, Rousseau offered women another prize that has received less attention: the repeal of the law of conjugal duty.

The *dû conjugal* had long been a cornerstone of Catholic marriage doctrine. Although in other respects the male prerogative dominated (*mulieres subjectae sint viris suis*), in regard to sexual union husband and wife were held to exercise equal rights. In the first Epistle to the Corinthians, Saint Paul insisted that "The wife has no authority over her proper body, it's the husband, and in the same way, the husband has no authority over his own body, it's the wife,"[40] and this theoretical parity was maintained through the eighteenth century. Flandrin believed that the equality of the two rights was only apparent, since the husband was entrusted with discerning the signs of desire in a wife who, for reasons of propriety, could not express such wishes directly.[41] François-Xavier Cuche, on the other hand, however, claimed that "generally speaking the Catholic church has defended the wife against the husband in conjugal matters."[42] This was not the language of theologians of the early modern period, who made the false symmetry of the conjugal debt abundantly clear. The payment of conjugal debt placed many women in the cruelest of quandaries, for around six months postpartum she ran the risk of getting pregnant again and having to cease breast-feeding, putting the life of her newborn child in danger. The negative effects on her own health of such frequent pregnancies posed another threat. The Church was adamant on the point, however, maintaining that the husband's sexual needs took priority over the health of the child or the mother, because if frustrated he might be led into mortal sin.

Blessèd Saint François Xavier (1506–52) made it clear to père Barze that women penitents should not be excused from their marital duty:

> When women swear to you that they'll live much more happily and pay more attention to the service of God if they can be rid of their husband's company, don't believe it . . . the husbands would have a right to be offended . . . take care not be seen as too much the partisan of women (that would be a very dangerous imprudence). I would demonstrate to women the respect that they owe husbands and describe the great punishments that God is preparing for those whose immodesty and arrogance forget such a holy and legitimate duty [as conjugal sex], in any case it's up to them to digest and suffer all the ills of it.[43]

Père Jacques-Joseph Duguet responded to the penitent consulting him about the possibility of time off from her spouse's embrace. He explained to her that while Paul did exhort married people to refrain from intercourse altogether, the Saint demanded "that the consent to abstain be mutual; without that condition what appears to be a virtue is a crime and one becomes impure in God's eyes in wishing to be chaste against [the husband's] will. There is no doubt that you offend God if you resist the natural law that submits you to a husband and if you afflict him with your disobedience. Your husband should never have anything to complain of, to you or anyone else, concerning your resistance. Otherwise you are out of order."[44]

Numerous Catholic texts hammered home the point that women were obliged to be sexually available to their husbands, no matter what. "May they refuse when they are menstruating?" a young priest asks père Féline in his *Cathéchisme des gens mariés*. "No, they can and must consent if they are pressed," Féline replies. During pregnancy? "No, most husbands would have trouble containing themselves during an entire pregnancy." How about if she has just given birth? "No, it is in vain that they invoke the suffering they would have to endure, they only prove that the Action of Marriage can become annoying and inconvenient, not that they are permitted to refuse." *No* also to the excuses of breast-feeding, age, illness, a "great number of children," and poverty. "No," père Féline patiently explains, "Providence enjoys blessing the families of the poor while those of the rich perish." All these injunctions have a firm natalist purpose, he points out, because the first finality of marriage is "to give citizens to the State, children to the Church, inhabitants to paradise."[45] Féline's tripartite natalist mission statement gave patriotism precedence over Catholicism, while the notion that heaven itself needed more souls came in last. The Church upheld the legitimacy of the conjugal debt with great fidelity throughout the centuries, even though the rationale for its existence evolved from an explicitly prudent male solidarity to an extraterrestrial populationism.

However enthusiastically Rousseau may have supported natalist causes elsewhere, on the question of conjugal debt he parts company dramatically with his sometime allies. While he disapproves of contraception,[46] he stoutly maintains that spouses are not obliged to engage in sexual relations when they do not wish to. "In marriage the hearts are joined but the bodies are not enslaved. You owe each other fidelity," he tells Sophie and Emile, "not accommodation [*complaisance*]" (4:862). "Knots break when we try to tie them too tightly. That's what happens to marriage when we attempt to give it more force than it should have. The fidelity that it imposes on the two spouses is the holiest of duties but the power it gives each one over the other is excessive. Obligation and love go poorly together and pleasure cannot be demanded. How can they make a duty of the most tender caresses and a right out of love's sweetest signs?" (4:863).

Rousseau's principle resonated not only with his emotional championship of breast-feeding, so compromised by the conjugal duty, but also with his reaction to a ticklish personal problem. In the *Confessions*, he recounted finding himself more than once embarrassingly unequal to a partner's romantic advances. Apropos of his fiasco with Zulietta, the beautiful if imperious Venetian courtesan whom he was unable to possess, he remarked, "Nature did not make me for taking pleasure. She poisoned this ineffable happiness for me as she placed a hunger for it in my heart" (1:320). In negating the conjugal debt, Rousseau not only liberated women from excessive connubial attentions but also relieved men of a sometimes unwelcome obligation. His strongly worded affirmation of the couple's physical autonomy was insistent: "Let the two of them, masters of their persons and their caresses, have the right not to yield them except when the desire is mutual" (4:863).

This would appear to be an antipopulationist stance. After all, forgiving the conjugal debt would presumably lead to less frequent sexual relations and hence fewer births. This, however, was not Rousseau's view. In addition to denying the necessity of sexual obedience, he offered a whole theory of relations between the sexes that demonstrated how infrequent sexual contact actually served to enhance, not reduce, fecundity. The worst enemy of the erotic impulse, according to Rousseau, was sexual satisfaction, and in order to preserve the fructifying attraction between spouses, they should enjoy relations very parsimoniously. "If love is a desire that is exacerbated by obstacles . . . it's not good for it to be satisfied; it's better for it to endure and be thwarted than to expire in the bosom of pleasure" (2:320), Claire d'Orbe tells Julie. The less intimacy couples engage in, the better their reproductive success and the more intense their connubial bliss. The preceptor warns Sophie, "You will long reign through love if you make your favors rare and precious. Do you want your husband ever at your feet? Always keep him at a distance from your person." So Julie goes to bed an hour after her husband and gets up an hour later as well. The same principle applies to nations as to households. Rousseau admonishes the Corsicans: "All things being equal, the most chaste women, those whose senses are the least inflamed by the use of pleasure make more babies than the others, and it is no less certain that men enervated by debauchery . . . are less suited to generation than those rendered more sober by a life of labor" (3:905).

Not only should sexual relations be infrequent, but women and men should be separated most of the rest of the time as well. At Clarens "there is little communication between the two sexes: this article is viewed as very important. Overly intimate liaisons between the sexes never produce anything but ill." This is the natural situation, unlike the artificial promiscuity, fostered by scheming women, that was endemic in France. "Savages are not to be seen indiscriminately mixed, the men and the women. The universality of this order shows it to be the most natural" (4:449–50).

Rousseau's mixed bag of arguments—his denial and subsequent affirmation of the family, his view of the naturalness of incest and rape, his scheme to stem depopulation by putting the woman "in her place," and his repeal of conjugal debt—offered something to, if not everybody, at least a great number of French men and women, who were swept up in a vast wave of enthusiasm for the sage's moving formulations. The incoherencies bothered a few sticklers for logic, but mainly his disciples seemed to take what they needed from the corpus of his works, elaborate upon it, and ignore the rest. His enemies, on the other hand, attacked each of his postulates.

The Unnatural Family

The implications of Rousseau's early, baleful view of procreation were not lost on either the conservative or radical factions. Many authors took issue with Rousseau's original denial of the bonds between father, mother, and child almost immediately upon the publication of the *Second Discours*. In Rousseau's essay he had made frequent use of Georges-Louis Leclerc de Buffon's great study of natural science, *Histoire naturelle, générale et particulière* (1749–67), the first four volumes of which appeared between 1749 and 1753. Buffon was often cited admiringly by Rousseau, who relied heavily on his expertise in animal physiology and the resultant authority it conferred. As Jean Starobinski noted in his commentary for Rousseau's *Oeuvres complètes*, "he furnished Rousseau with a scientific guarantor" (3:1360n). While Buffon claimed in a famous passage of 1753 that "in love, only what's physical is any good, the moral is worthless,"[47] a few pages later he described a whole range of postcopulatory animal behavior, both physical and moral. From monogamous birds to promiscuous beasts who, like the men of Sparta, "have no care for their posterity" (342), Buffon traced the paths of many different types of natural behavior. Buffon claimed that it was essential to hew as scrupulously as possible to observation in formulating generalizations about the behavior of a species.[48]

In response to Rousseau's *Premier Discours*, under the rubric "Carnivores," Buffon attacked his admirer's assumption that original man was unlike contemporary primitive peoples, who were observed living in families. "We do not go along with a Philosophe, one of the proudest censors of our humanity, that there is a greater distance between man in pure nature and the savage than between the savage and us . . . because it seems to me that when one wishes to reason about the facts, one should stay away from suppositions. Thus the state of pure nature is known, it is the savage living in the wilderness, but living in the family" (373–74).

Buffon did not reciprocate Rousseau's esteem, noting that he could "pardon Jean-Jacques neither his contradictions nor his paradoxes." He claimed to find the soul of the author of the *Confessions* "revolting."[49] Clearly dismayed by Rousseau's principle that the child in nature was capable of fending for himself right after being weaned, he called attention to biological evidence of prolonged childhood dependancy: "Unless it is claimed that the body used to be constituted differently from the way it is today and that its growth was much more rapid, it is not possible to maintain that man has ever existed without forming families, since children would perish if they were not helped and taken care of for some years . . . the union of fathers and mothers is natural since it is necessary." Nor was man a vegetarian, as Rousseau had claimed. Rather, according to Buffon, his teeth and intestines demonstrated that he foraged widely, ingesting both meat and plants. Buffon conceded that by the age of four, five, or six, a child might survive if abandoned, but in general the union between mating human beings "cannot fail to produce a respectful and durable attachment between the parents and the child" (374).

Like Buffon, Voltaire rejected the Rousseauvian thesis of natural solitude while also targeting Rousseau personally: "Except for a few barbarous and entirely brutalized souls, or perhaps a Philosophe more brutalized yet, the most hardened men love the unborn child by blind instinct, the womb that carries him and the mother, who redoubles her love for the one from whom she received the germ of a being like herself."[50] While Voltaire and père Castel seldom saw eye to eye, the Jesuit joined the philosophe in taking issue with Rousseau's celebration of the single state: "You should be trembling, monsieur Rousseau, from the savage solitude where you want to lead us, remote from our very selves. *Non est bonum, non est bonum hominem esse solum, solum, solum.*" According to Genesis, said Castel, Adam was never absolutely alone, he had the company of Eve. "Such an intimate society, more moral that physical, reverses all the doctrine and pretensions of M. Rousseau's book." The only source of discord, in Castel's view, was the result of Eve's entering into a "society of reason, philosophy and theology with the animals."[51] The distinction between man and beast, so unnervingly blurred by Montesquieu and Rousseau, was one Castel was anxious to maintain. He found Rousseau guilty of a sin related to Eve's, in that he established a parallel between human sexuality and that of the lower species. "Monsieur Rousseau has insulted and dishonored the image of man in treating the commerce of the two sexes as a *purely animal act.*"[52]

The elusive "Cerfvol," on the other hand, uttered a Newtonian-Rousseauvian warning against associating procreation with paternal responsibility. "The necessity to reproduce is imposed on individuals like gravity on weighty bodies," he announced. However, "it's possible that the law uniting the sexes extends beyond the physical goal of procreation, but I don't see it in the natural order. Let us remain aware that this obligation to raise one's posterity . . . is subject to infinite exceptions."[53]

In 1783, the year after Choderlos de Laclos published his sulfurously successful novel, *Les Liaisons dangereuses*, he composed a curious work treating the natural history of woman. A sort of cross between Buffon's *Histoire naturelle* and a version of the *Second Discours* told from the female perspective, "De l'éducation des femmes" defended Jean-Jacques and his thesis. Laclos takes on both Buffon and Voltaire, claiming that: "The union of fathers to the mothers seems to us absolutely useless, even following M. de Buffon's system, and as for mothers . . . their union with their children ceases to be natural as soon as it is not necessary."[54] He responded to Voltaire's familial effusion by noting that it was impossible to understand "how men (hardened or not) can love by blind instinct a baby they do not know will be born, the womb that they do not know is full, (etc.)" (432).

Laclos set about computing the rapport between life expectancy and the age of weaning. He calculated that if a female wolf lives twenty years and nurses her baby one year, "a woman who lives sixty or eighty years may well devote three years to this task, and when this time has passed, abandon her child" (427–28). Laclos's own illegitimate son, Etienne Fargeau, was a year old as his father penned those lines.

Like Rousseau's theory of the original unparental father, Laclos's ideas about the paternal state and the single mother fell on fertile ground in the decades preceding the Revolution. Numerous male writers proposed schemes by which population would increase, both in quantity and quality, if responsibility for the children could only be transferred from fathers either to the government or to the mothers. These authors took various of Rousseau's ideas, stripped them of nuance, and conflated them into increasingly radical schemes.

Augustin de Rouillé d'Orfeuil, in his resolutely Rousseauvian *Alambic des lois* (1773), spoke out for the complete equality of men, claiming it was an "incontestable principle . . . that all well-constituted men are equal."[55] Within that context of complete masculine parity, Rouillé saw a possibility of improving the human race while liberating the male sex from the servitude of fatherhood and bringing children back to nature. If only the child could be raised far from civilization, "This child would know only his mother and himself . . . his research would consist of finding nourishment and conservation for these two beings who are the whole universe for him. Suppose that two . . . three . . . a thousand women would be good enough mothers to have this desire and enough strength to execute this project, without giving their children any principles nor any notions . . . my little republicans would be vegetarians" (19–21).

While waiting for this experiment to begin, Rouillé outlines his plans for putting women in their place. Like Rousseau, he wants to increase population by redressing the balance of power in favor of his sex. He proposes to eliminate the already slender property rights of women.

> I promised to examine the rights our beauties hold over our belongings, since they already have all the rights over our souls and bodies, they won't leave us with anything; we will end up being but their most humble slaves. In my view a girl must never possess anything because her fate must depend absolutely on her husband . . . that's the only way to keep women in the subordination that is absolutely necessary to counter-balance the enormous advantage they have over men because of the imperious sensation excited by their natural charms (43–44).

Not only should women be financially dependent on men, but they also ought to live under constant surveillance: "One can't keep an eye on women too much," Rouillé warned (44). He built upon Rousseau's argument about the healthiest men being born from the most reserved mothers, constructing a whole physiological theory to explain the phenomenon. His findings showed:

> 1. That our nerves, our muscles, our fibers, our flesh and even our bones are nothing but forms of the mother's different liquids, which assume different degrees of hardness . . .
>
> 2. That a man's greater or lesser strength, his mental health, merit, honesty and consequently happiness depend absolutely on the good or bad composition of his mother's liquids, since the operations of the soul depend on the good or bad qualities of our physique.
>
> 3. That women cannot be too attentive about themselves & too scrupulous about their diet, conduct, etc.
>
> 4. That you cannot accustom girls too soon to a sedentary, calm, tranquil life with little dissipation and the greatest sobriety.
>
> 6. Finally that the education of girls must be regarded as an affair of State . . . parents who neglect their duties are guilty of *lèse société*.

Rouillé's tone is typical of those wishing to reform French reproduction in Rousseau's wake; he envisages not only demographic benefits from a male-centered society but eugenic ones as well.

While Rouillé was basically reactionary in his approach to women and property, François Boissel's 1789 *Cathéchisme du genre humain,* published on the very eve of Revolution, used the same points to advance a radical agenda. Boissel's dialogue, vulgarizing certain Rousseauvian themes pushed to their ultimate extreme, took Rousseau's theoretical delegitimation of marriage and of private property in the *Second Discours* and applied it literally to the society of his day. Marriage, or the sole enjoyment of a woman, since it was analogous to private property, or sole access to land, was the great cause of depopulation. The results were demographically dramatic, according to Boissel: "Dividing up the land gave birth to its exclusive usage and consequently the banishment of future races from the terrestrial globe, killing of hunger, thirst, and cold those who have no property unless they want to become the slaves of property owners."[56] On the same principle, "by means of the ownership and exclusive enjoyment of women, the most imperious penchant of men and women's natural constitution becomes irritated and rebels against the limitations and barriers imposed on it" (100).

The fatal conjunction of sex drive and property rights has created families wracked with enmity: "Fathers have no worse enemies than their children and wives," Boissel claims, "once they come to the age of gratification [*jouissance*], children wish only for the death of the father" (100–101).

The whole social construction of fatherhood repels Boissel anyway; he sees, like Rousseau in the *Second Discours,* that it is artificial: "Natural authority is that of the mothers . . . until the age when [children] can graze with their teeth for solid food. What does the father do during this period? Nature has not placed the same resources or the same feelings for children in him as in women (note: paternity is unknown in the physical order). The mother takes care of the child. What does the father do during this period? What does a man do during his virile years? If he likes women he takes hold of the ones who appeal to him" (155, 160).

Paradoxically enough, despite his endorsement of liberating sexuality from the conjugal bond, Boissel, like Rousseau, sees pleasure as dangerous. Although the "Author of all beings" endowed us with the "most imperious penchant," it was only for the perpetuation of the species and not "for us that this pleasure was established in our natural constitution." In point of fact, "the more people give themselves to this pleasure, the more they become enervated, or rather they are destroyed." Boissel explains further that overly sensual parents are responsible for their offspring's rickets and other "vices of their constitution" (165–66).

Not all Revolutionary figures accepted the Rousseauvian vision of man's bachelor past and ideal child-free future. Condorcet contradicted almost every argument that Rousseau made concerning family, demographics, and women. In the text written while he was threatened with arrest, *Prospectus d'un tableau historique des progrès de l'esprit humain* (1793), he maintains that "the society of the family seems natural to man. Formed from the beginning by the children's need for their parents, by the tenderness of their mothers and fathers, although [his is] less general and less lively, the long duration of the child's need allows enough time for the creation and the developement of a feeling tending to perpetuate their union."[57]

Challenging Taboos

In some ways the entire oeuvre of Rousseau and that of his *frère-ennemi*, Diderot, could be read as a three-decades-long fractious dialogue, as each man challenged, reflected upon, and responded to the other's works. Long after their enmity had ended all direct communication between them, they continued to goad and refute each other in print, often apparently driven to assume antithetical postures. Diderot, devoted father, editor of the *Encyclopédie*, and earnest missionary of Western civilization at the court of Catherine II, seemed virtually to embody the cultural and technological forces Rousseau so virulently denounced; whereas for Diderot the self-absorption, the primitivism, and the radicalism of his former friend acted as so many irritatingly constant temptations and provocations.

In his *Supplément au voyage de Bougainville* (1774), Diderot produced his own version of the story of "natural" man and his role as procreator. In this, his most Rousseauvian work, he ruminates on what human reproduction could be in a more "natural" world. Tahiti, as his example, stood in constant need of a high birthrate because a neighboring isle demanded an annual tribute of young men. But while France, also desperately natalist, dithered back and forth between sexual impulse, Catholic puritanism, and economic prudence, accomplishing little demographically, Tahiti matter-of-factly accepted that reproduction was its highest priority. Couples mated and parted with little ceremony, according to Diderot, their offspring valued by their parents and treasured by the whole island. In this context of communal populationism, any barrier to fruitful coupling, including rules against incest, was seen as irrational, unpatriotic, and contrary to nature.

The chaplain on board Bougainville's vessel is stunned to learn that the unspoiled Tahitians are indifferent to the taboo considered so powerful in Europe. He asks Orou, the elder spokesman for Tahitian ways:

A father can go to bed with his daughter, a mother with a son, a brother with a sister, a husband with somebody else's wife?

Orou
Why not?

Chaplain
Skip the fornication, but incest! But adultery!

Orou
What do you mean by your words, *fornication, incest, adultery?*

Chaplain
Crimes, enormous crimes, for one of which they burn people in my country.

Orou
Whether or not they burn people in your country doesn't matter to me.[58]

Orou goes on to state that the only rules governing behavior in Tahiti are "the general good and individual utility." He asks the chaplain to explain "in what way does your crime *incest* contradict these two objectives?" The chaplain sputters and is stumped. Orou obliquely raises the problem for Western theology posed by Adam and Eve and their two sons, and the chaplain is forced to admit: "You're embarrassing me, but no matter what you say, *incest* is an abominable crime and let's talk about something else." Pushed to the wall by Orou's relentless logic, the priest finally concedes: "I accept that perhaps incest does no harm in nature, but does it not threaten the political constitution? What would become of the security of a head of state if a whole nation composed of several million men found themselves assembled around fifty or so *pères de famille?*" (495–98), asks the chaplain, abandoning morality and falling back on the consequences for the sovereign, the father of his people, if an oligarchy of extrapotent patriarchs were to form.

Diderot's presentation of the incest issue within a natalist society is rigorously rational, once the initial premise is acknowledged. Every detail, every moral or political factor is worked out carefully and consistently. Unlike Rousseau's state (or states) of nature, and unlike France, Tahiti knows exactly what it values. Ambivalence has been banished, the natives love and care for their children, and not only that, they approve any sexual contact that might prove fruitful. A glow of nostalgic regret illuminates the blessed isle, as Diderot's interlocutors stoically determine that, as Europeans, they must nonetheless live by the conflicted codes of their own society, however irrational and counterproductive those codes are compared to Tahiti's primitive sanity. "Let us tell ourselves, let us preach incessantly that shame, punishment and ignominy have been attached to actions in themselves innocent; but let us not commit them," they conclude (515). Battling France's irrational laws against changing spouses and incest while continuing to obey them was Diderot's solution to his discontent with civilization, the opposite of Rousseau's advocacy of radical break. Both men, however, expressed agreement on one thing: the supreme value of population growth.

Since the incest taboo placed limits on desire, it was dismissed as "superstition" by other late-eighteenth-century writers as well, both propopulationists like Rétif de la Bretonne, whose work Georges Benrekessa describes as "dominated by the silent obsession with incestuous relations,"[59] and such proponents of sterility as the marquis de Sade in *Eugénie de Franval*.[60]

Rousseau's demonstration that male violence, far from being an aberration, was actually an integral part of fruitful sexuality, became a popular pseudoscientific truism in the years before the Revolution. The implacable logic approving all sexual acts providing they lead to conception impelled more than one writer to conclude that the decriminalization of rape ought to be considered.[61] In *Le Radoteur*, for example, Cerfvol mulled over whether a man should have to take no for an answer: "Violence has become a problem," he noted. "Should a man take a reasonable defence for a refusal? Should he pay no attention? Two questions it is important to answer: [women's] tears and their laughter are often uncertain signs." In nature, as opposed to effete Western society, "a savage, satiated after the hunt, feels the sweet emotion we call love, if he notices a female he chases her, attacks her and subdues her," Cerfvol points out approvingly, "the only scruple that could stop him might be her age."[62]

Dr. Pierre Roussel's famous *Système physique et moral de la femme* (1775; Paris, 1809) also appeared under the sign of Rousseauvian orthodoxy. J.-L. Alibert declared in the introduction: "Celebrated artists have depicted the author of *Emile* being crowned by children; I would like to see the author of the *Système physique et moral de la femme* receive the same homage from this enchanting sex, whose organism he unveils with so much finesse and such penetration" (ix). Roussel announces that his medical credentials permit him to make scientific moral pronouncements. His findings confirm Rousseau's principles, while his language outdoes that of his master in suave,

4. Louis Binet. "La Vertu inutile" (the useless virtue).
From Réstif de la Bretonne, *Les Contemporaines* (Paris, 1785).
The caption read, "C'est votre sort; il faut le subir."

periphrastic constructions.[63] Unveiling the "connections between women's physical and moral constitutions," Roussel notes: "In this regard I have doubtless recalled medicine to its true rights . . . in its bosom are to be found the foundations of true morality" (xli). Women, the doctor reveals, are constitutionally "delicate and tender, they preserve something of the child in their temperament"(4).

The study of medicine has taught Roussel the morality of sexual violence: "If strength is essential to the man, it seems that a certain weakness suits the perfection of women. This is even truer morally than physically: resistance excites [men]; [women,] as they give in, add the appearance of virtue to the natural ascendancy of their charms, in this way destroying the superiority strength confers on men" (11). Once again the use of male force is necessitated by the power of female "charms," and her coy struggles only add to the pleasure of the encounter.

As a lawyer (*avocat au parlement*), on the other hand, François de Menassier de l'Estre was concerned about the honor of fathers whose daughters were the objects of sexual violence. All too often, according to Menassier, young women were kidnapped, raped, and forced to marry their aggressors, who could then enjoy both the bride and her dowry with impunity. Although it was held that "the abused woman is *insensible* to the ultimate outrage, that she is *incapable* of registering a complaint about it, and that she ought to be rendered *inactive* in the pursuit of vengeance . . . fathers claim that they have been doubly offended because daughters are their fathers' belongings, *pater et filia sunt eadem persona*." The solution to this social problem, Menassier maintained, was to abolish dowries. Without that financial incentive, Menassier maintained, daughters of well-off families would be less subject to male violence motivated by greed.[64]

Louis-Sébastien Mercier's twelve-volume *Tableau de Paris* owes much to Rousseau's example, as does the author himself. Mercier even named his illegitimate daughter, born in 1792, Héloïse. In the *Tableau de Paris* Mercier shows how women's growing intolerance of natural male violence has undermined men's virility with unfortunate consequences. "Women these days are independent; they don't even want to be scolded, still less beaten. The poor things! They don't know the value of a blow struck in loving anger, the inestimable advantage of a torn dress. They are losing out on inconceivable love kisses. At the least reprimand they scream *separation;* and for not being beaten, they are reduced to the languors of cold gallantry which will never replace the vehement transports of passion."[65]

For Jérôme Pétion de Villeneuve, struggles and resistance were nature's own way of readying reproductive physiology: "Whether a woman wishes or does not wish to give in to the desire of the aggressor, she rebuffs him anyway, but not always with the same firmness . . . her refusals are only feigned, with no other object than making his advances more lively. This kind of flirtatiousness is such a constant law among the animals that one must conclude that it is a necessary prelude for preparing the great deed and rendering it fruitful."[66]

Even Diderot speculates in the *Supplément* that society has placed an inordinate opprobrium on rape. "Women's resistance has been consecrated, ignominy has been attached to male violence," his interlocutor complains concerning mores in underpopulated France, so that "violence which would be the merest insult in Tahiti becomes a crime in our cities."[67]

The New Domesticity

Exciting as were the redefinitions of incest and rape, they were marginal issues for the generation coming of age at the end of the eighteenth century compared to Rousseau's great vision of marriage reform. Although other authors referred to oppositions between the sexes, it was his formulation of their physical and moral polarities, so necessary for procreation, that deeply engaged the imagination of many writers, beginning with the publication of the *Second Dicours*.

Immediately following the appearance of Rousseau's *Discours sur l'inéga-lité*, Philippe-Laurent Withof published his *Dissertation sur les eunuques* (Duisbourg, 1756), extolling the providential hand of nature in the contrasting constitutions of the sexes. "Look at man," he told his readers, "full of courage, magnanimity, audacity and intrepidity, terrible in his anger, ardent for glory, indefatigable in his work. A robust body, an assured posture, a rough skin covered with hair, a serious face, a long thick beard, a loud voice, all that announces a formidable, majestic being." Unfortunately, however, a pernicious, antipopulationist custom had sprung up among certain peoples, depriving this exemplary being of his reproductive apparatus. Once he has been "separated from the sweet consolation of producing his fellow being," his admirable qualities all disappear. Now, according to Withof, he is but "a cowardly soul, timid, inconstant, lazy (etc.), his organs are soft, his senses inaccessible to vigorous pleasures . . . his eyes without fire," and so forth; in other words, he is a woman.[68]

Who invented this terrible practice? It seems it was the queen Semiramis, who, wishing to secure her position by "surrounding herself with women," unmanned her retinue. The custom quickly spread, and soon eunuchs were being put to all sorts of ignoble purposes, to the detriment of morals and population. Far wiser than these decadent despots, the author claims, are the most primitive of peoples, the Hottentots. The Hottentots split the difference, sagely removing only one testicle. As a result they are "neither fat nor thin, there are few hunchbacks or cripples. They are the most chaste of peoples. They even have a certain contempt for women so that they won't eat with them." Best of all, says Withof, according the Hottentots the ultimate Enlightenment accolade, "they engender very well" (208–9).

From the 1760s through the Revolution, all kinds of textual strategies were deployed to advocate the new rationale for domesticity, in which men's virility was uneasily policed and women were strictly kept in their place. In one publication, *Les Ephémérides du citoyen,*[69] begun by the marquis de Mirabeau, Nicolas Baudeau, and Dupont de Nemours the year after *L'Emile,* concerns about depopulation, especially its effects on agriculture, were a constant theme. Deploring the drain on rural manpower inflicted by "war, the navy, finance, justice, commerce, the arts, and even the Church," the authors took issue with the truism, "axiomatic among military men, that one day's births in Paris fills the void the bloodiest battles cost the State," pointing out that "there is no greater error, it's men you are killing, it's babies that are being born" (1:231–32). From its inception, the publication featured a rubric called the "Universal History of Women," allegedly the work of "a society of women" (1:185), who, like Rousseau, saw the weaker sex as responsible for a depopulationary decline in morals. While the *citoyennes* supposedly expressing themselves laid claim to a feminist perspective, wanting to know "who does not have a history? No one has written history for women, the history of women themselves" (1:187), their view of the subject was even more misogynistic than Rousseau's. Their "history" of their own sex began at the beginning, with the revelation that "Adam could not resist the prayers and caresses of his spouse: he became the accomplice in the same crime & soon he shared her punishment. Thus the sacred annals recount the origins of the human race: perhaps it's all too easy to recognize Eve's posterity in every generation. Everything one reads in Genesis (before the deluge) shows the dangerous influence of our sex on public morals and on the happiness of men united in society" (1:188).

We should only realize that women's natures, principles of honor, and moral rules were totally different from men's, the *citoyennes* urged, and that lacking "a male & inflexible courage," women should relinquish ambition and reading, except for "a few brochures carelessly piled on the marble top of a commode, next to the scent-sachet and a box of fans—a few papers scattered amidst the crystals and porcelains of their toilette" (1:110). Rather than claiming independent intellectual status, posed in this appropriately

5. Jacques Thouron. "La Famille Méret de Sérilly." Musée du Louvre.

frivolous setting, women would become more attractive, and thus more pregnable and more useful to the State. Here the apparently affluent spokespersons for the doctrines of female subservience are represented as women themselves. It is instructive to note that while the disapproval of intellectual women echoed a theme close to Rousseau's heart, the little display of luxury objects flung on a side table exemplified the kind of wasteful female exhibitionism he found deeply offensive. Rousseau's admirers took

6. Jean-Baptiste Greuze. "La Mère bien-aimée"
(the well-loved mother). 1765.
Bibliothèque Nationale.

certain themes from their master and ignored the rest, all the easier since he
presented such an eclectic assortment of ideas. The *citoyennes* of the
Ephémérides, with their references to Genesis and their box of fans, had not
yet completely mastered the new style of Rousseauvian domestic gospel.

The enigmatic chevalier de Cerfvol came closer to the correct paternalistic, benevolent tone. He responded to *L'Emile* by composing a complemen-
tary educational manual, this one destined for Sophie. While Rousseau's
version of Emile's marriage ended tragically, in *La Gamologie* Cerfvol
brings things off better. As self-felicitating as Emile's preceptor, Sophie's

tutor tells her, "My wish was to be useful to you, and I congratulate myself every day on the success of my efforts. You are the happiest woman in the world and your husband enjoys a happiness equal to yours."[70] Cerfvol, like Rousseau, depicts conjugal bliss as inextricably linked to procreation. Sophie's marital well-being depends on her uncontrolled fertility: "the more children you have the more your happiness will increase, you can take this maxim as a certainty" (5), he exhorts his pupil. While Cerfvol, as is his wont, approves of divorce, especially in instances where the wife is sterile, in this work he focuses on women who wish to control their fertility voluntarily, "of all absurdities, the most palpable." Cerfvol explains the medical basis of this judgment: "Women produce humours that must be devoured by pregnancies. Thus, my dear Sophie, your sex exposes itself to the most fearful accidents in trying to avoid a few passing inconveniences, whose effects are limited to giving us the strength to desire. The system of nature is so admirably linked together" (74). Like the doctor Benjamin Bablot, Cerfvol presents childbearing as heightening, not diminishing, sensual gratification. Not only is giving birth much less difficult than women like to pretend, it provides pleasures superior to those of love: "I do not fear being contradicted by fruitful women when I state that the sensations a MOTHER feels as she becomes one are of a kind superior to all those she receives under other circumstances. Without that wise reward nature would have failed her objective" (72).

Nevertheless, like Rousseau, Cerfvol warns the happy, fecund Sophie not to overdo it, because "if too frequent the pleasures of love soften the organs, thus the sober use of erotic enjoyment makes them more piquant" (72). The case of Cerfvol, given the doubt cast on his very existence, is particularly telling as a demonstration of the fashionable new Rousseauvian ideology, combining the cooption of female identity, hard-core natalism, and perverse eroticism—the whole message larded with sentimentality.

Bertrand Barère de Vieuzac (1755–1841) had mastered the new demographic moralism by the time he claimed that "of all the plagues that can trouble the order and the harmony of society, the dissoluteness of women is in effect the most damaging; it enervates the State in all its parts, it brings with it depopulation."[71]

Pétion de Villeneuve devoted much of his *Essai sur le mariage* (1785) to a long, careful attempt to reconcile Rousseau's early antifamilial stance with his later endorsements of populationism and the new domesticity, producing a coherent, seamless narrative. Pétion's text, now lyrical, now didactic, already belongs to the world of Revolutionary liberties; he shrugs off the strictures of the ancien régime as he asserts his right to express himself freely. Populationism is central to Pétion, who depicts the old regime as doomed by its feeble reproductive performance. "The way things are going now, in fifty years there will be two million fewer souls in France. The calculation is of little importance for the egoist who thinks only of himself, who lives only for himself, who would sacrifice the whole universe for a passing fancy; but the true citizen, who loves his fellow beings, does not think that way. If there were ever a moment to encourage marriages and population, it's now, there's no time to lose: already too much time has gone by."[72]

While Pétion is an ardent proponent of freedom, it is not to be granted to the potential mothers of the race. Girls must be "the slaves of public propriety, [they must be made] to taste the delights of private, sedentary life; Rousseau recommended it in almost all his works" (81). Pétion's reconstruction of the idyllic past predictably places male supremacy under nature's wing. According to his tableau, in primitive times, before the confusion of roles introduced by civilization, "the man was the revered head of the family; his authority was without limits, because it was as just as it was necessary" (21). Like so many Rousseauists, Pétion scorned the notion of equality between the sexes because, since conflicting wills always exist, "one of the two parties must prevail." To which partner should the ascendancy be granted? "To the man," he reasoned, "he is the stronger, his health is more regular, exposed to less inconvenience; these are his titles, they are incontestable" (22). Women, kept indoors as Rousseau wished, were once "entirely occupied with their children & the happiness of their husbands" (23). As civilization and its materialistic preoccupations advanced, however, "the sweetest of attachments has become the heaviest burden for the man" (32).

Marriage has sunk to such a vexed state, its obligations so much more abundant than its pleasures, that while "in the old days a numerous family offered man delights, now it causes his despair" (38). A virile State, untainted by monarchical gender confusion, would revitalize the family by reverting to the strict subordination of women perfected in Republican Rome. Pétion advises "the perpetual guardianship [*tutelle*] of women. Let this word *guardianship* not frighten a timid, easily alarmed sex: far from any idea of slavery and oppression, I understand by the word guardianship that gentle, benevolent inspection a father has of his children. A young girl stays in the family until she passes into the arms of her spouse; she dies without suspecting that she has been under *guardianship* all her life" (95). Domestic arrangements ought to be based on the citizen's highest calling: "What is more sublime than giving life to one's fellow being, children to the State! The act of generation is ennobled in the eyes of the Citizen and the Observer of Nature!" (18–19).

Within a few years Barère and Pétion, these two disciples of Jean-Jacques and his doctrine of fruitful female subservience, found themselves thrust onto the world stage, to exert, if only briefly, enormous power over laws and men, not just on paper but in the crucible of Revolutionary France. Barère, who called Rousseau his "master and model," was to become, in Leo Gershoy's words, "a reluctant terrorist"[73]—a member of the Revolution's extraconstitutional ruling body, the Committee of Public Safety, where for a time he was in an unusual position to put his ideas into action. The same was true of Pétion, who was elected mayor of Paris on 18 November 1790 and served for a short time on the Committee of Public Safety, until he fell afoul of Robespierre in April 1793. Pétion was placed under arrest and died in hiding in July.

A generation imbued with Rousseau's ideas to a marked degree, contradictions included, was involved in the efforts to create a more just society during the last decade of the eighteenth century. As the Revolution attempted to regulate the reproductive life of the nation, pitting patriotic natalism against other priorities, issues of Rousseauvian domesticity, celibacy, divorce, polygamy, and liberated sexuality went from the realm of speculation and rhetoric to the real world of legislation.

CHAPTER SEVEN

Population Politics
in Revolution

Le mariage est un des premiers devoirs du citoyen. M. GOHIER, 1792

The predominant evil of the kingdom [France] is having so great a population, that she can neither employ nor feed it, why then encourage marriage? ARTHUR YOUNG, *Travels in France,* 1792

Legislating National Procreation

The Enlightenment's long populationist campaign entered a new phase in 1789 when the nation's elected representatives became active participants in discharging the duties of government, both drafting the laws and taking responsibility for their consequences. The "number of subjects," which had been used to weigh the merits of Bourbon kings and found them wanting throughout the century, inevitably became the new regime's "number of citizens"; procreation had to be an explicit promise of the Revolution. In the process of stripping the Catholic Church of its established power, the old natalist causes of celibacy, divorce, polygamy, and "women's place" were finally put on the table for legal regulation by the secularized nation's representatives. For them, as Anita Fage comments, starting in 1789, "two preoccupations—reforming a defective morality and favoring procreation—always were to be found intimately linked."[1]

While Catholic strictures on sexual behavior lost State support, by and large the Revolutionary government nonetheless considered the regulation of sexuality and reproduction to be rightly under its purview because population was vital to the national interest. According to Pierre-Victorin Vergniaud (1753–93), member of the committee charged with drafting the constitution in 1792, it was up to the State to govern procreative unions, since "marriage . . . exerts an influence upon the power and splendor of empires; upon their power by increasing population."[2]

Under the reigns of Louis XV and Louis XVI, concerns about population, reliable statistical and demographic data, and public health gradually became internalized and moved into the function of government itself.[3] The Revolution continued the tradition of the old regime's important technocratic bureaucracy, but a new element was present: deputies using population to buttress their causes in public debates over legislation. The old separation between affairs of State and an opinionated public was largely effaced. In restructuring the nation with a high patriotic purpose, populationism was revealed as a shared value, explicit or otherwise. As J. Dupâquier notes, "the Revolutionaries will mainly favor an openly populationist policy."[4] It was above all the radical left, more than the centrists or the forces of Catholic and monarchic reaction, that expressed the most doctrinaire commitment to the natalist cause. According to Louis-Antoine Saint-Just, for example, "the world as we know it is almost depopulated, it always has been. I dare not say what a prodigious number of inhabitants it could nourish."[5]

As the fortunes of the Church sank throughout the years of the Revolution, Tridentine moral strictures seemed to lose their authority over many segments of the French people, at least in the short term. The new legislative bodies were, in theory, free to stipulate relations between men and women in a rational way, free from the "superstition and fanaticism" of religion. They found themselves increasingly under pressure to take advantage of that liberty.

To be sure, these questions were not debated in the abstract; they arose in the context of specific issues having to do with control over the registration of acts, the gathering of vital statistics, existent marriage law, inheritance rights, legitimacy, and traditional male conjugal prerogative. How should such matters be approached in a secular State that was to be dedicated to the "liberty, equality, and fraternity" of its citizenry? The solutions turned out to be far from obvious, for no sooner was one antiquated usage or taboo undone by law than another conundrum was revealed. Eventually the issues not only of celibacy, marriage, divorce, and polygamy, but also of paternity, legitimacy, abandoned children, inheritance, and adoption revealed themselves to be inextricably intertwined; a tug at one end of the tangle threatened to unravel the whole web of society.

The first important Revolutionary legislation concerning marriage was drafted on 20 September 1792, the last day of the monarchy and the Legislative Assembly, on the eve of the National Convention and the First Republic. The legislators dedicated the new government to a trinity of values, "the most precious gifts that heaven can bestow on men: liberty, the laws and peace."[6] To Francis Ronsin, the one constant ideal actually motivating the deputies drafting the marriage laws was "the one which, in their eyes, summed up, dominated, and eclipsed all the others, the one which visibly inspired and directed their work: respect for liberty."[7]

While liberty was the one principle of the three always present in the numerous variations of the eventual slogan, it by no means offered a clear structure for governing marriage, family, and divorce. Liberty, in the context of a commitment to equality, for example, would appear theoretically to present a symmetrical vision of male-female coupling and separation. Many authors saw divorce in terms of liberating women as well as men from dissolute spouses in order to form new, fruitful unions. But for other commentators looking at the new reign of liberty, marriage itself was an unwarranted impingement on man's procreative freedom. A customs agent from Longwy, referred to simply as Noé, wrote to his representative asking why supposedly liberated men should be subject to regulation in this area at all: "Cannot excellent citizens be formed without the law interfering in sexual relations? And is man . . . to be less free than the other animals to follow the instincts of nature?" he asked.[8]

Not only was the application of equality itself problematic where women were concerned, but the concept was also full of pitfalls in discussions about the important issues of legitimacy. The ancien régime had institutionalized two unequal classes of citizens—the privileged, born in wedlock, and the disfavored bastard. The distinction worried many delegates, as did the increasing numbers of neglected, fatherless children who in principle should have been treasured as the nation's demographic asset but were in fact living on the streets in misery. The number of out-of-wedlock children had been on the rise in France since the beginning of the eighteenth century. Between the 1740s and the years of the Revolution, it approximately tripled.[9]

Besides liberty and equality, the perhaps preconscious association of fraternity with masculine solidarity also cast a troubling light on bastardy. Were unwed mothers to be honored and supported as procreative contributors to the nation, or castigated as immoral criminals? And what of the fathers? Were they to be held legally responsible for their children's upbringing or were they in fact innocent fellow men, probably needing protection from predatory females?

More than one Revolutionary commented on the contradiction between fraternity as an inalterable male bond and the other two terms of the Revolutionary credo. In the words of Philippe Juges: "In the National Assembly most of the deputies are fathers and however virtuous a father may be, it is rare that in wishing to destroy political despotism he does not wish to preserve domestic despotism."[10] Every question having to do with marriage, sexuality, and children brought up the universalism of Revolutionary principles, for if men and women were to be treated alike under the law, as was decided on the night of 4 August 1789, the consequences threatened age-old procreative custom, sowing conflicts in the minds and souls of many deputies.[11]

Committed to incompatibilities but struggling to create a transcendent polity, deputies of the first governing bodies faced their legislative tasks by and large adhering, at least publicly, to a common cultural value beyond the Revolutionary triad: population.

Celibacy

Jacqueline Hecht points out that "the Revolution, in its early years, realized much of the Enlightenment's dream of liberating reproduction from artificial constraints, but in a more authoritarian manner than might have been expected."[12] Among the reproductive issues faced by the Revolution, as the Church's influence waned and family was more and more elevated to a patriotic piety, the problems of religious chastity vows and selfish bachelors were among the first to galvanize partisanship. Revolutionaries were, by and large, innocent of the theory that celibacy and late marriage were mainly what kept the population in balance, and the rhetoric was largely on the side of natalism.[13]

The status of chastity vows was immediately challenged from the convocation of the Estates General, culminating in the legislation of 1792–93 and in the often violent demonstrations against the clergy and religious orders marking the movement toward dechristianization. The story of the abolition of religious celibacy is included in that of the radical disestablishment of the Church. On the other hand, the struggle to force the laity into matrimony actually often received ecclesiastical support.

Dechristianization, as Michel Vovelle points out, is an aspect of the Revolution which has traditionally presented special problems of interpretation to historians, from positivists like Alphonse Aulard to those like Albert Mathiez,[14] who was sympathetic to the Jacobins. The meaning of the

movement, the violence it unleashed, and the resurgence of faith it provoked remain divisive issues and are subject to conflicting interpretations.
Isolating the sanctions against religious vows from the tumultuous context
of the popular phenomenon that Vovelle compares in intensity to "the
Great Fear" reveals a complex, piecemeal affair, one that moved inexorably
toward the abolition of those sanctions.

Demands for changes in the laws began appearing early in the *Cahiers de
doléances* as well as in other unofficial publications of 1789. In June of that
year, the abbé Taillard published his *Plaintes et doléances de M.L. L'Abbé
T*** concernant le célibat ecclésiastique*. In this letter, the Canon of Beaujeu
requested the abolition of civil law enforcing religious chastity, thus separating ecclesiastical jurisdiction from that of the State. The same month,
G.-J. B. Target's more radical *Esprit des Cahiers presentés aux Etats-Génér-
aux* demanded the outright suppression of all chastity vows. Anonymous
pamphlets such as the *Motions adressées à l'Assemblée en faveur du sexe* implored the deputies to throw open the doors of the nation's convents: "If we
are all born free, if you propose to break all bonds of servitude, you cannot
abandon these expiring prisoners [nuns] who were also born for liberty,"[15]
wrote the purported former nun. A *Cahier pour le Tiers-Etat du district de
l'Eglise des Théatins* (1789) went further than invalidating vows by calling
for obligatory clerical marriage. On October 28 the National Assembly
voted the provisional suspension of perpetual vows.

The following year saw the publication of numerous pamphlets taking a
more menacing tone toward religious chastity. Dominique Darimayou, for
example, blamed the Church's unrealistic vow for the scandalous behavior
of licentious clerics in *La Chasteté du clergé dévoilée* (1790), consisting of police accounts supposedly filed for the edification of Louis XV and the information of the Archbishop of Paris. The reviewer in the *Moniteur universel* chided the editor for having "lifted the veil covering these scandalous
scenes" (1132), while an anonymous *Considérations politiques et religieuses sur
le célibat ecclésiastique* (1790), carefully summarizing all the arguments for a
married clergy, concluded that priests would occupy their time more fruit-
fully educating their own children for the fatherland than pursuing the
"meaningless pastimes" of their religion.[16]

Diderot had accused convents of sins against population in his clandestine novel, *La Religieuse* (1761), asking when the nation would close up
these "abysses" destroying future generations.[17] His question was answered
some thirty years later, when the cloister itself, as well as perpetual monas-

tic vows, was in effect abolished by the laws of 13–19 February 1790: "The constitutional law of the kingdom no longer recognizes the solemn monastic vows of either sex. Consequently, the orders and congregations where such vows are taken are, and shall remain, abolished in France and no more such establishments are to be permitted in the future."[18]

At this point, the old balance of power between the Church and the French people flipped. Whereas under the ancien régime, State and Church had engaged in centuries-long struggles over the status of monasteries and convents, now the Revolution abruptly "closed up the abyss," supposedly rescuing potentially fruitful citizens from involuntary celibacy. For some nuns and monks, however, the abolition of monachism carried the opposite meaning: the holy cloister, long the shelter for chastity and spirituality, was being violated by a profane state. Reversing the values of the ancien régime, what had been seen as the oppressive cult and the liberating Revolution could now be depicted as the martyred religion and the tyrannical new government.

The latter view was of course embraced by traditional Catholics. The prioresses of the Carmelites of France, for example, signed an "Address to the National Assembly" on "behalf of all the monasteries of France," drawn up by mère Nathalie de Jésus, expressing the Carmel's rejection of the government's rescission of their vows: "These days worldly people like to say that monasteries enclose only victims slowly consumed by regrets; but we protest before God that if there is true happiness on earth, it is ours in the shadow of our sanctuary. . . . After having solemnly declared that man is free, would you oblige us to think that we are free no more?"[19] Thus the "liberty" to *abjure* vows of celibacy demanded by generations of Enlightenment authors and claimed by Revolutionaries was now recast as the liberty to *observe* such vows, to remain in religious orders, as the Catholic Church dropped the role of persecutor and took on that of victim.[20] It could be argued that nothing did more to reinvigorate a languishing Catholicism than its Revolutionary status as a martyred faith.

Nevertheless, many priests did endorse the new law, citing its advantages for national procreation. Curé Blanchet, in an address to the Assembly of 12 June 1790, praised the newly voted decree, denouncing the negative demographic effects of "the cruel law of celibacy" on regular clergy, as well as the alleged dangers to health it posed.[21] The dialectics of liberty followed their own logic as the nullification of religious chastity vows quickly evolved into demands for obligatory marriage of clergy. Later the same year, an actual motion on the matter came before the Assembly, the speaker insisting that the nation no longer tolerate clerical celibacy "for reasons both moral and demographic . . . there are 100,000 young women who must be married."[22]

The year 1791 saw the themes of rights and of population increasingly joined in numerous pamphlets, including Fr.-E. Bernet de Boislorette's *Réclamation du Droit le plus cher à l'homme*, where, quoting Rousseau, procreation was labeled both a "right and a duty," as it was in H. Morel's *Le Coup d'oeil de ma raison sur le célibat ecclésiastique* (Paris, 1791) and H. Hermes's *Entretiens d'un acolythe avec son directeur sur le célibat* (Paris, 1791), to mention only a few of the numerous writings urging reproduction as somehow at once an entitlement and a responsibility for all citizens. The Legislative Assembly voted in October in answer to direct petition that a married priest could continue to be salaried.

Still, despite the resentment expressed toward unprolific immoral bachelors, the Convention did not mount a separate campaign against the unmarried laity of the magnitude of the one leading to the suppression of religious vows. Yet there still remained the nagging problem of confirmed bachelors, as loathe to spawn for the Republic as they had been for the monarchy. Ordinary citizens who remained unwed frequently became the object of Revolutionary rhetorical disparagement and discriminatory legislation. The deputy Louis Dupuy contemplated going beyond even obligatory marriage; he envisaged a State in which the individual's reproductive capacities would be totally under government control: "The citizen is the property of the Fatherland and a part of its wealth," he claimed in his *Observations philosophiques sur le célibat*. "His person, his life, his liberty, his belongings, his repose, his legitimate pleasures, his happiness are under the safeguard of Society."[23] In this context, Dupuy claimed, Rousseau had demonstrated that "the abolition of celibacy is perfectly in agreement with the views of the nation" (28), and, furthermore, childless unions should be invalid. This last point, rational enough in a natality-obsessed context, was often urged although never proposed as legislation.

It was not ultimately sterile marriages that citizen Dupuy was targeting; his anger was mainly directed against those who refused to get married at all. The Church's continuing efforts to protect legions of "lazy, good-for-nothing monks," and "virgins condemned to a futile way of life when [the State] needs industrious mothers of families"(3) could not be berated too harshly. The nonprocreative themselves, whether religious or secular, married or single, were not even to be considered human. Instead they were "gnawing worms" and "insatiable, devouring hornets" (9).[24]

The tradition of judging monarchies by the number of their subjects was now applied to the Revolutionaries themselves. At this point, France had been virtually in the hands of its elected representatives for more than three years; should not the old monarchical generative sloth have given way to democratic procreative vigor? "A government where a great number of individuals are reduced to the physical necessity of living celibate is detestable. . . . Celibacy is still permitted [by law], therefore the government is detestable," according to Dupuy. He rehearsed the old list of ills visited on society and on women by self-centered bachelors, finding "100,000 unmarried men reducing at least 100,000 others to live in celibacy as well" (5).

The decree of 13 January 1791, concerning personal taxes (*la contribution mobilière*), offered a financial incentive to fathers by reducing taxes according to the number of children, with breaks for those families with more than three or more than six offspring.[25] The *Moniteur* (27 October 1791) describes a debate in the Assembly about whether "bachelors over the age of 36 will be placed in the highest income-tax bracket." The deputy Charles F. Bouche, one of the most ardent dechristianizers, contemptuously denounced all unmarried persons, lay or religious, as "parasites, in general corrupt or corrupting . . . a useless weight on the face of the earth." There was agreement on that count, but certain deputies were concerned about whether it was fair that unmarried *women* should be taxed as punitively as their male counterparts. M. Fermond asked whether *celibate* referred to females as well as males. Despite lip service to the principle of equality, the monarchist Louis Foucault [de Lardimalie] opposed taxing single women at the same rate as men, because, he believed, women were not unmarried by choice. He posed the question to his colleagues: "Has any of you ever known a girl to refuse an offer of marriage?" (*Moniteur* 6:226).

Foucault and Dupuy were not alone in blaming celibate men for denying equal numbers of women the opportunity to marry, but at this point in the debate the discussion was abruptly terminated, a vote was taken, and article 17 was approved, stipulating higher taxes for the unmarried, men and women alike (*Moniteur* 6:226). Apparently the swamp of gender injustice was not one the majority of the deputies elected to navigate at that point.

An anonymous pamphlet appeared shortly thereafter, entitled *Observations de deux soeurs célibataires sur la discussion du décret du célibat.*[26] The "two sisters" who purportedly authored the piece were hurt by Bouche's con-

temptuous remarks, describing themselves as "honest and peaceful unmarried citizens, never harming the least of our fellow citizens, supporting our
mother to her last days and still taking care of our nephews and nieces" (1).
They were not writing, they hastened to add, to avoid paying the celibate
tax, but rather "to combat the insulting and demeaning notions which have
been put forward on this subject" (4). Indeed, aggressive populationist
propaganda against sterile "parasites" took no notice of the often indispensable contributions of kinship to the raising of children, indiscriminately
condemning devoted maiden aunts along with profligate rakes.

Cautious Revolutionaries were not anxious to get into the key question
of the Church's control over sexuality and marriage. It was forced upon
them, in a way, by the petition of a great luminary of the French stage. On
12 July 1790, Fr.-Joseph Talma (1763–1826) complained that the priest of
Saint-Sulpice had declined to publish his bans of marriage or to bestow the
nuptial benediction on his wedding because under ecclesiastical law men
and women of the theater were refused the sacraments.[27] Durand de Maillane and Lanjuinais were charged with drawing up legislation to deal with
Church intransigence in granting dispensations for cases such as Talma's, as
well as those involving the more frequent impediment of "incest." Their report, which included recommendations regarding impediments, dispensations, forms of marriage, and their registration, was rational, consistent
with Revolutionary principles of secularization, and very alarming to mod-
erates. Pétion de Villeneuve, whose *Traité sur le mariage* had contained so
many hair-raising suggestions, now became cautious regarding the reform
of marriage. He moved to adjourn the meeting discussing the report, "few
delegates being ready to talk about such matters." Bouche conceded that
these questions were "delicate, thorny and dangerous to discuss." Yet the
questions continued to come up, occasioning sharp and fundamental dis-
agreement, with one side insisting on the State's right to regulate marriages
and births, independent of religion, and the other warning that tampering
with such basics of life would "raise counterrevolution."[28]

Another major debate over all aspects of the regulation of vital acts—
birth, marriage, death—took place in June 1792. The marquis Cl.-Emman-
uel de Pastoret (1755–1840), charged with drafting a decree, attacked "the religious idea that has been the most destructive of civil order, the perfection
of the celibate state . . . a chimeric perfection that would have quickly depopulated Europe."[29]

On 10 September, the Legislative Assembly passed legislation permit-

ting nuns to marry; on 20 September, the day before the Republic was declared, the major law regulating marriage and civil status explicitly denied
the validity of "spiritual impediments," in effect opening the door to marriage for all in religious orders. On 19 October, the deputies voted a still
more specific proposition that no civil law could prevent priests from marrying, and in mid-February of 1793 it was decreed that the Republic no
longer recognized any vows of celibacy as legally binding in the civic
sphere. The tone of the discussion began to grow more threatening later
that year as the Terror gained force, when P.-C.-F Bert proposed that
priests should not receive a stipend from the nation and that they should be
forced to get married. If not, he warned them: "You will be cut out like useless and dangerous undergrowth." To priests who protested that they could
not support a family without a State salary, Bert recommended fertile pen-
ury: "The rich man has few children, or none at all; the poor man, on the
other hand, multiplies prodigiously."[30] Pierre-M. Lenoble presented a project for a law about marriage to the National Assembly that would punish
all bachelors, not just obdurate priests, by taxing them heavily. He also
brought forth another proposal that would have helped to resolve a different procreative issue. Since many children in France were without parental
support, he demanded that the unmarried "fulfill their social duty by adopting a citizen" (art. 6). Adoption, which had been rare and difficult under the
ancien régime, would be facilitated by the law of 12 brumaire an II (2 November 1793).[31]

Amid the Terror (July 1793), the Convention decided that not only were
clergy allowed to marry, but bishops who "put forth any obstacle to the
marriage of priests would be deported and replaced."[32] After the decree of
25 brumaire–12 frimaire an II (15 November–2 December 1793), priests who
did get married or those whose bans were published were no longer themselves subject to deportation or arrest.

One of the Revolution's most infamous episodes, immortalized by the
Georges Bernanos–François Poulenc opera, *Les Dialogues des Carmélites*,
took place on 22 July 1794, just a few days before Thermidor (the fall of the
Jacobin government). Sixteen Carmelite nuns from Compiègne, in accord
with the beliefs of mère Nathalie de Jésus, refused to abjure their vows and
chose instead to die. Condemned by the Revolutionary tribunal, they
mounted the scaffold and were beheaded.[33] The menacing language of anticelibacy propagandists was thus actualized in the execution of nuns who
remained faithful to their vows.

In the period between 1792 and Thermidor, the end of Jacobin hegemony, it was much more frequently ecclesiastical rather than "egotistical" celibacy being publicly castigated. Was the issue more or less pushed to the back burner during this time, despite the flowering of Republican family sentiment, because attacking the Church was politically more useful? Or could the fact that the Jacobin leaders, Robespierre and Saint-Just, were unmarried, have played a role in the relative reticence during the Terror concerning the threat posed by "selfish bachelors"?

As the Terror reached its climax and Jacobin authority became ever more embattled, voices again began to call for the punishment of the secular unmarried. One could speculate over whether the motion brought forth on 4 March 1793 (14 ventose, an II) by the People's Society of Dunkerque had special reference to the Jacobin leadership. Were the winds of Thermidor beginning to blow with the demand: "Send them away . . . let the nature-cheating celibates go expiate their crime in the army, with no place for them available anywhere else; how could they, without being husbands or fathers, pronounce equitably on the fate of families? They're the scourge of society, they eventually destroy it; let them serve in the army and let them expiate their fear of family life by some courage."[34]

After Thermidor and the execution of the single Jacobin leaders, the rhetoric against secular bachelors picked up strength. [Pierre] Platon Blanchard (1772–1840), although opposed to dechristianization, articulated an increasingly popular belief that nature, morality, and the law of the land should all speak the same language, in this case demanding that the secular bachelor be stripped of his citizenship altogether: "since he has contempt for the first duty of man, he can no longer be a citizen."[35]

In March 1794, the popular society of Condom addressed the Convention. Despite five years having passed since the Revolution and the salutary reordering of values it had wrought, "regenerated France is still crawling with bachelors," the petitioners complained. Besides refractory priests and nuns, the most threatening celibates were those frivolous, overdressed, sterile idlers known as "muscadins," who were secretly contemptuous of Republican society and the *sans-culottes* and who "to the detriment of the future race and public decency would rather live with one or two mistresses than with a legitimate wife." The Convention must "declare by a solemn law that celibacy is a political crime and inflict a heavy punishment upon those guilty of it." The honor of being a French citizen imposed two duties: "the first is to love the Fatherland, the second is to transmit one's being to posterity by the means prescribed by the law and good morals." The society envisaged a way to encourage marriage and reproduction while finally removing that thorny old barrier, the dowry. They demanded in the same decree that a rich female citizen must marry "a poor *sans-culotte,* and that a rich Muscadin will have to fix his choice on a poor *sans-culotte* woman." In this way the legislators would be able to "taste the pleasure of propagating the population" and simultaneously efface traces of the prevalent "excessive inequality of wealth."[36] Marriage could thus be a mechanism both for increasing the number of citizens and for leveling fortunes.

The post-Terror constitution of year III (1795) maintained the anticelibate attitude of previous governments but now aimed legislation more at the laity than the clergy. It included a provision declaring that "no one may be elected to the *Conseil des Anciens* . . . unless he is married or widowed." According to the former Jacobin deputy and enemy of Robespierre, E.-L.-A. Dubois [de] Crancy (1747–1814), it was "a joke to claim that men can reach the age of thirty without feeling the need to get married. Any man at that age who is not in a state to give life to another, is not capable of being a legislator."[37] Thus, while the left had frequently targeted religious celibacy, post-Thermidorian legislators would get after the parentally unproductive by restricting the governing body exclusively to family men. The stipulation was voted in, although apparently without effect on the composition of the governing body, which continued to make room for confirmed bachelors.

It appears that the campaign against lay celibacy did bear some fruit in the legislation of the Revolution—at least on paper, although the demographic results, if any, were ambiguous. According to Jacques Dupâquier, the Revolutionary decade as a whole set a record for marriages (2,693,000) that would not be matched until 1840–49.[38]

Estimates of the numbers of religious chastity vows broached during the period of dechristianization vary. According to Michel Vovelle, approximately six thousand priests married, willingly or under duress.[39] Ruth Graham put the number at five thousand, out of around 135,000 ecclesiastics.[40] About a third of these unions were said to have been blessed with issue.

The Enlightenment project of undermining religious celibacy, largely channeled into the more general effort to strip the Catholic Church of its prerogatives, property, and prestige, achieved the anticlerical goals of so many eighteenth-century populationists, although its actual demographic effects were dubious and the cost was high.

Unwanted Children

Celibacy had another disturbing face for the legislators to consider: the fate of children born to the unmarried. It was one thing to punish bachelors and rail against priests, but reforming the very concept of legitimacy threw the meaning of marriage into doubt, a troubling development for many deputies. On the one hand, any birth in the Republic ought to be an occasion to be celebrated by ardent natalists, but babies born out of wedlock, having almost no legal right to family,[41] suffered serious deprivation and were frequently abandoned. The issue was all the more troubling in that illegitimacy was rising precipitously. Not only were famous writers like Rousseau, Laclos, Rétif, Mercier, and Beaumarchais known to have fathered children out of wedlock, but the disruptions of Revolution and the freedom "in the air" also seemed to have spurred many men and women from all classes to dispense with the cumbersome rites of Catholic conjugality, even as married couples were limiting the number of their offspring. Dupâquier notes, "In 20 years [after 1789] the frequency of illegitimate births doubles while legitimate fecundity drops to an extraordinary degree."[42]

Jacques Peuchet (1758–1830) was a lawyer and journalist before the Revolution, as well as an editor of the *Gazette de France* and the *Moniteur*.[43] In 1789 he became police chief of the Paris commune and recommended many reforms based on carefully compiled economic statistics. His ideas tended to be less visionary schemes than seriously constructed programs. In 1790 he proposed that the category of bastardy be simply abolished: "It is time to end this injustice, to give children back to their fathers and fathers back to their children, to declare finally that there cannot be two categories of men where there is but one law, one power and one judge."[44]

One of the unintended consequences of attacking religious orders was the disruption of the vital system of Catholic aid to the needy, including abandoned children. Could the Republic be less generous toward its offspring than the Church? François Chabot pled for the rights of children born out of wedlock: "The declaration that all men are born equal before the law guarantees the rights [*titres*] of natural children. Bastards have fought just like you for liberty and equality," he told his fellow deputies, "they must enjoy the benefits, can we deprive them of these advantages?"[45]

Cl.-Emmanuel de Pastoret claimed that the laws of the ancien régime protected men at the expense of children. Baptismal certificates attesting to illegitimacy "punished the innocent son for the sins of the father." Under the Revolution, however, according to Pastoret, "society cannot reject as its son the one it accepts as its citizen. It is all the more absurd to keep the child of nature from being the child of the laws because if ever there were a being whose fate demanded the protection of the laws, it is the bastard."[46]

Title three, "Birth," of the law of 20–25 September 1792, outlined procedures for the care of abandoned children, but the issue of legitimacy was approached in a much more gingerly way than the fire-breathing rhetoric of Pastoret and Chabot would suggest. It was sincerely felt that children of a just Republic should not be punished for the sins of their parents, but in practical terms it was very difficult to protect bastards in law without undoing the whole concept of marriage. Could the Revolution force a father to become a husband whether he wished to or not, thus abolishing the concept of legitimacy, regardless of the "Rights of Man"? And what if the father were already married?

The report of the committee to extinguish beggary (*comité pour l'extinction de la mendicité*), incorporated into the law of 26 June 1793 (eventually the *Code des enfants trouvés*), emphasized not only the suffering and injustice of abandoned children but the demographic loss they represented. Marie-Cl. Phan comments on the committee's sympathy for the children as well as its indignation over "the formidable human and financial waste" of so many lost citizens. "This concern was inscribed in the framework of a populationist project aiming at the augmentation of the number of citizens who ought to be the strength of the Republic and its future."[47] The law offered illegitimate children certain rights to subsistence and inheritance, provided their fathers recognized them. If not, bastards were expressly forbidden to try to discover the father's identity, nor could the mother launch a paternity suit, since such acts were, according to Théophile Berlier, precluded by "nature's wish for secrecy."[48] If Nature wished for fatherhood to be apparent, according to Berlier, She would have given a clear sign. The new law neatly synthesized the deputies' noble egalitarian sentiments, their respect for nature's intentions, and their caution in regard to male responsibility. But despite its sometimes moving language, the new law did not resolve the problem of caring for the nation's unwanted children.

Divorce

Like celibacy, indissolubility made the transition from Enlightenment populationist reproach against the throne and the Church to subject of actual governmental debate and legislation during the Revolution. A burst of writings appeared between 1789 and 1792 calling for the legalization of divorce. Whereas the debates about celibacy constantly invoked a natalist rationale, the extent to which the prodivorce campaign was really linked to concerns about population has been subject to question. According to Anita Fage, legislative arguments focused on the common objectives of both demographic and moral reform. Yet Alfred Sauvy perceived a diminution of natalism at this time, observing that the depopulation scare began to fade during the Revolution. "When despotism and all its evils will have disappeared, said the liberals, population will increase all by itself, and there will no longer be a reason to worry about depopulation or surpopulation either."[49]

A study of the discourse of the period—the *Cahiers de doléances,* the debates in the assemblies, the proposals and the texts of laws—reveals the presence of both tendencies. As direct political action on deep-seated problems like privilege and taxation became possible, the need for using demographic propaganda to attack the government indirectly seemed to lessen. Meanwhile, population increase continued in great measure to be the given referent, explicit or understood, by which ideas for marriage reform were evaluated, whether orators and authors were sincerely preoccupied with French fertility or merely waving it about as a shibboleth.

Divorce, linked to natalism or not, had scarcely figured in the *Cahiers de doléances* (it was mentioned in only 4 out of 600 *cahiers généraux* presented to the king). The convocation of the Estates General, however, triggered an explosion of prodivorce sentiment. As Giacomo Francini has pointed out, "from 1789 on, a mass of brochures, pamphlets, letters, memoirs, treatises and collections flooded the streets of the capital, provoking an unprecedented debate in the framework of a new vision of the family and the State. The Revolution gave voice, expression and legitimacy to divorce."[50]

The prodivorce writings of the Revolutionary era differ from those of the 1760s to the 1770s. The assault on indissolubility is more direct, with by and large little of the tangled literary subterfuge marking the works of Cerfvol.[51] By 1789, the project of legalization had passed from the realm of private fantasy and literary artifice to the comparatively sober arena of legislation.

A nation involved in articulating the Rights of Man and of the Citizen addressed, not without ambivalence, sexual engagements and their human and legal consequences. As Berquin, in *L'Ami des enfants* remarked, "Divorce is a natural consequence of the rights of man." In his pamphlet of 1790, *Les Mariages heureux, ou l'Empire du divorce,* Philippe Juges declared:

"The laws of divorce must be engendered by the declaration of the rights of man."[52]

Although the era produced a spate of publications, one work dominated the divorce debate in the early years after the Revolution. *Du Divorce* (1789), the magisterial study of Albert-Joseph Hennet (1758–1828), became the Revolutionaries' reference of choice. Hennet, who received an honorary mention from the National Assembly in 1789 for his work, began his treatise by describing his own initial ignorance: "Accustomed to seeing the most ill-suited unions subsist, I said to myself: undoubtedly divorce is impossible!"[53] In his subsequent studies, however, Hennet claimed to learn that "man had enjoyed the right to correct a mistake, in all times and in all countries; it has only been for a few centuries that it has been taken away from a small portion of Europe" (2). The crucial factor was whether the so-called objective of marriage,—reproduction—was taking place. This technique of shrinking Catholicism in time and space while enlarging other cultures to universal proportions was the one favored strategy of writers urging the end of indissolubility. What all peoples, save benighted Western Catholics, held in common was respect for reproduction, according to Hennet and so many others.

Like a number of Revolutionary commentators, Hennet saw the abolition of the divorce prohibition inevitably linked to the end of privilege. "When the National Assembly, during the memorable night of August 4, wielded the hatchet in the forest of antique abuses that covered France, I no longer doubted that the abuse of indissolubility would fall with the others" (vij).[54]

In Hennet's *Du Divorce,* he attempted a synthesis of populationism and individualism in fashioning a rationale for divorce. He began traditionally enough, drawing his argument from Genesis, noting that after God created Adam, He said: "it is not good for man to be alone, let us make him a companion like himself. When He had formed the two spouses, the Eternal One said to them: Be fruitful and multiply, thus announcing the two great aims of nature, the conservation and reproduction of human beings" (7–8). Thus, Hennet argued, when a couple had no children, the marriage ceased to exist: "there is no more wife, there is no more marriage, and one may not keep a meaningless title, an ineffectual attachment" (8–9). Hennet, in keeping with popular belief, saw sterility, implicitly that of the wife,[55] as tantamount to divorce. He favored other grounds as well, including the all-purpose, no-fault incompatibility of temperament that was to be incorporated in the law of 1792.

Although Hennet repeatedly invokes demographics as a rationale for permitting divorce, one senses that individual happiness and the moral integrity of the family were perhaps really closer to his heart. He describes with great poignancy the misery of people caught in the unbreakable chains of an ill-sorted union. "The criminal actions that can result from a hated marriage are incalculable" (81). He mentions humble acceptance and prayer, the traditional Catholic answers to such despair, only to dismiss them as anachronisms of a bygone era. "It will be objected that sanctity is born of persecution; that the more a husband or a wife is unhappy, the more they earn the merit of being blameless. This assertion carried more authority in the past; these days, however, people no longer believe in useless virtues: those anchorites who martyr themselves for the human race inspire more pity than admiration" (82).

Resolutely modern in certain ways, Hennet's discussion of the benefits divorce would confer on individuals is nonetheless grounded in the context of its demographic consequences.

> There is an object that particularly concerns the government upon which marriage has special influence; it is population. Conjugal indissolubility is harmful to population by rendering marriages less fruitful. How many spouses do we not see who live in the same house, bear the same name, but have nothing else in common? How many others are completely separated by the law? These fragmented marriages produce at most one child and are then lost as far as population is concerned. (94)

Indissolubility also led men to avoid an irrevocable commitment that so frequently turned out to be disastrous. "Reestablish divorce," Hennet implored, "and I would walk to the wedding temple assured that if I found the Furies waiting there I could also find a way to escape their homicidal rage" (94). Hennet emphasized the economic and military advantages that divorce would offer the nation, which could "never have too many hands to cultivate and defend its land" (95). Recruitment for the military and for the police imposed great hardship on Catholic countries, already drained by what Hennet called their "three types of celibacy, lay, ecclesiastic and conjugal" (96).

> Who could defend France, Spain, and Italy against the immense emigrations of peoples from the North, happily exempt from these three scourges? What will it serve a France, thinly sprinkled with men, to be sovereign and

free at home if she becomes subjected and enslaved by a nation bristling with soldiers? Therefore neglect nothing, French legislators, so that the strength of the nation equals its wisdom. Fix your gaze on population; accept with eagerness all means to encourage it. The freest nation ought to be the most populated. Realize that an institution tending to augment the number and the fertility of marriages, to embellish your countryside with laborers and your frontiers with soldiers is necessarily one of the best political institutions. (96)[56]

Like Hennet, reproductive utilitarians in general favored divorce in order to render sexuality more procreative, but, all commentators hastened to agree, not to facilitate erotic variety. Diderot had suggested to Catherine of Russia that people be limited to two changes of spouse. During the Revolution, Philippe Juges recommended laws permitting "three divorces but one must stop with the fourth marriage which may be dissolved by nature alone. It is important that the laws of divorce not authorize capriciousness."[57]

In *Réflexions d'un bon citoyen en faveur du divorce,* the anonymous author explained, "In demanding divorce, we are far from wishing to favor those flighty, inconstant, libertine tastes where a change of pleasures would play a larger role than solid reasons."[58] Contented, procreative family life, not hedonist indulgence, was most frequently mentioned to support legalizing divorce, although clearly other sub-rosa agendas were often at stake. In the otherwise feminist array of arguments put forth by Mme de Cailli, she remarked that if divorce were legal, "how many sterile spouses would become fertile!" Divorce, she concluded, would restore dignity to marriage and "double the population,"[59] yet the rest of her pamphlet shows no interest at all in reproduction.

The "bon citoyen," like Maurice de Saxe, claimed that France was suffering in contrast with neighboring countries where divorce was legal, echoing Montesquieu's intimations of a population race with the Germanic states that was to play such an important role in ninteenth- and twentieth-century politics. "Just consider what's going on among Protestants in Switzerland, in Holland, and in several cantons of Germany . . . and you'll see how superior their population is to ours," he warned (6), urging France to catch up with the Protestants by permitting men to change spouses.

The credo that divorce favored population did not go unchallenged. It was contradicted, for example, by abbé Armand-Anne Chapt de Rastignac in his refutation of Hennet's work, *Accord de la révélation et de la raison contre le divorce* (1790): "They say States where divorce is permitted are more populated,—that is what they say but they do not prove it. It remains to be proven that the largest population has as its unique or partial cause the various principles and usages relative to divorce. Divorce is permitted in Greece for adultery, yet the population is much less numerous than in other countries. As the indissolubility of marriage supports morals it can only be favorable to population."[60]

Even a conservative Catholic defense of indissolubility rarely challenged the principle that population increase was a top priority. It was not Chapt's contention that demographic considerations were secondary to eternal moral truths, merely that Hennet had not demonstrated the reproductive superiority of countries permitting divorce. Since morals and population were inseparable, according to Chapt, divorce must be contrary to both. The Church was no longer claiming indifference to the propagation of the species, as Louis Cornaro had done in the period of the Reform; it had taken up the cause and was shaping it to Catholic ends.[61]

To pass any divorce decree on 20 September 1792, as the Republic itself was being born, in the midst of a society in political, religious, and economic turmoil, was a major achievement. In its modernity the bill transcended the flux of Revolution to such an extent, as many later historians have noted, that the provisions went far beyond the modest reforms desired by the nation and its deputies.[62] Its most radical provisions, permitting divorce on the grounds of mutual consent or incompatibility of temperament, were light-years ahead of the French mentality in 1792. Although two of its clauses, one depriving women of rights and benefits in the common holdings if the woman was found guilty of certain crimes (III, V) and the other forbidding women to remarry in less than a year, accorded privilege to masculinity, the law was fundamentally egalitarian. The great traditional inequality, the one that punished a wife for adultery but not a husband,[63] was absent from the new legislation.

Tensions between the founding principle of equality and a widespread sentiment that women needed to be kept under male control erupted definitively in October of 1793, when women were conclusively denied active citizenship and participation in the political life of the nation.[64] The rhetoric of nationalist natalism, however, consistently took pride of place over the thorny gender problems of individual freedom, remaining an almost invariable referent in most prodivorce writings until nearly the end of the Revolution. Juges's utilitarianism was typical: "Divorce is the most fertile seed of population . . . the population will become prodigious in France because divorce will suppress the waste of pleasure."[65]

However, an important shift did take place in the treatment of the divorce-population connection as it moved from object of speculation to actual legal reform. Starting in 1789, many speeches and pamphlets tended to rely less on hard-core natalist ideas and instead concentrate, as we have seen, on the well-being of children already born. When d'Antraigues reasoned about divorce and population at the beginning of the Revolution, he contemplated the effects upon the existent children more than the births that might result from a switch in partners. Attempting to reconcile the traditional punishment of the adulterous wife with the new sense of responsibility toward family cohesiveness and the needs of children, his struggle to find formulations shows his conflicts concerning divorce legislation. His remarks deserve to be quoted at some length because they reveal so clearly the turbulent conflicts of Revolutionary thought about marriage, its legal dissolution, and the effect on children. "Divorce is an absolute necessity" he begins, however,

> if children already exist . . . indissolubility must reign as long as the children of the marriage exist. No, no, the fathers must not be separated from their children. Heaven joined them, as long as such mediators exits, no hatred is eternal, marriage is thus indissoluble. But if the fruits of adultery have soiled your home through the infidelity of your wife, then . . . I admit, if there are no children other than those born of adultery, the father is bound by no obligation. But if there are children left over from the days when the mother was virtuous, marriage is indissoluble . . . [etc.][66]

From the tortured tergiversating of d'Antraigues to the cries of the pamphlet press, publications appearing throughout the Revolution, aimed at every readership, increasingly discussed divorce in terms of protecting real children rather than multiplying hypothetical offspring.

In arguing for divorce on fertility considerations, as so many apologists from Montesquieu through Hennet had done, a certain mental barrier had been crossed. For if marriage ought to be structured for maximum reproductive efficiency, if the old Catholic strictures were to be disregarded in favor of more "natural" and therefore fruitful conjunctions of men and women, why stop with divorce and remarriage? If the objective was to "be fruitful and multiply" for the good of the nation, and liberty was the means, why should men be bound by the old prejudices, as for example, the law obliging them to have but one wife? As Francis Ronsin comments, "Deciding that procreation was the sufficient cause of marriage introduced another litigious issue: polygamy . . . the idea was in the air!"[67]

The Primitive Right of Man

Polygamy polemics erupted from time to time throughout the Revolution, as the terms of the arguments evolved with changing circumstances. Although some commentators claimed the permissive divorce law of 1792 legalized "serial" polygamy, simultaneous polygamy was basically not on the legislative agenda. The rhetorical enthusiasm that had been expressed over this "primitive right of man" prior to the Revolution nonetheless made its way to the floor of the Assembly in other guises. While some deputies argued that polygamy was a natural masculine entitlement, others urged it as a way of doing justice to unwed mothers and their offspring.

Ch.-Fr. Oudot (1755–1841), deputy from the Cote d'Or, commenting on Vergniaud's plan for registering births, marriages, and deaths (9 April 1792), presented an elaborate proposal intended mainly to obliterate the difference between legitimate children and bastards and thus, in a way, between the married and the unmarried.[68] Oudot favored an alternative "free union," to be celebrated in secret, in which the parental couple were not exactly legally obliged to each other but their children would be considered legitimate for purposes of inheritance.

These issues of defining and regulating celibacy, marriage, legitimacy, the transfer of property, and the status and rights of children and women were filled with pitfalls for Revolutionary leaders. However, unlike twentieth-century debates in France over the legalization of alternative partnerships, agreement was general among Revolutionaries that, in Oudot's words: "laws relative to marriage and the birth of citizens must obviously aim towards favoring population, which is the wealth and strength of empires."[69]

Oudot went still further in his demographic fervor, urging the denial of inheritance rights to the childless, thus making the transfer of property for widows and widowers dependent on their reproductive performance. He argued that after all, "in being born, does one not contract the obligation to reproduce, and to give the State at least one child to replace oneself?—for free men, population is the wealth of the State" (16–18). In their efforts to disestablish Catholic marriage, however, while at the same time debating legislation to eliminate the stigma of illegitimacy (eventual law of 12 brumaire an II), the Revolutionaries found themselves faced with the possibility of a kind of de facto polygamy after all. In Oudot's *Essai,* he proposed two forms of State-recognized marriage: one to be "solemn," the other "private." While article 8 of his projected law stated that polygamy would be forbidden, by permitting a man as many "private" marriages as he wished, a system of informal polygamy would in effect be established. Oudot recognized the contradiction but commented philosophically that the "law ought not forbid what it cannot prevent . . . since other unions exist, independent of the law, how can the law not recognize the results and how can it refuse to protect the children that are the consequences?" (123). Oudot's plan was of course not accepted, but the possibilities that he raised continued to be treated seriously by various citizens from time to time during the period of the Convention.

Rivolet, mayor of Montbard in Burgandy, wrote to the legislative committee on 7 June 1793, letting his *concitoyens* know that "last March 4 a bastard son was born to me whom I recognized the next day. I gave him his mother's first name and mine for his family name; he's a superb boy, although I am in my 65th year. . . . I hope he will have his share of my inheritance, like the four children of my so-called legitimate marriage."[70]

Egalitarian movements to obliterate all distinctions between legitimate, natural, adulterous, and incestuous children were poised on a slippery slope, threatening to destroy the protection traditionally accorded to marriage. Yet from a different perspective, it was argued that without the strictures of the discredited Catholic Church, there was no reason for the State to intervene in a personal matter at all.

On 10 frimaire, an II (30 November 1793), Citizen Fleurant, from Soissons in the North of France, addressed the representatives of the Nation: "The Rights of Man permit doing whatever does not harm others. That is the fundamental basis upon which the Republic rests. [This being the case] . . . how is it that this bizarre slavery, following the barbarous usage of the old despotism, forces man to marry only one woman? What a contradiction! Either man is entirely free or he is a slave, there's nothing in between; in the first case he can . . . have as many spouses as he desires." Fleurant invokes the sex ratio again, claiming that more women are born than men and that because of "supernatural laws," an abundance of women are "abandoned," among whom are to be found "the number of mistresses who destroy the best families, women of ill repute who entirely ruin our youth both spiritually and corporally." Since the law supposedly protects natural children, says Fleurant, "polygamy will solve the problem of illegitimacy."[71]

Deputies were uncomfortable with the inconsistency of abolishing the distinction between nobles and commoners while perpetuating a privileged class based on whether one's mother was married. In a collection of notes published after his death, Saint-Just speculated over means of reconciling the rights of all children with the freedom of men and some sort of not necessarily exclusive legal marriage. He imagined splitting the difference by reserving one kind of wedlock only to those bearing children. The law would read: "The man and the woman who love each other are spouses but if the wife gets pregnant, they are obliged to declare their marriage before the magistrate."[72]

Despite the various speculative approaches imagined by Revolutionaries, formal plural marriage was never really an option for the deputies of France's assemblies. Far from conforming to the principles of the Revolution, in the final analysis, as Montesquieu had observed, the institution of multiple wives was associated with despotism or the privilege exercised by one man at the expense of others.[73] By the end of the Revolutionary era, polygamy had by and large quit the sphere of public discourse, retiring discreetly to haunt the domain of private life in the centuries to come. The Napoleonic Code firmly eliminated the temporary theoretical equality of bastards and legitimate children wrought by the intermediate legislation; its provisions remained virtually unchanged for almost two centuries, until 3 January 1972. The old Catholic incest taboo was sharply reduced but not eliminated: "Marriage is prohibited between natural and legitimate relatives of direct lineage, between allies of that lineage, and between brothers and sisters,"[74] stated the law of 20 September 1792. The radical divorce legislation did not long outlast the Revolution—it was drastically truncated under the Restoration in 1816 (law of May 8), then moderately liberalized in 1884. Its essence was not to be restored in full until 1975 (law of July 11).

From 1789 until the fall of the Jacobin faction and the seating of a reactionary government, women, with a few exceptions, were equal under the law, if not necessarily in the Revolutionary mentality, except in the administration of the financial assets they held in common with their husbands. This kind of equality between the sexes was the subject of heated argument. J.-J. Régis de Cambacérès's first two egalitarian drafts of a civil code would have granted women the right to codirect their family finances under certain circumstances. Although on 27 October 1793 the Convention voted in favor of granting women equal control over communal marital property, unless their marriage contract stipulated otherwise, the first two drafts of the civil code had to be abandoned. By the time of the third, finally successful project, eventually incorporated into the Napoleonic Civil Code of 1804, Rousseauvian ideology, based on the putative law of nature, had finally triumphed over the Revolutionary principle of equality. In this third draft, the ever-supple Cambacérès reversed his previous position, stating that "although equality ought to be the rule in all acts of social organization, it is not a deviation to maintain the natural order and thus prevent arguments that would destroy the charms of domestic life." Cambacérès explained his reasoning frankly: if women could share household financial management with their husbands, "nothing would prevent the administration of finances from falling exclusively into the woman's hands: would such an arrangement not contravene natural law and wouldn't it make people suppose the husband to be an imbecile?"[75]

Cambacérès's argument reflected the dominant Rousseauvian tone of family legislation from October 1793 through the period of post-Thermidorean reaction following the fall of Robespierre and the Jacobins. Whereas Rousseau's politically radical stances against private property, representation, and the division of power went down along with Jacobin hegemony, a Rousseauvian version of nature's will in family matters finally succeeded in being put into law. It was Rousseau the domestic advisor, whose teachings would keep husbands from looking "like imbeciles," not Rousseau, the rabble-rousing menace to entrenched authority, who was blessed by Joseph Lakanal at the moment of the sage's pantheonization. Rousseau was to be thanked for his salutary impact on family life since he "brought mothers, until then lost in dissipation, to the tribunal of nature, and back to their duties," according to Lakanal.[76] Women, in strict accordance with Rousseau's doctrine, were enjoined to repopulate France by adopting a demure, unthreatening, breast-feeding persona that would lure men back to their familial duties. According to Etienne-Ch. Maignet, speaking for the Committee of Public Assistance (*Comité de Secours publics*), "Once women become mothers again, soon men will become fathers and husbands. A numerous population is the wealth of the State."[77]

7. "La Mère à la mode—la mère telle que toutes devraient être" (the fashionable mother—the mother such as they all should be). Bibliothèque Nationale.

The Voice of Nature

Across the eighteenth century "Nature" assumed a capital role in legitimizing reproductive politics, as authors vied with each other to be Her anointed spokesman.[78] During the Revolution, Nature's voice, speaking in Rousseauvian tones, filled the vacuum left by the collapse of monarchical and religious consensus and lent weight to the dictates of those seeking power—on all sides of the political aisle but especially the left.[79] Nature replaced God and king as the ultimate authority, whose will could be articulated by the writer or speaker. Fundamental to much debate over marriage-related issues was the primacy accorded to natural law, however defined, over positive law. The Revolutionaries generally saw themselves not as anarchists demolishing the State but rather as restorers of an antecedent Providential order. Saint-Just commented, "I am not breaking the bonds of society, but rather it is society that has broken the bonds of nature; I am not attempting to establish innovations but to destroy innovations."[80]

From both sides of the aisle, original, untainted "Nature" was frequently heard to urge female dependency, paternalistic authority, and vigorous reproduction. Abbé Claude Fauchet, disciple of Rousseau, in his eccentric Revolutionary publication, *La Bouche de fer* (6 January 1791), endlessly reiterated Rousseau's thesis that "a woman's throne is in the midst of her family, her glory is in the glory of the children she has raised for the State."[81] He took issue with Condorcet's plea for female equality under the law: "Civil and political liberty is useless to women and thus must remain foreign to them." The abbé does not base his authority on the discredited teachings of the Church but relies on nature to validate his blunt political message: "Nature . . . has prescribed to each sex its respective functions. A household must never be deserted a single instant. Destined to pass their lives under the paternal roof or within the marital home, born for perpetual dependency from the first moment of their lives until their death, they are endowed with private virtues only. Women! Don't compete with us, don't let a misplaced jealousy alienate you from us" (76).

Joseph Presevot agreed with Fauchet, arguing for encouraging population by curbing women. "The way not to get lost in politics is to fix one's mind on the intentions of nature," he reminded his readers. Women should not own property because "the more they possess the less is left for the Citizen."[82]

During the Terror, doctor François Lanthenas, deputy to the Convention from Rhône-et-Loire, urged the establishment of a *Censure publique pour la surveillance des moeurs et la morale publique,* to exert constant vigilance over women's behavior and thus ensure maximal motherhood, "such an important object for the happiness of the people, the improvement of society and the *propagation of the species.*"[83]

Presevot, Fauchet, and Lanthenas were not alone in conceiving of the Republic as a wholly masculine State, embodying a patriarchal natural law, one which produced, distributed and protected mothers, wives, and daughters but did not include them. Sylvain Maréchal's use of the word *man* demonstrates this thinking, as he dismisses the legislators' complicated wrangling: "You don't need all that to make 25 million men happy and good, all it takes is instinct," he assured his readers: "child, husband and father. This is where man begins and this is where he must return."[84] Man, *homme,* morphed effortlessly between *homo* and *vir* in the discourse of many Revolutionary commentators, depending on whether the speaker was arguing a universalist or patriarchal cause.

Since the number of citizens determined the value of the government, the left necessarily had to vaunt the superior reproductivity of Republics.

Pastoret introduced his draft of laws concerning marriage by pointing out the demographic differences between governments: "A well-known relation exists between the liberty of peoples and the population of empires. Reliable calculations tell us that Holland, with its Republican forms of government, had one marriage for every 64 persons each year. There is one for 100 in England, where the monarchy is mixed, but only one in a 125 in France, where the government was akin to despotism."[85]

Not just the citizen's government but also his political allegiances within the nation determined his reproductive vigor. The left embodied paternal virility: "What does a sans-culotte need with getting rich?" asked Louis Prudhomme in his publication, *Révolutions de Paris*. "His fortune is a big family." Jacobin husbands "love their spouses with more energy" than aristocrats, among whom "a cold politeness takes the place of a real attachment." The result is that "fecundity & happiness are to be found in most [Jacobin] households" as opposed to the chilly, childless establishments of the rich.[86]

Rousseau, who swore by population as the criterion of good government, was invoked with predictable regularity on all sides of the political fray, and ultimately it was his vision of the restructured family—animated with populationist sentiment, dominated by the protective father, dependent on the submissive, fertile mother, and underwritten by the providential State— that emerged as the triumphant ideology enshrined in the *Codes civils* (1804, 1812), which formally prescribed the legal aspects of the husband's superior status in the home.[87] Clerical celibacy, with certain modifications, was reestablished in France after the Concordat of 1801, the scope of the modern divorce law of 1792 was sharply reduced in the *Codes civils* of 1804 and 1812, and polygamy never really stood a chance of being legalized. Yet Rousseau's overt formula for the fruitful family triumphed over political vicissitudes of the era, surviving, despite changes in regime, to provide not only the Revolution but much of the nineteenth century with a logically murky but emotionally compelling ideology. In Madelyn Gutwirth's words, "After Thermidor . . . the regime of compulsory female conjugality was firmly in place . . . the wife and mother was relentlessly installed as the sole acceptable ideal for women." Well after the Revolution, throughout the nineteenth century, according to Jacques Dupâquier, "the wife, deprived of civil status, is more strictly subordinated to the husband than under the ancien regime."[88]

The effects of Revolutionary natalism on France's population, if any, are difficult to ascertain. The statistics are incomplete and further distorted by the incidence of the Terror, war, and emigration. The government asked for demographic data from municipalities, but the responses were erratic and unreliable. Dupâquier points outs that "of seven census projects prescribed during the period, not one was completely published." From the available data, it appears that departments and regions differed enormously in their demographic fate; the Seine lost 68,000 inhabitants, while the Vosges gained 40,000. According to Dupâquier, the population of France overall was 28,260,000 in 1791, decreasing slightly to 28,159,000 in 1801.[89]

From Too Few to Too Many

While populationism continued to dominate mentalities through the end of the ancien régime and during the Revolution, a dark antithetical cloud was beginning to gather on the horizon. Starting at midcentury, a new kind of demographic anxiety had begun to make itself felt, first faintly and then with increasing insistence among certain observers. As J. Hecht has shown, two related theories were emerging that linked population growth less with national grandeur than with a diminished standard of living. A number of authors were observing that salaries decreased in proportion to the size of the available work force.[90] In the countryside, the so-called law of diminishing returns or inevitable limits to the growth of agricultural production was starting to attract attention.[91] It was beginning to occur to some commentators that, far from suffering from a dearth of people, France was actually beset with the problems posed by too much poverty. According to Dupâquier, in the 1770s and 1780s, the numerical disequilibrium between generations was exerting serious pressures on the economic and social structures of the nation. Grain prices were rising along with unemployment and the average age of marriage (to 28.5 years of age for men, 26.5 for women). André Burguière refers to the last decades of the century as marked by "stagnation of prices, contraction of rural or manufacturing industry, an increase in poverty, the reappearance of grain riots, and the increasing paralysis of governmental action." He comments that "two decades of economic stagnation [were] exacerbated and crowned by the classical but unusually severe subsistence crisis (the bad harvests) of 1788 and 1789."[92]

The harsh conditions of the last decades before the Revolution stressed the capacities of Catholic institutions like the *Hôtel-Dieu* and the *hôpital général,* where Sisters of Charity, founded by Vincent de Paul and Louise de Marillac, cared for the poor nobody else would help—the orphans, the handicapped, the retarded, and the elderly. Olwen Hufton describes the numerous orders of nuns serving the sick, as well as such organizations of pious women as the Blessed (*béates*) of Le Puy, who performed a whole range of vital services in small communities, from providing day-care to helping working girls amass a dowry. In Hufton's words, the *béate* "is one of the best instances of the spirit of Catholic solidarity, in which the lowly helped the lowlier as well as the aristocrat the poor."[93]

Despite the best efforts of so many struggling religious foundations in Paris and other cities of France, the latest victims of the economic crunch began to swell the ranks of beggars alarmingly. The poorhouses established to accommodate them, the *Dépôts de Mendicité*, operated at once to offer relief to the desperate and to keep them off the streets. This uneasy double function of the government—simultaneously a last resort for the destitute and a lockup for the undesirable—turned the *Dépôts de Mendicité* into the hellholes they were known to be.

The plight of the needy had engaged the attention of France's forward-looking Minister of finance, the encyclopedist and physiocrat baron A.-R.-J. Turgot (1727–81). During his brief term of office (1774–76), he had attempted to alleviate the misery by abolishing the poorhouses and engaging municipal governments in constructive programs at the local level. He also tried to tear away the vast web of restrictions impeding all aspects of French economic life, from the guilds' strangleholds over manufacturing to the governmental control of the sale of grain, in the belief that "laissez-passer laissez-faire" would resolve the nation's recurrent subsistence crises. Rather than simply providing welfare, Turgot established a kind of public works program, including employment for women, since he recognized the reality that all women and children were not necessarily under the protection of a male provider. Emma Rothschild summarizes his projects as basically being part of a strategy "to provide political guidelines and public finance for short-term income security."[94] But Turgot's reforms came to an end when he was driven from office in 1776, and even most of the wretched *Dépôts de Mendicité* were reopened soon thereafter.

The food shortages and frequent dislocations of the period coincided with increased abandonment of children, bastards and legitimate alike. Sébastien Mercier wrote about the ominous situation in Paris in 1788, where "six to seven thousand children were abandoned by their parents and thrown into the orphans home [*enfants trouvés*]. What more terrible and striking image could one have of the people and of the degradation of the species?" The government was considering plans to finance provincial shelters to keep the "orphans" from being dumped in the Paris *enfants trouvés*, where "9/10ths of the children died before the age of 10." A. Burguière notes that many historians have wondered whether abandonment was not in reality "the new face of infanticide."[95]

The average working man's salary was estimated as being just adequate to support a wife and one child. It was the birth of the second child that drove working families over the edge. Many working women resorted to wet nurses willing to nurse the baby for a few sous less than the mother could earn.[96] Mercier describes the processions of destitute fathers, unable to pay their children's wet nurses, whose debts and fines were being relieved by Catholic charity. They were marched from debtors' prison through the streets, accompanied by "bishops in violet robes. Poor humiliated fathers!" Mercier comments. "And this word 'government' really means something?"[97]

The little vignette illustrates the tangle of reponsibility, blame, and guilt characterizing the natalist imperative. The fathers were married men, not feckless bachelors, and therefore they were shouldering legal responsibility for their children's support. Despite their obedience to the injunction to be fruitful and multiply, they were put in jail, from which they could not feed their families. The mothers sent their babies out to nurse, in defiance of the vast public relations campaign urging maternal breast-feeding, but they did so to be able to put bread on the table for other children. The Church, hurtling anathema at the "fatal secrets" used by some couples to prevent conception, both came to their aid as victims and publicly shamed them as deadbeats. More and more voices were joining Mercier in blaming the government for all social ills and supplicating it for relief.

The same year Mercier's tableau was published, 1788, one of the figures most consistently concerned with remedying the plight of the marginal, M. J.-A.-N. de Caritat, marquis de Condorcet, friend of Turgot, philosophe, mathematician, statistician, and tragically unsuccessful Revolutionary leader, published his *Essai sur la constitution et les fonctions des assemblées provinciales,* examining the theoretical bases of eligibility and elections as well as concrete issues such as taxation, justice, public works, and aid to the poor. While affirming the rights of private property, he also recommended State assistance to the needy, especially the children. His vision of a proper institution was a far cry, however, from the lethal *enfants trouvés* of Paris: "Asylums [*maisons de secours*] for abandoned children could be greatly useful. Some belong to parents who lack the means or the will to raise them; others are what is called *illegitimate*. The State must provide for the existence of both and if the support were well-directed, it would have to be regarded less as a drain on the public treasury than as an investment from which the nation would receive great advantages."[98]

Thus Condorcet called for the State to heal itself by helping its children, above all through education. According to Condorcet, only one out of fifty French children received an education "capable of developing the natural strength of their minds." By instituting free universal schooling, the nation would increase fiftyfold the number of people "whose intelligence and superior learning can help the progress of human knowledge and public happiness." Condorcet wanted the nation's girls to be educated in the same way as its boys (8:465, 472).

Vauban, Boisguilbert, Montesquieu, and so many others had insisted on the symbolic and utilitarian importance of France's population, but they had accorded ultimate primacy to the betterment of people's lives, to the objective of individual happiness. On the other hand, many eighteenth-century authors, like Mirabeau and Rantzow, seemed to go along with Rousseau's dictum about the superiority of the poor but populous State. An intermediate approach was taken by protoeugenicists like Turmeau de la Morandière, who, warning that "not only are Frenchmen fewer than in the past but the species has greatly degenerated," urged "wise but severe" government measures to improve the "quality of the race," basically for the sake of the ascendant classes and only incidentally for the people themselves.[99] Somewhere on this spectrum of gradations between Frenchman as object of national value and Frenchman as eudemonic subject, there was a moral split between those idealists who favored State aid to poor children and other unfortunates and the conservative utilitarians whose interest focused on the numbers.

Condorcet reiterated the thesis that human happiness, not sheer numbers, was the only real good, beyond even that of life itself: "Great philosophers have said that ... if the whole world embraced [celibacy] the human race would be extinguished tomorrow; if the human race is unhappy its destruction would be a blessing. Economists claim that the more men there are in a State the more powerful it is. They should show that those who inhabit it are happier." Like Montesquieu and Voltaire before him, Condorcet defied the populationist piety that the number of people in the State took precedence over their well-being. For him, "the objective of the

human race is not existence but happiness and not the puerile idea of load-
ing down the earth with useless and unhappy beings."[100]

On this issue, however, Condorcet went further than other eighteenth-
century liberals, approaching the one topic that even his most free-thinking
fellow countrymen could not bring themselves to discuss: obviating poverty
by controlling natality. He put forth an argument for the value of avoiding
unwanted pregnancies.[101] How could individuals limit their fertility in instances where they could not find work, where they could feed no more
mouths, where they were watching their present children starve? "Nature
has attached the greatest of all pleasures to the reproductive act and that
motive alone suffices to maintain the races of animals but it's different for
men, they have invented the means to enjoy the same pleasure without any
consequences and the little sacrifices they have to make are more than compensated by the inconveniences they avoid" (345).

Rather than righteously denouncing these means, these "fatal secrets" of
taking pleasure while avoiding consequences, as his fellow philosophes had
done, Condorcet frankly addressed the subject of artificial contraception
(not just coitus interruptus), a subject that Diderot, Rousseau, Mirabeau,
and so many others had claimed to find too horrible to contemplate. The
condom, offering protection against venereal disease as well as control of
fertility, was Condorcet's answer to unwanted pregnancies and, in effect,
what was being perceived as the real problem: population in excess of resources. The individual man, not the State, could control his reproduction,
limiting his offspring to the number he was prepared to raise with care.
Condorcet, with the primacy he accorded human happiness, recommended
a means of enjoying one of the few pleasures of life available to poor working people in a way that would not burden them with insuperable responsibilities. It was only a question of a simple device, if such an object could be
discussed without hysteria. Condorcet posed the question: "How is it that
they have attached shame to what has no other purpose than saving men
and preventing the birth of individuals destined for the suffering that almost infallibly awaits the unwanted child?"[102]

Condorcet's specific blueprint for realizing Montesquieu's admonition to
"raise men like plants" called for public relief programs, structural leveling
mechanisms, equality between the sexes, and active personal assumption of
responsibility for reproduction. In his view, neither Christian charity nor
public relief programs nor prolonged celibacy were acceptably humane responses to the recurrent problem of excessive births.

The logic of the Revolution and the social upheaval it unleashed forced these issues to be faced in ways that tested the capacities of the State. The institution of the *Hôtel-Dieu,* under royal patronage and much the same since the middle-ages, was the last resort for the terminally ill, the insane, women giving birth, the wounded, and those struck with communicable diseases, all of whom were thrust together in overcrowded and unsanitary conditions. The doctor Pierre-J.-G. Cabanis sounded the alarm about its deplorable state in 1790,[103] and his horrific account of conditions among the most unfortunate members of society spurred a movement toward reform. Desmaisons, Paris police administrator, commented: "I have never thought of these abysses of destruction without horror, where all ills are piled on top of each other, as if the objective was to make each one incurable by the complications of all the others. One might say that this institution owed its existence to an atrocious policy, which claims that in a great State there must be some means of diminishing an overly abundant population."[104] Was Desmaisons merely waxing hyperbolic, or did the morally bankrupt *hôpital* serve the same unconscious social purpose as the *enfants trouvés?*

In the winter of 1790, poor women, denied their traditional right to certain kinds of employment, began demanding beds at the *hôpitaux,* as did increasing numbers of beggars. Turned away at the door, the women rioted and were quelled only by police intervention. Women thereafter were required to present a certificate of "good morals" in order to be admitted to the facility, and if they tried to force their way in without it they could be imprisoned for a month. The National Assemby stripped the *hôpitaux* of their ecclesiastical assets on 3 December 1790 and attempted to organize help for the poor, the sick, and children along secular, Revolutionary principles. The enormity of the task continued to defeat the legislators' best efforts.

With the influx of destitute children from the provinces, the widespread Catholic network of programs assisting the needy was deeply disrupted, just as royal establishments were deprived of revenues.[105] Although orphan homes and charitable establishments had been temporarily excepted from the repression of religious orders in February 1790, they were unable to cope with the flood of needy people, the loss of traditional sources of revenue, and the atmosphere of hostility against clergy and nuns. The National Assembly was repeatedly petitioned by overwhelmed nuns asking for help in caring for the orphans and the dying. More and more beggars and vagabonds swarmed into the capital, and after an explosion of violent incidents, including murders, the Assembly formed the Beggary Commission (*comité de mendicité*), under the leadership of the duke of Rochefoucauld-Lian-court, to assess the plight of the swelling numbers of poor and hungry people all over France.[106]

The Beggary Commission was supposed to find solutions for the emergency. The decrees of that spring (30 May, 6 and 12 June) authorized the establishment of workshops for the able-bodied, including women and children, reserving *dépôts de mendicité* for the sick and those who refused to work. Not only Catholic charities but also many institutions formerly under royal patronage, like the institute for deaf and dumb children, fell into financial and administrative chaos, their charges adding to the swarms on the streets. The Beggary Commission was beset with difficulties on all fronts. For example, the mayor of Paris asked to have two convents evacuated (Récollets of the faubourg St.-Laurent and Dominicains of the rue St.-Jacques) in order to turn the entire space over to the homeless. But the question arose among the representatives of the Commune de Paris: what then would become of the ejected nuns? Would they not in turn become homeless? The municipal government was charged with providing beds for them, but then what of the children they had succored?

On 11 June 1790, Jacques Necker asked the National Assembly who was going to pay for giving work to all the needy of the nation. Their number far exceeded what programs in Paris could absorb, and it seemed that the more the capital tried to accommodate, the more came. The money accorded the poverty-stricken to discourage begging, although a pittance, prompted ever more desperate wretches to pour in from the provinces. The Assembly was forced to consider whether these masses could legitimately be kept from entering Paris, forcibly sent back to the provinces whence they came, or imprisoned. Necker spelled out the plight of the king's finances: the royal treasury was nearly depleted but "the king presently is supporting 12,000 men in public workshops in Paris besides the substantial manufacturing subsidies his Majesty provides every week." Government aid was being abused, and, according to Necker, "the needs are increasing as means diminish. If all these unemployed do not quit pouring into the capital, the safety and tranquillity of Paris are not assured."[107]

The problem cut to the heart of Revolutionary ideals. Could the Nation's representatives really punish the indigent for not finding work that was unavailable? What about the swarms of homeless children? The old system was unraveling fast, but a new system was not in place. A motion was proposed to suppress the tithe (*dixme*), one of the Church's principle sources of income. The State took on the responsibility for priests' salaries, but how were the clergy to continue their tradition of "good works"? Despite the wishes of many deputies to avoid totally alienating Catholic France from the Revolution, the logic of the secular State pushed extreme measures with unpredictable consequences. As these crises were being negotiated, the destitute crowds continued to invade the capital, violence erupted in the streets around the *salle de manège,* and the national guard under La Fayette was called to keep order. The other side of "the population crisis" was starting to make itself felt with a vengeance.

By 1791 the Beggary Commission was warning that "in order for the augmentation of the population to assure the happiness of the State, it must be accompanied by employment and France today does not find itself in that proportion . . . the disproportion between the French population and available employment is the first and essential cause of indigence."[108] The commission proclaimed a right to work, reserving relief to assistance to those who could not find a job. On 31 January 1791, it presented a multipart plan for assisting the poor, including "constitutional recognition of a right to aid; measures in favor of the sick, abandoned children, elderly, disabled and families." As Jacqueline Hecht points out, however, "in its reports, the commission never invoked overpopulation nor did it imagine recommending birth limitations to the lower classes."[109]

In the midst of the Terror, the situation of homeless children had become a crisis. A decree of 4 July 1793 stipulated that all abandoned children be called *enfants de la patrie* and be "adopted" by the nation. During the ensuing year, the actual implementation of the law encountered grave difficulties, despite the emotional solidarity and support of so many delegates. The Convention was presented with a petition from the wet nurses of the State-supported Hospice for Children of the Fatherland. According to Dumas, these women, charged with breast-feeding numerous abandoned babies, were themselves severely undernourished. "At five in the evening, they are given a rather small portion of dry legumes of the worst quality and they take no other nourishment until the next day at eight, although during this long interval they are obliged to satisfy the constant demands of their nurslings."[110]

The Jacobins were horrified by this revelation, but whatever measures they may have taken were forestalled by Thermidor. Subsequently, under the directory a decree was issued (20 March 1794) regulating the care of *les enfants de la patrie,* but it too was doomed to failure. The problems were as easy to resolve in theory as they were intractable in reality.

An observer who had no stake in France's nationalistic natalism, the British agronomist Arthur Young, was traveling in the country at the end of the 1780s. He published a description of his experiences and an account of the Revolution in 1792. Like Vauban, Young had the opportunity to observe close-up the realities of rural France, and he was shocked by what he saw: "Couples marry and procreate on the idea, not the reality, of a maintenance," he commented, "they increase beyond the demand of town and manufactures; and the consequence is distress, and numbers dying of diseases arising from insufficient nourishment." Unlike Vauban, however, Young blamed overpopulation. "I am clearly of the opinion, from the observations I made in every province of the kingdom, that her population is so much beyond the proportion of her industry and labour, that she would be much more powerful and infinitely more flourishing, if she had 5 or 6 millions less of inhabitants. From her too great population she presents in every quarter such spectacles of wretchedness, as are absolutely inconsistent with that degree of national felicity which she was capable of attaining, even under the old government."[111]

Young's comments attest to the conditions in many parts of France, pressuring the poor to migrate to Paris, as well as to the explosive prospect of the Revolutionary government being judged unfavorably in comparison to the monarchy on the grounds of national happiness. Revolutionary legislators had to face the expectations aroused by the new rules of society that proclaimed the solidarity of all citizens under a theoretically egalitarian regime. Young signals the alternative view of population: its increase is a curse to the government, not a blessing.

For the government, the problems of dealing with penurious, dangerous, pullulating masses became increasingly central to the integrity of the Revolution, and, although a number of admirable reforms were proposed and voted into law, no functioning system was ever implemented. Condorcet's generous and far-reaching project to reform the education of children in such a way as to abolish the structural causes of poverty and its ills, not just alleviate its effects, met with no success in his lifetime either, although some of its principles were incorporated into the legislation of the year III (1795–96), only to be lost in the chaos of the Terror.

The Revolution itself, for all its populationist propaganda, was responsible for the deaths of many thousands of citizens in the course of the war with the foreign powers, the political purges, the devastating campaigns against counterrevolution, and the mass drownings at Lyon and Nantes. All the Jacobin natalist rhetoric notwithstanding, both the image and the reality of death were increasingly associated with the cause of the radical left. Maignet, who was so insistent on Republican women's fruitfulness, was accused of having the entire population of the village of Bedouin "exterminated." He was also said to have had another two thousand traitors guillotined in Orange, on the orders of the Committee of Public Safety, a charge denied by Décembre-Allonnier (2:347). Other radical champions of population demanded the massive executions of their political enemies, like Marat who wanted to see "another 300,000 heads roll!" Dupâquier quotes the sanguinary exhortations of Jacobin leaders like Carrier, Collot d'Herbois, and Geoffroy, the last demanding "that the guillotine be in constant use in the entire Republic: five million inhabitants will be enough for France." Dupâquier comments that these statements were not really anti-populationist but rather only "passing comments" (*propos de circumstance*).[112]

The radical leader of the so-called conspiracy of equals, friend and then enemy of Robespierre, Gracchus (Fr.-Noël) Babeuf, (1764–97) thought otherwise. Horrified by the Terror and its systematic massacres, especially Carrier's atrocities in Nantes, Babeuf published a pamphlet entitled *Du Système de dépopulation*, charging that the Jacobins were conspiring to rid France of its excess citizens because the government could not deal with public demands for subsistence. In this indictment, Babeuf depicted the mounting spirals of violence of the Terror not as the result of factionalism and political struggles for dominance but as a deliberate plot to reduce the population in order to realize the social program preached by Jean-Jacques Rousseau. According to "Jean-Jacques," said Babeuf,

> All citizens must have enough and no citizen should have too much. From this premise derived the following considerations and consequences . . . that among us men were crowding in on each other too much for each one to be able to live comfortably . . . that with the superabundant population being able to increase to such a degree . . . there would have to be a sacrifice of a portion of the sans-culottes. With the system of depopulation and the new redistribution of riches among the survivors everything can be explained,— the war in the Vendée, the foreign war, the proscriptions, the guillotining, the drownings (etc.), Jacobins are also guilty of the system of poverty and

shortages, the other monstrous child of the government . . . that starved the entire Republic.[113]

Thus the Jacobin ideology of extreme populationism was denounced as a hypocritical sham in a nation decimated by subsistence crises, political mass murders, and war. The long-favored doctrine that measured the value of the nation's government by the number of the inhabitants now was used to accuse the Jacobins of deliberately destroying the *sans-culottes,* and Rousseau, patron saint of large Republican families, was now charged with inspiring systematic genocide. Population growth was being increasingly associated with violence and famine as the coping mechanisms of the old order, however inefficient, gave way.

Malthus

The dismaying idea, raised by Arthur Young and Desmaisons, attributed to the Jacobins by Babeuf, that France needed to rid itself of superfluous population was not an isolated eccentricity in the late 1790s. The Enlightenment's long fixation on population, juxtaposed against the terrifying realities of Revolutionary mass despair and violence, as well as Condorcet's ideas and the recommendations of the Beggary Commission, was to provoke the theory behind the most famous—or infamous—demographic text of the eighteenth century.

Thomas Robert Malthus was the son of Daniel Malthus, cultivated English country gentleman, admirer of Condorcet and the protosocialist optimist William Godwin,[114] and good friend of Jean-Jacques Rousseau. So devoted was Daniel Malthus to Rousseau, who had visited him when Malthus's son was three weeks old, that he raised the boy following the precepts of *Emile.* As has often been noted, when Robert Malthus grew up he resoundingly repudiated Rousseau's theories, mocked Godwin's optimism, and condemned Condorcet's programs for dealing with the unfortunate of the earth, setting forth the ultimate antinatalist argument in his *Essay on the Principle of Population.*[115] Malthus's *Essay* described a whole nightmare world not unlike Paris in the 1790s, where burgeoning humanity was always on the brink of destruction—a world where children of poor parents were destined to die of hunger. As for those abandoned by their parents, "these children must necessarily fall for support upon the society, or starve."[116] Unlike the representatives of the French nation, who were torn between feelings of responsibility and overwhelming obstacles in dealing with the homeless, Malthus expressed no solidarity with society's hungry waifs. Social efforts to care for such children, in Malthus's view, were wrong-headed, sentimental interference in a natural law and would only encourage more surplus population while unjustly taxing private property to keep them alive.

Unwanted children, the dispossessed, the elderly, the sick, and the poverty-stricken could only receive public assistance by dipping into the pockets of the well-off. Between the rights of the needy and those of the propertied class, the Christian clergyman Malthus did not hesitate to decide, opting for the law establishing private property which "must not be defeated by the concession of a right of full support to all that might be born. . . . The concession of such a right, and a right of property, are absolutely incompatible, and cannot exist together." Malthus conceded that charity was the one way of relieving one's conscience at the sight of human starvation, provided the decision to give was strictly up to the individual, since charity "loses its essence the moment it ceases to be voluntary" (3:532). Charity is based on the donor's relationship to God, not to the State. It permits a measure of control over the object of one's largesse, whereas governmental poor relief not only bleeds the solid citizenry, it obliterates the moral superiority of the contributor over the recipient. The difference between the grateful but powerless and the arrogant entitled was one Malthus was very intent on preserving.

Like so many of the century's population experts, Malthus claimed to understand the secret workings of nature. "It has appeared, that from the inevitable laws of our nature some human beings must suffer from want. These are the unhappy persons who, in the great lottery of life, have drawn a blank." Anyway, if given assistance, "the number of these claimants would soon exceed the ability of the surplus produce to supply" (1:74), a conclusion it was not difficult to buttress with the evidence of the French Beggary Commission. In his second edition of the *Essay* (1803), Malthus's lottery metaphor evolved into his famous image of rightful exclusion, the banquet with limited seating. Once proprietorship of the earth has been divided up among families, "there is no vacant cover at nature's mighty feast," Malthus observed. Like Paris in the Revolution, the table of life was only so big. Admit the starving "and the happiness of the guests is destroyed by the spectacle of misery and dependence in every part of the hall . . . the guests learn too late their error in counteracting those strict orders to all intruders, issued by the great mistress of the feast," Nature, "who, wishing that all her guests should have plenty, and knowing that she could not provide for unlimited numbers, humanely refused to admit fresh comers when her table was already full" (3:505–6). Besides, Malthus claimed, the sufferings of the desperate are not just natural but divinely intended, the necessary spurs to industry and mental development, the "instruments with which the Supreme Being forms matter into mind" (1:135).[117]

Malthus came to other conclusions from the French example as well as that of the British Poor Laws, pointing out an additional defect in grandiose governmental plans to help the needy: they were seldom adequately implemented. "The grand objection to the language used respecting the 'right of the poor to support' is, that, as a matter of fact, we do not perform what we promise, and the poor may justly accuse us of deceiving them" (1:38).

While Condorcet, before Malthus, had foreseen an eventual disproportion "between the natural increase of population and food," his contraceptive solution was too much for the English clergyman. Malthus expressed shock that Condorcet: "proceeds to remove the difficulty in a manner which I profess not to understand . . . he alludes . . . to something . . . unnatural. To remove the difficulty in this way will, surely, in the opinions of most men, be to destroy that virtue and purity of manners, which the advocates of equality, and of the perfectibility of man, profess to be the end and object of their views" (1:57).[118] And in the 1826 edition he claims: "I would always reprobate any artificial and unnatural modes of checking population" (2:479).

Malthus seemed to be able to countenance, with resigned equanimity, the spectacle of millions of starving children who had "drawn a blank" or found themselves without a place at "nature's banquet." The notion of a condom, on the other hand, was so unnerving to him that he had to "profess not to understand" it. In the second version of his *Essay,* he recommended the austere regime of delayed marriage and premarital chastity as the only morally acceptable ways of avoiding unwanted births, once again putting caution above gratification. In so doing he was urging as an individual, conscious choice the means of population limitation that had been operative as a silent social control mechanism in France and other parts of Europe for centuries. Continued adherence to this prudent way of life would avoid the kind of disaster that had so recently wracked France. "A mob," Malthus warned, "which is generally the growth of a redundant population goaded by resentment for real sufferings . . . is of all monsters the most fatal to freedom" (8:501).

The power of the eighteenth-century "depopulation delusion" lies in its resonances with anxieties ranging from the most abstract to the most visceral. God had commanded fruitfulness and multiplication, He condemned infertile sex, the king needed more subjects, national security depended on demographic strength, the Republic had to be more fertile than the monarchy, true happiness required a large family, without fatherhood men were not men, women without children were worse than useless beings—the string of directives invoked all the major sources of authority, from divine will to social norms. After the Revolution, however, with its nightmarish eruptions of uncontrollable masses at once demanding subsistence and destroying life and property, after the frank appeal to class solidarity of Malthus's *Essay*, after the Directory's regrouping of forces and the Napoleonic takeover, France's chronic population apprehension underwent a new series of metamorphoses. Hard-core natalism continued to command loyalties, especially among the socialists and the Napoleonically rehabilitated Catholic church. A prudent Malthusianism, however, was distinctively making itself felt not only in the boudoir but eventually in public discourse. Less cautious voices soon also were heard, as advocates for artificial birth-control attempted to bring the great taboo subject to public attention. Openly political debates raged over the issues during the nineteenth century: whether it was immoral to prevent conception or to bring children into the world who could not be fed; whether the government was instituted to protect property or to provide for the needs of the less fortunate classes; whether service to the State or happiness, including sexual pleasure, was the legitimate goal of human existence.[119]

It took another defeat for the French government, this one at the hands of the procreatively robust Prussians in 1871, to regenerate the cause of ardent natalism as the nation's comparative demographic position in Europe continued its long decline.

NOTES

Chapter One: The Value of Kings

1. Baker, "Politics and Public Opinion," 210.

2. Thau, *Raison d'Etat et pensée politique,* 245.

3. Merrick, "The Religious *Police* of the Ancien Régime," 3.

4. Roche, *France and the Enlightenment,* 423. Habermas's 1962 study, *The Structural Transformation of the Public Sphere,* which investigates means of communication, social networks, and various institutions of the ancien régime, continues to generate fruitful controversy over the nature of the "public sphere," its class and gender parameters, and the reality of its unity. See Maza, "Women, the Bourgeoisie, and the Public Sphere," for a discussion of the contributions of J. Landes, D. Gordon, D. Bell, D. Goodman, and K. M. Baker to the ongoing debate. Darnton has investigated the culture of subversive publications and their influence and distribution before the Revolution in a series of studies, including *The Literary Underground of the Old Regime* and *Gens de lettres, gens du livre.*

5. For a historical analysis of this topos, see J.-Cl. Perrot, "Les Economistes, les philosophes et la population," 499–551, and Hasquin, "Le Débat sur la dépopulation," in Moheau, *Recherches et considérations,* 397–424.

6. Dupâquier, introduction to *Histoire de la population française,* 2:2–4.

7. Michel Foucault frames the development of populationist discourse in terms of the question: "Cette mise en discours du sexe n'est-elle pas ordonnée à la tâche de chasser de la réalité les formes de sexualité qui ne sont pas soumises à l'économie stricte de la reproduction?"—only to cast doubt on this hypothesis because it does not, in his view, adequately explain why the repressive measures were not differentially applied to the working classes. He concludes that it was perhaps less an effort of the "classes dirigeantes" to limit the pleasure of others than an experiment "they tried out first on themselves." *Histoire de la sexualité,* 1:62–63; 1:158–68. As this study demonstrates, the period's innumerable populationist texts spring from a variety of sources and incorporate a whole range of often conflicting concerns, difficult to attribute to a single mentality looking to further only one agenda.

8. J.-Cl. Perrot, "Les Economistes, les philosophes et la population," 2:545. Among numerous other studies devoted to this question, see Spengler's pioneering

work, *French Predecessors of Malthus,* and Riley, *Population Thought in the Age of the Demographic Revolution.*

9. Among the scientific advances achieved under the pressure of demographic concerns, J. Hecht traces the origins of the census and its relations to government and sacred practices dating from the dawn of civilization. She discusses sources of demographic information in Europe from the eighth century through the Enlightenment in "L'Idée de dénombrement jusqu'à la Révolution." The development of demography is treated by M. Dupâquier and J. Dupâquier in *Histoire de la démographie;* this development is framed in relation to agriculture by G. Weulersse, *Le Mouvement physiocratique en France, 1756–1770* (Paris, 1910); A. Landry, *François Quesnay et la physiocratie* (Paris, 1958); E. Boserup, *Evolution agraire et pression démographique* (Paris, 1970); in relation to economics by E. Labrousse, *La Crise de l'économie française à la fin de l'Ancien Régime et au début de la Révolution* (Paris, 1944); J. J. Spengler, *French Predecessors of Malthus: A Study of Eighteenth-Century Wage and Population Theory* (New York, 1965); and in relation to political science by E. Brian, *La Mesure de l'Etat.*

10. Tomaselli, "Moral Philosophy and Population Questions," 7.

11. Chastellux, *De La Félicité publique,* 128. In Chastellux's view, the question "depuis longtemps aurait dû être décidée par des dénombrements," but instead it "n'a guère été jugée que par l'humeur et la flatterie."

12. Messance, *Tableau de la population de la France;* Moheau, *Recherches et considérations;* Expilly, *Tableau de la population de la France;* Chastellux, *De La Félicité publique,* 128.

13. It was not until the 1870s that the reality of a falling population in France caught up with the widely held misconception of the preceding century. Questions related to demographics, particularly those concerning natalism, contraception, and immigration continue to provoke bitter controversies in France. See Dupâquier et al., *Histoire de la population française,* vol. 3, especially Charbit and Béjin, "La Pensée démographique," 465–501. Ronsin describes the struggles in nineteenth- and twentieth-century France between proponents of populationism and advocates of family planning in *La Grève des ventres.* The more recent antinatalist salvo launched by Hervé le Bras in *Marianne et les lapins, l'obsession démographique* (Paris, 1991) elicited much political and scientific controversy.

14. Delon, "The Priest, the Philosopher, and Homosexuality," in Maccubbin, ed., *Unauthorized Sexual Behavior,* 3:124.

15. Cassan, *La Recherche des droits du Roy,* 2. Marc Bloch, *Les Rois thaumaturges,* his study of the supernatural attributes of the Bourbon monarchy, including the king's power to heal scrofula by his touch, remains the essential text in this area.

16. Frazier goes on to note: "the complete failure of that power in [the king] would involve a corresponding failure in men, animals, and plants, and would

thereby entail at no distant date the entire extinction of all life, whether human, animal, or vegetable." *The Golden Bough,* 4:27.

17. Kantorowicz, *The King's Two Bodies,* 22. According to Georges Dumézil there were three functions common to Indo-European royal ideologies: "sovereignty (magico-religious and juridico-religious), physical strength (principally that of a warrior) and fertility (with its numerous harmonics: abundance, riches, health). "Le Rex et les flamines maiores." Le Roy Ladurie, in *L'Ancien Régime,* 1:30, points out that the French ritual of coronation specifically emphasized those three functions, the last of which "covers the vast area of fecundity, fertility, productivity, prosperity."

18. Le Roy Ladurie, *Mémoires de Louis XIV,* 1:272.

19. Goubert, *Louis XIV,* 9–21.

20. In "Extrait des Eloges," 382–440.

21. Fénelon, *Ecrits et lettres politiques,* 149.

22. Rothkrug, *Opposition to Louis XIV,* 257. According to Urbain (editor of *Fénelon's Remonstrances*), 16, the letter was probably received by the king. Keohane believes that Mme de Maintenant suppressed the letter. *Philosophy and the State,* 334, n. 6.

23. Quoted by Vilquin in "Vauban," 207–57.

24. Rebelliau, *Vauban,* 293–96.

25. According to the authors, this census "constitue sans doute l'unique recensement national de toute l'histoire de l'Ancien Régime." Hecht, "L'Idée de dénombrement jusqu'à la Révolution," 1:85. See Desrosières, *La Politique des grands nombres,* for an account of the development and usage of the census and its statistical analysis.

26. Hecht and Sauvy discuss the Revolutionary modernity and scientific value of Vauban's ideas in "Le Grand Homme du 'Grand Siècle,'" 15:33.

27. Dupâquier and Vilquin, "Le Pouvoir royal et la statistique démographique," 1:86.

28. Hecht discusses Boisguilbert's debt to Vauban in "La Vie de . . . Boisguilbert." Boisguilbert was born in 1646 and died in 1714.

29. Boisguibert, *Détail de la France,* 1014–15 (159).

30. Saint-Simon, *Le Roi soleil* (Paris, 1992), 15, 25.

31. See Boislisle, *Mémoires des intendants,* and Esmonin, "*Les Mémoires* des intendants pour l'instruction du duc de Bourgogne," for discussions of this and other early efforts at arriving at an objective evaluation of France's population. According to Esmonin, the skeptical De Brou, Intendant de Bourgogne, commented: "tout cela ne servira qu'à barbouiller du papier" (30).

32. Goubert, *Louis XIV,* 14–15.

33. Bernstein, "Sur la Diffusion des oeuvres de Boisguilbert et de Vauban," 163–65.

34. Hecht comments on public curiosity concerning demographic information in

principle accessible only to the King and his aides: "Ce souci d'information et de publicité statistique est très vif à une époque ou, dans la plupart des pays, le secret pesait sur les différentes opérations comme sur les archives des gouvernements, particulièrement en matière de finances et de population." "L'Idée du dénombrement," 56. Dupâquier and Vilquin discuss various other projects for arriving at a numerical representation of the population, including contrôleur général Dodun's effort to exempt the very poor from the salt tax; Bertin's project in 1762; the abbé Expilly's revision of Saugrain in 1762; and the "*enquête* of Averdy in 1764." "Le Pouvoir royal et la statistique démographique," 88.

35. Brian, *La Mesure de l'Etat*, 155.

Chapter Two: Montesquieu and the "Depopulation Letters"

1. Among the most successful novels in letter form featuring political satire and foreign locales before Montesquieu were J.-P. Marana's *L'Espion du Grand Seigneur, et les relations secrètes envoyées au Divan de Constantinople* (Amsterdam, 1664), reedited as *L'Espion dans les cours des princes chrétiens* or *Lettres d'un espion turc* in numerous editions until 1756, and J. F. Bernard, *Réflexions morales, satiriques et comiques* (Amsterdam, 1711). For a discussion of this literature, see Van Roosbroeck, *Persian Letters before Montesquieu.*

2. Dupâquier, *La Population française aux XVII et XVIIIe siècles*, 43–45.

3. For studies of the critique of monarchy in Montesquieu's novel, see Ehrard, *Politique de Montesquieu.*

4. J.-C. Perrot, "Les Economistes, les philosophes et la population," 517.

5. Montesquieu, *Pensées*, first published 1899 and 1901, *Oeuvres complètes*, 1:1228.

6. Montesquieu's comments that in his work "l'auteur s'est donné l'avantage de pouvoir joindre de la philosophie, de la politique et de la morale, à un roman, et de lier le tout par une chaîne secrète et, en quelque façon, inconnue" (*Oeuvres complètes*, 1:130). This "secret charm" has provoked considerable speculation as to the significance of the metaphor. Pauline Kra was among the first to call attention to its meaning in "The Invisible Chain of the *Lettres persanes*," *SVEC* 102 (1973): 121–41. Kra's article provoked a long series of ripostes, discussed by Diana J. Schaub in *Erotic Liberalism: The Feminized Philosophy of Montesquieu's Persian Letters* (London, 1995),163–64. See also Grosrichard, *Structure du sérail* (Paris, 1979), 34–39.

7. According to the Koran, however, "vous ne pourrez jamais traiter également vos femmes, quand bien même vous le désireriez ardemment" (4:28); and, further, "jamais vous ne pourrez être équitables envers [vos] épouses, même si vous vous efforcez de l'être" (4:129).

8. See Goody, *Development of the Family*, 146–56.

9. Leibacher-Ouvrard analyzes the purposes that the figure of the eunuch was made to serve in various Enlightenment causes in "L'Eunuque, anathème et prétexte," 11–26.

10. Dupâquier, *La Population française,* 26.

11. Dupâquier and B. Lepetit, "Le Peuplement," in Dupâquier et al., *Histoire de la population française,* 2:62.

12. "Pour le Philosophe ce sont le fer et le bled qui ont civilisé les hommes et perdu le Genre-humain." *Oeuvres complètes* 3:171–72.

13. See Guy, *The French Image of China* and R. Etiemble's three-volume *L'Orient philosophique au XVIIIe siècle* (Paris, 1956–59). Voltaire devotes a long essay to attacking the myth of populous China as an example of all the virtues, commenting sarcastically: "La population prodigieuse de cet empire, en comparaison duquel notre Europe n'est qu'un désert, suffit pour prouver infailliblement que ce peuple est le plus sage et le plus heureux de la terre" in "Lettre de Ferney," 13 June 1766, *Correspondance littéraire,* 5:287.

14. Cantillion, "La Multiplication et le décroissement des peuples," in *Essai sur la nature du commerce,* 1755, 47.

15. Malthus, *An Essay on the Principle of Population* [1798] 1:104.

Chapter Three: Celibacy

1. "La société du temps n'ayant absolument pas conscience de sa surpopulation relative, les contemporains n'ont pas saisi les aspects positifs de ce mécanisme prémalthusien, facteur essentiel de régulation démographique et de croissance économique." Hecht, "Célibat, stratégies familiales et essor du capitalisme," 7:282. For an analysis of the question of "surpopulation" in seventeenth-century France, see J. Dupâquier, "La France de Louis XIV était-elle surpeuplé?" *Annales de Démographie,* 1975, 43.

2. Hecht notes that the term *célibat* appears in French around 1549, *célibataire* in 1711, Hecht, "Célibat, stratégies familiales et essor du capitalisme," 7:259. See also Knibiehler, "Le Célibat," 78.

3. Goody, *Development of the Family,* 95.

4. Dupâquier argues that in reality the ascendant class controlled the birthrate more than the Church did, by means of three *social* taboos more powerful than either civil law or religious dogma: no extramarital conception, no cohabitation of married couples, and no marriage without the means to set up a household ("La France de Louis XIV," 40). These interdictions do not appear to contradict legal or ecclesiastical strictures.

5. *Oeuvres sur la virginité* (Paris, 1729), 381.

6. *Treatises on Marriage* (Washington, D.C., 1955), 10.

7. Goody, *Development of the Family,* 78–82.

8. *Tametsi* [Paris, 1686], in Sarpi, *Histoire du Concile de Trente,* 1:524–30.

9. Luther, *Mémoires* (Paris, 1974), 323, 214. Luther also composed numerous tracts against celibacy, including "An Exhortation to the Knights of the Teutonic Order that they lay aside False Chastity and Assume the True Chastity of Wedlock" (1523),

in Luther, *Works,* trans. W. Brandt (Philadelphia 1962). A list of these writings appears in 45:143, n. 3. Lyndal Roper discusses the views of Luther and Calvin regarding chastity vows in *The Holy Household: Women and Morals in Reformation Ausberg,* (Oxford, 1989).

10. Schulte van Kessel, "Vièrges et mères," 3:145.

11. Grandier, *Traité du célibat des prêtres,* 32; Bayle, *Dictionnaire,* 2:590–91.

12. This work was first published in Padoue, 1558, and reprinted in Utrecht, 1750.

13. See Hufton, *The Prospect before Her,* 1:367.

14. In Rufus Bishop, *Testimonies of . . . Mother Ann Lee* (Hancock, Vt., 1816),12.

15. In Flo Morse's *The Shakers and the World's People* (Hanover, 1987), the suspicion is voiced that in the course of the ecstatic trembling dance that gave the sect its name, certain pleasurable, if nonprocreative, erotic satisfactions were to be enjoyed.

16. Charron, *De la Sagesse, trois livres,* 98.

17. Puffendorf, *On the Duty of Man and Citizen according to Natural Law,* 120.

18. Moheau, *Recherches et considérations,* 99. In the Académie française, Moheau points out, "on compte trois célibataires contre un homme marié," (99, n. a).

19. Goody discusses the economic history of primogeniture in *Death, Property and the Ancestors.*

20. Cantillion, *Essai sur la nature du commerce,* 43. Mysteries surround the life and work of this millionaire Irish economist, who probably born between 1680 and 1690 and disappeared in 1734. See the comments in the 1997 edition of Cantillion's *Essai sur la nature du commerce* of C. Théré, E. Brian, A. E. Murphy, A. Fage, A. Sauvy, A. Fanfani, J. J. Spengler, and L. Salleron on his demographic and economic thought, i–lxxiii. The major studies of Cantillon are those of Murphy.

21. Verzure, *Réflexions hazardées d'une femme ignorante,* 143.

22. Mercier, *Le Tableau de Paris,* 2:440.

23. See Flandrin, *Le Sexe et l'Occident.*

24. According to Bernos, "Pour ne pas avoir à s'abstenir totalement, les garçons au moins disposent d'un autre moyen: le mariage des autres . . . Ils y trouvent des partenaires commodes, pour qui une éventuelle gravidité ne serait plus une catastrophe remettant en cause leur statut social et leur avenir, puisqu'elles sont 'casées.'" *Le Fruit défendu,* 175.

25. Gutwirth, *The Twilight of the Goddesses,* 40–41.

26. Foucault's observation is discussed by G. S. Rousseau in "The Pursuit of Homosexuality in the Eighteenth Century," 132–68, in Maccubbin, ed., *Unauthorized Sexual Behavior.* This collection contains a number of other relevant pieces, especially those of J.-M. Goulemot, M. Delon, M. Rey, and R. Trumbach. Numerous aspects of eighteenth-century unconsecrated sexual behavior have been treated in illuminating ways in recent years. A few works dealing with subjects most germane to this study include J. Merrick and B. T. Ragan, eds. *Homosexuality in Modern France,* and G. S. Rousseau and R. Porter, eds., *Sexual Undergrounds of the Enlightenment.*

27. According to the *coûtume de Paris* (Paris custom), women who enjoyed some level of emancipation included certain categories of widows, "public merchants," and those few who had succeeded in obtaining legal separations.

28. Verzure, *Réflexions hazardées d'une femme ignorante*, 150. However, it is true that, beginning in the late sixteenth century, certain religious teaching, missionary, and nursing orders offered "filles séculières" the possibility of attenuated vows and greater freedom in conjunction with career responsibilities in the world. See Jean de Viguerie, "Une Forme nouvelle de la vie consacrée," 175−95.

29. Suchon, *Du Célibat volontaire ou la vie sans engagement*, 134.

30. Mercier, *Le Tableau de Paris*, 2:165.

31. According to an edict of 1556, an unmarried pregnant woman was obliged to declare her pregnancy before a magistrate. If she failed to do so and the child died unbaptized, she could be put to death. For a discussion of the legal and theological aspects of this law, see Hufton, *The Prospect before Her*, 1:271−76. Linguet, *Du Plus Heureux Gouvernement*, 60−61. For a discussion of Linguet's probing analysis of the relationship between property and the status of women, see D. G. Levy, *The Ideas and Careers of Simon-Nicolas Linguet*, 62−64.

32. "L'opinion de L.S. Mercier est nette: la dot est une 'empêcheuse' de mariages; puisqu'elle augmente le nombre de célibataires, il faut la supprimer." Farge, *La Vie fragile*, 33. A. Farge and C. Klapisch also bring together a group of texts representing the conflicted self-images of women alone in *Madame ou Mademoiselle?* (Paris, 1984).

33. Fauve-Chamoux, "Le Surplus urbain des femmes" 368.

34. According to Jean Astruc, "Professeur en droit français de l'université de Toulouse," the fiscal burdens imposed on the widow who remarries or "misbehaves" (*malverse*), especially within a year of her husband's decease, are far heavier than those suffered by the widower because "of a kind of prerogative or preeminence accorded the dignity of the viril sex." Astruc, *Traité des peines des secondes noces* (Toulouse, 1774), 370. G. de la Champagne's *Traité des . . . secondes noces* (Paris, 1720), P. Dupin's *Traité des peines de secondes noces* (Paris, 1743), and J. Le Scène des Maison's *Contrat conjugal* (Neuchâtel, 1783) all present the impediments imposed upon the remarriage of widows. According to A. Burguière, 50 percent of widowers remarried compared with 20 percent of widows. "Réticences et intégration," 41−48.

35. Jacques Poumarède, discussing the various legal and social sanctions to which the widow was subject, points out that not until 1891 was a law passed permitting widows in France to be included in the order of inheritance of their husbands' estates. "Le Droit des veuves," 74.

36. Marat, *De L'Homme*, 1778, 98. Leviratic marriages were those under Jewish law by which the brother or other relative of a deceased man was obliged to marry the widow. Goody, *Development of the Family*, 60−68. Depending on whether a widow lived in "pays coûtumier" or "pays de droit écrit," various waiting periods and

certain other fiscal and legal restraints were applicable. Except for the youngest women (between the ages of twenty and twenty-nine years), most widows did not remarry. See Traer, *Marriage and the Family*.

37. On celibacy, "Jesus replied, 'Not everyone can accept this word, but only those to whom it has been given. For some are eunuchs because they were born that way; others were made that way by men; and others have renounced marriage because of the kingdom of heaven. The one who can accept this should accept it.'" *Matthew* 19:11–12.

38. E. A. Wrigley and R. S. Schofield, in *The Population History of England* (London, 1981), would seem to lend credit to Montesquieu's analysis by attributing the increase in English population in the early modern period to its prevailing matrimonial structures, or "nuptuality." Tomaselli comments that Montesquieu's argument was intended to promote "moving away from the absolutism of Louis XIV's reign and curbing the power of the Church. It meant following the English example." "Moral Philosophy," 15.

39. Hecht, "Célibat, stratégies familiales," 261.

40. Walter, "Le Complexe d'Abélard," 12:147.

41. In *Ouvrages de morale*, vols. 4–15.

42. The "Englishman" is a reference to W. Petty's *Political Arithmetick (sic)*. For a recent study of the emerging calculating mentality in England, as well as a rich bibliography, see R. E. Connor, "'Can You Apply Arithmetick to Everything?'," 169–94.

43. Perrot, "Les Economistes, les philosophes et la population," 2:512.

44. Melon, *Essai politique sur le commerce*, 50.

45. Cantillion, *Essai sur la nature du commerce*, 53.

46. Voltaire, *Oeuvres*, 21:481.

47. Meslier, "Mémoire," in *Oeuvres,* 499. Meslier is seriously engaging a theme with which libertine writings of the previous century had often toyed. For example, in B. Fontenelle's "Lettre sur la nudité," he assures the indulgent marquise, his correspondent, that far from being objects of shame, human reproductive organs are to be honored as "les parties naturelles, par lesquelles la Nature opérait le plus noble de ses ouvrages . . . la multiplication du genre humain." *La République des philosophes* (Geneva, 1768), 179. For a discussion of Thomas Pichon's critique of the danger posed by Meslier's manuscript, see G. Artigas-Menant, "Quatre Témoignages inédits sur le 'Testament,'" *Dix-huitième Siècle* 24 (1992): 83–94.

48. Voltaire, *Discours en vers sur l'homme, Oeuvres* (Paris, 1829), 12:84.

> [Dieu] ainsi qu'en son sérail un musulmane jaloux,
> Qui n'admet près de lui que ces monstres d'Asie,
> Que le fer a privé des sources de la vie.

49. In *L'Essai sur les moeurs*, for example, Voltaire demonstrates familiarity with the demographic estimates of the period, discounting the pessimistic calculations of his contemporaries and coming to a conclusion in harmony with Montesquieu's at

the end of the "depopulation letters": "qu'importe qu'il y ait beaucoup ou peu d'hommes sur la terre? L'essentiel est que cette pauvre espèce soit le moins malheureuse qu'il est possible." Voltaire, *Oeuvres*, 24:582.

50. Montesquieu, *Esprit des lois*, 2:683.

51. Prior to the Revolution, the principle that "the marriage demonstrates who is the father" (*pater est quem nuptiae demonstrant*) was respected, a rule to be reaffirmed by the decree of 19 floréal, an 2 [8 May 1794]. M. Lévy agrees with Montesquieu when he postulates that "the institution of marriage according to law is the answer to the impossibility of proving paternity," going on to examine how "the Church, then the *Code Civil*, then Social Security have claimed to deal with this matter and its consequences." Lévy, "Le Secret de la paternité," 1.

52. Montesquieu here joins Samuel Puffendorf, who held that "the obligation is that the propagation of the human race must absolutely not proceed by way of casual and promiscuous intercourse. It should always be bound by the laws of matrimony and therefore only practiced within marriage. Without this a decent and well-ordered society among men and the development of civil life are inconceivable." Puffendorf, *On the Duty of Man and Citizen according to Natural Law*, 120.

53. Toussaint was responsible for the article "Jurisprudence" in the *Encyclopédie* (vol. 14). The police description contained in the files of inspector Joseph d'Hémery, concerning this relatively unknown "*homme de lettres*" who five times was imprisoned in the Bastille for his writings, is included in the chapter "Les Encyclopédistes et la police" in Darnton's *Gens de lettres, gens du livre*, 82. According to the police dossier, Toussaint was "un homme estimable."

54. Toussaint, *Les Moeurs*, 232.

55. See, for example, the counterattacks of abbé J. Richard, *Réflexions critiques*, and abbé G. Gauchat, *Lettres critiques, ou Analyse et réfutation de divers écrits modernes contre la religion*, a series of 19 volumes, from 1755 to 1763, in which the abbé attempts to stem the rising tide of "impious" writings, including Toussaint's as well as those of Voltaire, Montesquieu, and others.

56. Grimm and Diderot, *Correspondance littéraire*, 2:365–66.

57. Eon de Beaumont, "Les Espérances d'un bon patriote," 52–53.

58. Eon de Beaumont, *Les Loisirs du chavalier d'Eon*, 274.

59. Rousseau, *Oeuvres complètes*, 2:668.

60. Wallace, *Dissertation historique et politique sur la population*, 103.

61. Fage provides this list in "Les Doctrines de population," 611.

62. Diderot and D'Alembert, *Encyclopédie* 14:56. Subsequent text references during this discussion are to the *Encyclopédie*.

63. Published in Morin, *Histoire critique du célibat*, in *Mémoires de l'Institut National de France*, 4:308–45. S.v. "Célibat" in Diderot and d'Alembert, *Encyclopédie*, 6:600–610.

64. Voltaire, *Dictionnaire philosophique*, in *Oeuvres*, 3:196–97.

65. *Oeuvres complètes* 26:531–60. For a collection of "Extraits relatifs au Mariage des Prêtres" in Voltaire, see *Oeuvres*, 26:559.

66. For a discussion of Voltaire's writings on population, see Hasquin, "Voltaire démographe."

67. For a discussion of Diderot's liberal populationism, see Hasquin, "Politique, économie et démographie chez Diderot," 107–22.

68. Diderot, *Correspondance*, 14:118; Walter, "Le Complexe d'Abélard ou le Célibat des gens de lettres," 12:147.

69. Diderot, *La Religieuse*, in *Oeuvres romanesques*, 311.

70. Ibid., 119; Diderot, *Correspondance*, 4:85. That Diderot knew a lot more about the complexities of human sexuality than he reveals in his most natalist texts is evident from the jealousy he displays toward Sophie's lesbian relationship with her sister, the married Mme Legendre (3:74–75), as well as the frank discussions of masturbation, bestiality, and sodomy in his "private writings," that is, *Le Rêve de D'Alembert*, *L'Entretien de D'Alembert* and *La Suite de l'Entretien*, composed in 1767 and circulated among a small group of friends. Diderot called this manuscript a "dangerous production," which, if it became publicly known, would "destroy my repose, my fortune, my life and my honor, or the just opinion people have conceived of my morals" (*Correspondance*, 9:157–58).

71. Hecht, "Malthus avant Malthus," 26:77.

72. D'Holbach, *La Politique naturelle*, 2:132.

73. Pilati di Tassulo, *Traité du mariage*. The aristocratic Pilati (1733–1802) was a *fils spirituel* of Montesquieu. "Il se proposait de parcourir les différents Etats de l'Europe pour en étudier les différentes formes du gouvernement et reconnaître leur influence sur le caractère et le bonheur du peuple," according to Michaud, *Biographie universelle*, 14:328.

74. Felice, *Le Code de l'humanité*, 2:210, 229; Capitani, "The *Encyclopédie* in Switzerland," 35–38.

75. Menassier de l'Estre, *De L'Honneur des deux sexes*; Mercier, *Tableau de Paris*, 1.

76. Anonymous, *Moyens proposés pour prévenir l'infanticide*, 48.

77. Groubert de Linière, *L'Antimoine*, 26.

78. Mirabeau, *L'Ami des hommes*, 3:172.

79. Ibid.; Cantillon, *Essai sur la nature du commerce*, 47.

80. Hume, *Political Discourses*, 398.

81. Expilly, *Dictionnaire géographique, historique et politique des Gaules et de la France*, 6 vols. (Amsterdam; rpt., Paris, 1973); Messance, *Recherches sur la population* (Paris, 1776; rpt., Paris, 1973); *Tableau de la population*, (Lyons, 1788); Chastellux, *De la Félicité publique*; Moheau, *Recherches et considérations*. Concerning the identities and attributions of Moheau and Montyon, see R. Le Mée, "Jean-Baptiste Moheau," and E. Brian, "Moyens de connaître les plumes," in Moheau, *Recherches et considérations*, 313–66; 383–96.

82. Brian, *La Mesure de l'Etat*, 169.

83. J. Dupâquier, in his introduction to Moheau's *Recherches et considérations* (xix), discusses how Moheau, while sharing many concerns with the philosophes, nevertheless defended such institutions of the ancien régime as the Church, the French monarchy, and the patriarchal family. He places Moheau among the little group of administrators wishing to reform and modernize rather than destroy the bases of the monarchy.

84. Moheau, *Recherches et considérations*, 112. According to Hajinal, high levels of celibacy have been characteristic of all European cultures, not just the French, since the sixteenth century. See Hajinal, *European Marriage Patterns*. For a discussion of this and alternate points of view, see Goody, *Development of the Family*, 8–9.

Hecht discusses various estimates of religious celibacy in eighteenth-century France, from a high of 500,000 (Plumat de Dangeul [John Nickolls], *Remarques sur les avantages et les désavantages de la France et de la Grande Bretagne* [Leiden, 1754]; Goudar, *Les Intérêts de la France*) to Moheau's evaluation of 194,214 in 1762 and only 130,000 in 1772. See Hecht, "Célibat," 263. In 1789, Brion de la Tour's summary of the numbers accorded to ecclesiastical celibacy in France are in agreement with Hecht's figures, although he attributes the 500,000 number to Linguet while choosing the figure of 250,000 himself. Abbé Sieyès, on the other hand, anxious to demonstrate the numerical superiority of the Third Estate, put the number at only 80,400, including nuns and monks, in *Qu'est-ce que le Tiers Etat?* (n.p., 1789; Paris, 1982), 45. Dr. Robert's estimate of "about 1/50th of the population before 1790" in *De l'Influence de la Révolution française*, 6, would tend to agree with the 500,000 of Goudar et al.

In regard to nuns, Henry and Houdaille conclude that: "around 1765, for 7,839,000 women 20 years and older, there would be about 57,000 nuns or around 7% of the female population" ("Célibat," 1:45). They see a gradual increase in female celibacy across the century: "From 6% to 7% in the generations born around 1676, the frequency of definitive celibacy rises to 12% among women born a hundred years later—all the way to 14% among women born around 1790" (1:60). According to Expilly, "there were about 80,000 nuns in France around 1754," or about 4% of the population (Expilly, *Tableau de la population*, 39). Hufton offers a survey of known statistical estimates of various categories of unmarried females in "Women without Men."

Knibiehler notes that celibacy was more prevalent in Europe (4%–20%) than in Asia or Africa (1%). "No religion," she comments, "has ever valorized chastity to the same degree as Christianity" (Knibiehler, "Le Célibat," 75–76).

85. Moy, *Discours*, 2–3.

86. Flandrin explores the evolution of Church doctrine between the value placed on chastity and the emphasis on procreation in "L'Attitude à l'égard du petit enfant et les conduites sexuelles dans la civilisation occidentale," *Annales de Démographie Historique* (1973), 143–210, and *Le Sexe et l'Occident*.

87. *Correspondance littéraire,*1755, 1:390–91; 5:318.

88. Hecht, "Malthus avant Malthus," 69–78.

89. Cantillion, *Essai sur la nature du commerce,* 42.

90. There has been an abundance of literature devoted to this question. J.-L. Flandrin's *L'Eglise et le contrôle des naissances* (Paris, 1970) is a good resume of J. T. Noonan's magisterial treatment of the problem in *Contraception, a History of Its Treatment by the Catholic Theologians* (New York, 1967). See also J. Hecht, "Malthus avant Malthus"; Le Roy-Ladurie, "Démographie et 'funestes secrets,' Le Languedoc (fin XVIIe début XIXe siècle)," *AHRF* 2 (1965); H. Bergues et al., "La Limitation des naissances dans la famille. Ses Origines dans les temps modernes," *Cahier* 35 (1960); Goody, *Production and Reproduction* (Cambridge, 1976); A. Bideau and J.-P. Bardet, "Fluctuations chronologiques ou début de la révolution contraceptive?" in Dupâquier, ed., *Histoire de la population française,* 2:373–78. Eighteenth-century authors frequently denounce the conjugal avoidance of pregnancy, often ambiguously referred to as "le célibat dans le mariage" ou "tromper la Nature." M. Bernos describes the various types of contraception in use before the French Revolution in *Le Fruit défendu,* 159–85. Also see E. Van de Walle and F. Van de Walle, "Allaitement, stérilité et contraception; les Opinions jusqu'au XIXe siècle," *Population* no. 27 (1972): 685–701. J.-M. Gouesse analyzes a cluster of texts from Normandy intended for the instruction of priests to assist them in their confessional duties. The seminar founded by the Bishop Claude Auvry and Saint Jean-Eudes in the middle of the eighteenth century examined many "cas de conscience" having to do with delicate questions of conjugal behavior and avoidance of pregnancy. According to Gouesse, contraceptive maneuvers in Normandy would have resulted from an increased attention to the well-being of children. "Le Refus de l'enfant au tribunal de la pénitence," *Annales de Démographie historique* (1973), 231–61. For a summary of women's opinions on the issue, see Théré, "Limitation des naissances."

91. Sabatier, *Odes nouvelles,* 6.

> Vous êtes plus cruels, vous Epoux inutiles,
> Qui contents d'un seul fils, osez être stériles,
> Jaloux de l'enrichir.
> Vous qui préoccupés de sa grandeur future,
> Dans vos embrassemens, arrêtez la Nature,
> Et trompez son désir.

92. Mirabeau, *L'Ami des hommes,* 1:99.

93. Gutton, *Domestiques et serviteurs,* 147.

94. Maza, *Servants and Masters,* 92–94.

95. Bernos, *Le Fruit défendu,* 191.

96. Messance, *Tableau de la population,* 84.

97. Of domestics, Moheau wrote: "Cette existence est particulièrement nuisible à la population en ce que la plupart des maîtres, pour jouir sans partage des services

des hommes gagés, préfèrent ceux qui se vouent au célibat. Quant aux femmes, elles sont forcées, par les embarras ou la dépense de la grossesse, de l'accouchement et de ses suites, de renoncer au mariage ou à la fécondité. Il serait à désirer que le nombre des domestiques des grandes villes fût connu et que des bornes fussent mises à leur multiplicité. Environ le douzième de la population est dans l'état de [domesticité]." Moheau, *Recherches et considérations*, 117.

98. Mirabeau, *L'Ami des hommes*, 1:101. Mirabeau may have found this observation in Cantillon, who pointed out the same phenomenon (*Essai sur la nature du commerce*, 41), less the polemical tone affected in *L'Ami des hommes*. Practical-minded Messance took issue with Mirabeau in this regard, pointing out that to have good harvests it takes manure (*Tableau de la population*, 85).

99. Butel-Dumont, *Théorie du luxe*, 98–99; Goudar, *Les Intérêts de la France mal entendus*, 272. Franco Venturi calls Goudar a "talented adventurer," describing his efforts to urge reform in the papal states in *Italy and the Enlightenment*, 242–44.

100. See Hasquin on the depopulation credo in "Le Débat sur la dépopulation dans l'Europe des Lumières," in Moheau, *Recherches et considérations*, 397.

101. Gutwirth describes the strange sexual ambiguities and gender uneasiness of salon life, where "French eighteenth-century upper-class men ape the trappings of cultural femaleness . . . both go about clad in satins and laces and wear abundant artificial hair." *The Twilight of the Goddesses*, 89. See also Delon, "Un Monde d'eunuques," 79–88. Houdaille showed that the number of children born to noble families fell from 5.3 among couples formed between 1650 and 1699, to 3.0 for couples formed between 1700 and 1749, to 2.0 for the period 1750–1799. "La Noblesse française, descendance 1600–1900."

102. Withof, *Dissertation sur les eunuqes*, 207.

103. Anonymous, *L'Homme en société*, 217, 323.

104. Duguet, *Lettres sur divers sujets*, 4:123. Féline, *Cathéchisme des gens mariés*, 26.

105. Cerfvol, *Le Radoteur*, 2:17.

106. Dutoit-Mambrini, *De l'Onanisme*. De Felice's description of "l'onanisme dans le mariage" is so vividly hyperbolic it merits being quoted at some length: "L'Onanisme s'oppose à la destination naturelle de la semence, l'onanisme détruit en peu de temps la machine de celui qui s'y livre & qui devient le meurtrier de lui-même. Une autre espèce d'onanisme encore plus criminelle que la précédente & qui est fort à la mode aujourd'hui, c'est celle qu'on commet dans le mariage même. Rien de plus ordinaire dans les compagnies des jeunes mariés, que d'entendre dire impudemment qu'ils ne veulent plus d'enfants, qu'ils ne sauraient en entretenir ou établir plus qu'ils n'en ont; que les grossesses sont pénibles. . . . pousserait-on l'impudence jusqu'à dire que leur union conjugale n'est qu'un onanisme horrible & une pédéraste révoltante? Cependant voilà le sens de ces propos." Felice, *Le Code de l'humanité*, 2:103.

107. Cited in H. Bergues, *La Prévention des naissances dans la famille, Ses Origines dans les temps modernes*, ed. Bergues et al. (Paris, 1960), 265.

108. Saint-Lambert, *Les Saisons*, 66.

109. For a discussion of the impact of military service on rates of marriage, see A. Corvisier, "Célibat et service militaire au XVIII siècle." L. Henry and J. Houdaille, in "Célibat," comment that the preponderance of celibacy in the aristocracy was mainly attributable to officers, returning at a certain age from the army, who did not marry.

110. Moheau, *Recherches et considérations*, 290.

111. Verzure, *Réflexions*, 150.

112. Diderot, *Oeuvres complètes*, 4:108, 253.

113. Leszczynski, *Pensées philosophiques*, 311.

114. Blondel, *Des Hommes*, 81.

115. Bablot, *Epître à Zulmis*, 5–6.

116. "Une seule chose m'a arrêté longtemps dans la publication de cette pièce de poésie, c'était la crainte ou j'étais que quelques oreilles chastes ne vinssent pas trop à s'accommoder du tableau de la jouissance & de ses préliminaires, quoique sous l'auguste & sacré noeud de l'Hymen" (ibid., 12).

117. Ibid., 21.

> Cher amant, tendre Epoux, ardent à te complaire,
> Tu ne me verras point, à tes désirs contraire,
> De nos plaisirs jamais interrompre le cours,
> Puissé-je en ta faveur les voir croître toujours!

118. Galtier, *Les Lettres persanes convaincues d'impiété*, 82–84.

119. Chaudon (though also attributed to the abbé Nonnotte and the abbé Coger), *Dictionnaire anti-philosophique*, viij.

120. Pichon, *Mémoire sur les abus du célibat*, 678–80. The following year Pichon also published a *Mémoire sur les Abus dans les mariages* (Amsterdam, 1766), in which he deplored the dominance of property considerations in marriage, urging legislation in France to curb "l'intérêt . . . y devenu la passion dominante" (10).

121. *Journal [Mémoire] de Trévoux* (Novembre 1765): 1176–87. For a discussion of Berthier and his editorship of the publication, see Pappas, *Berthier's 'Journal de Trévoux.'*

122. Moy, *Discours*, 31. The *Journal de Trévoux* described the freethinkers' literary assault upon the clergy: "Ils ont imaginé contre [la religion] un genre de persécution qui pourrait lui faire regretter le siècle des Nérons: ces lettres romanesques, ces fictions théâtrales, où les rôles sont tellement distribués que les plus odieux sont réservés aux Chrétiens de notre Communion, ou les plus vertueux personnages sont des Payens" (1757): 57.

123. Goudar, *Les Intérêts de la France mal entendus*, 272.

124. Pétion de Villeneuve, *Essai sur le mariage*, 143.

125. Robert, *De L'influence de la Révolution française sur la population*, 1:47. Dr. Robert expressed fear of masturbation as both a nonprocreative form of sexuality

and as an element in the decline of French virility, as did Dr. Hugues Maret (*Mémoire*) and Fr.-Cl. Leroy de Lozembrune, who in his *Anecdotes et remarques sur l'éducation publique,* described the damage beginning in the schools: "Le 'vice du college' . . . détruit le principe de production avant d'avoir atteint l'âge pour l'ordinaire ou l'on devient père . . . c'est la source du dépérissement humain." It was Dr. S. T. Tissot's popular *De L'Onanisme,* however, that most effectively sounded the alarm: he demanded that "les yeux de la jeunesse se dessillent, & qu'elle apprendra peu à peu à connaître le danger en même temps que le mal: ce serait un des plus sûrs moyens de prévenir cette décadence dont on se plaint dans la nature humaine, & peut-être de lui rendre, dans quelques générations, la force qu'avaient nos aieux, & que nous ne connaissons plus qu'historiquement, ou par les monuments qui nous en restent" (xviij). For a discussion of the onanism scare, see Thomas Laqueur, "Masturbation, Credit and the Novel."

126. Toussaint, *Les Moeurs,* ix; Linguet, *Du Plus Heureux Gouvernement,* xxvij.

127. See E. Walter, "Le Complexe d'Abélard." An occasional timid voice was still heard upholding intellectual bachelorhood's traditional apology, such as that of the anonymous author of *Réflexions philosophiques sur le plaisir, par un célibataire,* who maintained there existed "un petit nombre de gens vertueux que l'amour des lettres, le gout de la retraite et l'étude de la philosophie retiennent dans la solitude, incapables des embarras du Ménage et des devoirs qu'exige l'état du Mariage."

128. Flandrin observes that only Condorcet expressed wonder at the philosophes' refusal to challenge populationist pieties, although they rebelled at so many other interdictions. "Pourquoi . . . les philosophes, qui ont bravé la ligue des tyrans et des prêtres, craindraient-ils celle des mauvais plaisants et des hypocrites de morale?" *Familles, parentés, maison, sexualité,* 231.

129. I discuss Diderot's intense preoccupation with fatherhood in Carol Blum, *Diderot: The Virtue of a Philosopher* (New York, 1974).

130. Rousseau, "Ecrits sur l'Abbé de Saint-Pierre," *Oeuvres complètes,* 4:660.

131. H. de Jouvenel treats the marquis de Mirabeau's catastrophic family life in *La Vie orageuse de Mirabeau* (Paris, 1928), as does G. Henry in *Mirabeau père* (Paris, 1989).

132. Kors, *D'Holbach's Coterie,* 204. For an account of Mme d'Epinay's fraught relations with Grimm, as well as her unsung contribution to the *Correspondance littéraire,* see Weinreb, *Eagle in a Gauze Cage.*

133. Saint-Lambert was also the author of the six-volume *Principes des moeurs chez toutes les nations, ou Catéchisme universel,* which appeared during the Revolution (1798), of which volume six was particularly laudatory of marriage and the family.

134. Eon de Beaumont, "Les Espérances d'un bon patriote," 62–63. See Kates's informative account of the famous Chevalier's career in *Monsieur d'Eon Is a Woman.*

135. Voltaire, *Correspondance,* in *Oeuvres,* D13195, D12305. Was Diderot aware of this exchange when he portrayed his friend, in his *Rêve de d'Alembert,* ejaculating in

his sleep while dreaming of Mlle de l'Espinasse, murmuring: "On a planet where men multiplied like fish, where the sperm of a man pressed on the eggs of a woman . . . I would have fewer regrets," sentiments, in any event, apparently more typical of Diderot than his celibate colleague. Diderot, *Oeuvres philosophiques,* 301.

136. Voltaire, "Sur la Nature du plaisir," *Oeuvres,* 12:82. Concerning man and marriage, Saint-Lambert waxed lyrical:

> Vous le rendez heureux, volupté douce et pure! Attaché à l'Hymen, aux noeuds de la Nature,
>
> Ses enfants sont sa joie, ils feront sa richesse
>
> Si l'on veut du bonheur le voir accompagner
>
> Sous les lois de l'hymen il le faut enchaîner.
>
> (*Les Saisons,* Chant 2, 66)

137. Rétif de la Bretonne, *Monsieur Nicolas,* 11:321.

138. Bablot, *Epître à Zulmis,* 73, n. 1

139. Rousseau's theories of reproduction, society, and the State are discussed in chapter six.

140. Beaumarchais, "Un Mot sur *La Mère coupable,*" *Théâtre* (Paris, 1965), 248. Strangely enough, eight years earlier (1767) Beaumarchais had written a play called *Eugénie* about an out-of-wedlock pregnancy that culminates in marriage.

141. Laclos, *Lettres inédites,* 239.

Chapter Four: Divorce, the Demographic Spur

1. Charron, *De la Sagesse,* 217. Condorcet praises Charron as an early freethinker: "On ne peut nier que cet ouvrage de Charron ne respire le déïsme. Il a bien servi l'humanité contre la superstition." *L'Almanach anti-superstitieux,* 127.

2. J.-L. Flandrin notes that modern commentators frequently fail to understand the function of marriage under earlier economic systems: "Notre siècle, qui ne croit qu'aux mariages d'amour, rit ou s'indigne des 'mariages de raison' arrangés par les familles, dans lesquels il a tendance à ne voir que des 'mariages d'argent.' Mais dans une société où l'immense majorité des familles tiraient leur subsistance d'un capital petit ou grand . . . il était criminel à l'égard des enfants à naître de se marier sans avoir le capital nécessaire pour faire vivre une famille." *Familles, parentés, maison, sexualité,* 181–82.

3. Hufton, *The Prospect before Her,* 101.

4. The need for consent, the principle that *nuptias consensus nonconcubitas facit,* was the object of a long struggle between the monarchy and ecclesiastical authorities. See Hanley, "Engendering the State."

5. Antraigues, *Observations sur le divorce,* x. The multifaceted career of Emmanuel-Louis-Henri de Launez, comte d'Antraigues (1755–1812), spy under the ancien régime, deputy to the Estates General, and eventual émigré, is treated by Roger

Barny in *Le Comte d'Antraigues, un disciple aristocrate de J.-J. Rousseau: de la fascination au reniement, 1782–1797* (Oxford, 1991).

6. Toussaint, *Les Moeurs*, 232. The age of majority in most parts of France was fixed at thirty for a man, twenty-five for a woman.

7. Rouillé d'Orfeuil, *L'Alambic des lois*, 7.

8. Laclos, *Les Liaisons dangereuses*, 325.

9. Pétion de Villeneuve, *Essai sur le mariage*, 37–38.

10. Puisieux, *Les Caractères*, 216. For a study of this acerbic observer so intimately associated with Diderot, see Alice M. Laborde, *Diderot et Madame de Puisieux* (Saratoga, 1984).

11. Merrick describes the options available to the dissatisfied husband. He could "charge his wife with adultery, confine her to a convent, and then, after two years, either take her back or leave her there for the rest of her life and deprive her of her dowry, except for whatever pension he paid her. If he could not afford to pension her, she might end up imprisoned in the company of prostitutes." Merrick analyzes the accounts of separation suits brought before courts in various parts of France reported in the *Causes célèbres, curieuses, et intéressantes de toutes les cours souveraines du royaume*, edited by Nicolas-Toussaint Moyne (Desessarts), 179 volumes (Paris, 1775–89), in "Domestic Politics," 373–86. See also Arlette Farge and Michel Foucault, eds., *Le Désordre dans les familles, Lettres de cachet à Paris au XVIIIe siècle* (Paris, 1982).

12. Phillips, *Putting Asunder*, 306. Francini discusses the various categories of separation available under the ancien régime and their relative frequency in his two-volume thesis, *Moralia coniugalia*, 1:27–45; 177–205 passim.

13. Montesquieu, *Oeuvres complètes*, 1:1300.

14. Montesquieu describes how Christianity had at one point assumed a more egalitarian position in regard to marriage, adultery, and divorce than did the Romans, allowing either spouse to demand a separation in case of adultery because, for the church, "looking at marriage purely in spiritual terms and in connection with the life to come, the violation was the same." *Esprit des lois*, in *Oeuvres complètes*, 2:58. For a discussion of the difference between repudiation and divorce, see Ronsin, *Le Contrat sentimental*, 26–28.

15. Phillips discusses the deeply promarriage rationale for favoring divorce to be found in most eighteenth-century writings: "Each divorce was seen as nothing so much as a prelude to another marriage." *Putting Asunder*, 172.

16. Saxe, *Réflexions sur la propagation*, 37.

17. Süssmilch, *Die göttlichte Ordnung*, 2:16.

18. Turmeau de la Morandière, *Appel des étrangers*, 83. Sauvy discusses Turmeau's career in "Some Lesser Known French Demographers."

19. Diderot and D'Alembert, *Encyclopédie*, 11:139–40. Boucher d'Argis also con-

tributed "Concubinage" and "Divorce" to volume 6 of abbé Henri-Joseph Du Laurens's *Portefeuille d'un philosophe*, as well as authoring two works on marriage, one legal, *Traité des gains nuptiaux*, the other medical-juridical, *Principes sur la nullité du mariage pour cause d'impuissance.*

20. Besides the immense body of his writings on legal, political, and philosophical issues, Linguet is remembered especially for his relations, at first amicable and then adversarial, with the philosophes and for his *Mémoires sur la Bastille*. He was executed in 1794.

21. This case, involving an Alsatian Jewish carpenter, Borach Lévy, was decided in 1750 by the Parliament of Paris, which declared that marriage was an indissoluble contract, even between nonbelievers (*infidèles*). Voltaire discusses the case in his article "Mariage," *Dictionnaire philosophique, Oeuvres*, 31:132–35. See G. Francini, *Moralia coniugalia*, 1:46–72.

22. Quérard, *La France littéraire*, 101; Ronsin, *Le Contrat*, 49.

23. Quérard, *La France littéraire*, 2:100.

24. Ernest Lavisse offers a different version of the story, according to which it was the king who instigated an effort to have Madame Du Barry's marriage annulled. "Louis XV songeait à faire une fin et à l'épouser. Il y eut même des négociations entamées par Mme Louise avec le Saint-Siège pour obtenir l'annulation du mariage de la courtisane," Ernest Lavisse and Alfred Rambaud, *Histoire générale du IVe siècle à nos jours*, 12 vols. (Paris, 1893–1901), 7:342. See also A. Sauvy, "Some Lesser-Known Demographers."

25. Goncourt and Goncourt, *Mme du Barry* (Paris, 1878), 72. The Goncourts refer to a work of abbé Terray entitled *Mémoire concernant l'administration des finances sous Terray*, London, 1776 (also appearing as the *Mémoires de l'Abbé Terrai, Contrôleur-général des finances*, London, 1777). These latter *Mémoires* are labeled apocryphal in the preface by an unnamed editor who claims the work was written by a Monsieur Coquereau [Jean-Baptiste-Louis],"a promising young lawyer . . . who, unable to survive the destruction of Parliament, blew his brains out." (iv). The story of the Du Barry divorce scheme is repeated, although without further direct evidence for its reliability, in a number of works up to the present day, including the suspect *Mémoires de la Comtesse du Barry*, put together by Lamothe-Langon in 1829, the duke of Castries' *La Du Barry* (1986), and Daniel Baruch's *Linguet, l'irrécupérable* (1991). Ronsin notes that while the story is often mentioned, its truth has not been proven (*Le Contrat*, 47).

26. I owe Marcel Gutwirth thanks for calling this suggestive coincidence to my attention.

27. Biographical dictionaries of the period reveal nothing but the title "chevalier de" before the name and no solid information about him is available. In the pseudomemoires of Palissot, almost certainly written by the same person who wrote the rest of Cerfvol's oeuvre, however, it is stated that Cerfvol lived in Geneva, where di-

vorce was legal, and had recently died. The name is not mentioned in the eight-volume *Dictionnaire historique et biographique de la Suisse* (Neuchâtel, 1924), Hozier's index of noble families in France, the lists of members of the orders for which the title chevalier would be appropriate (i.e., du St. Esprit, de Saint Michel, and de Saint Louis), nor the *Grand Armorial de France,* listing noble families from 1660 to 1830.

28. Cited in Francini, 244, in Phil[i]bert/Palissot, *Oeuvres* 1:xiii–xv. Francini presents his arguments for identifying Cerfvol with Phil[i]bert/Palissot in "Il Divorzio nella Francia."

29. Grimm and Diderot, *Correspondance littéraire* (1772), 8:301. Grimm also excoriates Palissot for his satire of the Encyclopédistes and their friends in his 1760 play *Les philosophes,* 8:19–21.

30. Cerfvol, *Mémoire sur la population,* 29–30.

31. Voltaire also castigated the church for refusing to allow sterile couples to try their luck in other matches: "Ce culte proscrit le divorce que permettaient les anciens & en cela il devient un obstacle au mariage; ajoutez que la pureté de la morale réduit l'acte de la génération à l'insipidité du besoin physique & condamne rigoureusement les attractions du sentiment qui peuvent y inviter. . . . si l'un des deux n'est pas propre à la génération, la vertu prolifique de l'autre reste nulle." *L'essai sur l'histoire générale,* in *Oeuvres,*1:789.

32. Grimm and Diderot, *Correspondance littéraire,* March 1769, 6:352–53.

33. Riley, *Population Thought,* 55.

34. Diderot, "Du Divorce," *Mémoires pour Catherine II,* 204–5. For a description of Diderot's oeuvre during the crisis of the early 1770s, see A. Wilson, *Diderot* (New York, 1972), 571–93, and C. Blum, *Diderot: The Virtue of a Philosopher* (New York, 1974), 108–26.

35. Pilati di Tassulo, *Traité du mariage,* 74.

36. D'Holbach, *Ethocracie,* 209, 210.

37. Felice, *Le Code de l'humanité,* 10:xi, 290.

38. Catholic defenses of marriage as a perpetual bond continued to appear throughout the 1780s and 1790s, including a 1775 volume of *Conférences ecclésiastiques de Paris sur le mariage où l'on concile la discipline de la jurisprudence du royaume de France,* and abbé Pilé's 1778 *Dissertation sur l'indissolubilité absolue du lien conjugal,* 2 vols. (Paris, 1788).

Chapter Five: Polygamy

1. See John Cairncross, *After Polygamy Was Made a Sin,* chaps. 1, 2. Norman Cohn's *Pursuit of the Millennium* (Fairlawn, N.J.: 1957) places the Münster Kingdom of the Saints in the context of the era's theological preoccupations. Leo Miller traces the multiple strains of Western thinking on polygamy, including the views of Luther, Milton, and Puffendorf, in *John Milton among the Polygamophiles.*

2. J. Waterworth, trans., *Canons and Decrees of the Council of Trent* (London, 1983). Sarpi's *Histoire du concile* described the political stakes and the intricate jostling of personalities over *Tametsi*.

3. Cairncross comments about controversy over papal dispensations for royal bigamies still being granted in the sixteenth century: "This latitude, specially in relation to kings, is probably an echo of earlier practices when plural marriage was common among rulers. Emperors such as Charlemagne, Lothaor and Pepin had, officially, several wives." *When Polygamy Was Made a Sin,* 59. According to Claude Lévi-Strauss, "en concédant le privilège polygamique à son chef, le groupe échange les éléments individuels de sécurité garantis par la règle monogamique contre une sécurité collective, attendue de l'autorité." *Tristes Tropiques,* 363.

4. "L'adultère reste un péché motel dont le roi se rend coupable aux yeux de tous, il est donc au sens propre un péché scandaleux." M. Bernos, *Le Fruit défendu,* 194.

5. Henri comte de Boulainvilliers, "Touchant L'Affaire de Mrs. les princes du sang," in *Mémoires présentés à Monseigneur le duc d'Orléans, Régent de France,* 112–56. E. Le Roy Ladurie minimizes the significance of Louis's testament, pointing out that with the deaths of all heirs but the none too sturdy duke of Anjou, Louis XIV was attempting to ward off a divisive struggle for the throne after his death. *L'Ancien Régime,* 1:402.

That the ancient royal privilege is not completely forgotten, however, is illustrated by a remark in the *Nouvel Observateur,* in which Phillipe Sollers expressed his regret that the funeral of François Mitterand, attended by both the president's wife and his mistress, was such a modest affair. "Pourquoi pas cinq ou six . . . je trouve que deux femmes, cela fait un peu mesquin, petit-bourgeois. La France a une grande tradition de ce point de vue" (8–14 August 1996): 7.

6. Charron, *De la Sagesse,* 225–26.

7. Gilles Pison discusses whether polygamy, the most ancient form of matrimony, really does favor population growth more than monogamy, the modern system, in present-day Africa south of the Sahara, concluding that, by a slight margin, it does. See "La Démographie de la polygamie."

8. Milton, *The Doctrine and Discipline of Divorce.*

9. Laugier, *Tyrannie que les hommes ont exercé.* Laugier, unlike many of his contemporaries, attached a positive significance to the superior status accorded women in Western civilization. "Plus les peuples sont civilisés, comme en Europe, plus on rend à ces aimables objets la justice qu'ils méritent; cependant on s'y ressent encore . . . des usages de l'ancienne barbarie dans laquelle ils étaient ensevelis . . . car sur quel fondement & par quelle fatalité, quand un enfant vient de naître, demande-t-on d'abord s'il est mâle ou femelle? S'il est mâle, il semble qu'il apporte avec lui les trésors de Pérou, tandis que c'est souvent le contraire s'il est femelle, la joie ou l'on était dans l'espoir & dans l'attente que ce fut un mâle, se change en tiédeur" (45–46).

10. Marie-Jean-Nicolas de Caritat, marquis de Condorcet paid little attention to

the natural-law fundamentalists arguing for the return of family life to its primitive or even animal origins. "Les droits des hommes résultent uniquement de ce qu'ils sont des êtres sensibles, susceptibles d'acquérir des idées morales, et de raisonner sur ces idées. Ainsi les femmes ayant ces mêmes qualités, ont nécessairement des droits égaux. Ou aucun individu de l'espèce humaine n'a de véritables droits, ou tous ont les mêmes; et celui qui vote contre le droit de l'autre, quels que soient sa religion, sa couleur ou son sexe, a dès lors abjuré les siens." "Sur l'Admission des femmes," 5:54.

11. Leyser, *Polygamia Triumphatrix*. The author is also presented as Théophile Aletheus (Lizerus), which Bayle labels a "false name" in the *Nouvelles de la République des Lettres,* 256. The English edition appeared under the title *Reflections upon Polygamy, and the Encouragement given to that Practice in the Scriptures of the Old Testament,* by Phileleuthus Dubliniensis.

12. J. M. Gouesse notes that in 1708 an ecclesiastical conference in Normandy debated whether the *cresite et multiplicamini* of Genesis was an absolute obligation, concluding that it was only a benediction "ou tout au plus qu'un commandement *ad tempus* qui ne subsiste plus, comme tel . . . le Messie étant venu et le monde suffisament peuplé," "Le Refus de l'enfant," 237.

13. Oscar Kenshur analyzes Bayle's inventive format as a function of his skepticism in "Pierre Bayle," 314–15.

14. According to the Koran, deserving members of both sexes will enter paradise (4:123). For an overview of representations of Mohammed and Islam in eighteenth-century France, see D. van der Cruysse, "De Bayle à Raynal"; M. Dobie discusses the complexities and ambiguities of European male authors depicting the situation of oriental women in *Foreign Bodies.*

15. That Montesquieu knew Leyser's work is demonstrated by Usbek's reference to *Polygamia triumphatrix* in letter 35 of the *Lettres persanes.* He was of course familiar with Bayle, parrying accusations of having adopted Bayle's skepticism in his *Défense de l'Esprit des lois,* 2:1126–30. Besides Antoine Galland's famously successful *Mille et une nuits* (1704) a number of *contes* and novels with harems as settings appeared in the early decades of the eighteenth century, bearing such titles as Thomas-Simon Gueullette's *Aventures merveilleuses du mandarin Fum Hoam, contes Chinois* (1723) and *Sultanes de Guzarate, contes Mogols* (1732). See M.-L. Dufrenoy, *L'Orient romanesque en France, 1704–1789* (Montreal, 1946).

16. "Il fallut nous dépouiller de ces ornements qui t'étaient devenus incommodes; il fallut paraître à ta vue dans la simplicité de la nature. Je comptais pour rien la pudeur; je ne pensais qu'à ma gloire. Heureux Usbek, que de charmes furent étalés à tes yeux!" (1:135).

17. D. J. Schaub discusses the political implications of the collapse of Usbek's harem in *Erotic Liberalism: Women and Revolution in Montesquieu's Persian Letters* (Lanham, Mich.: 1995).

18. "Pourquoi aurions-nous . . . un privilège? Est-ce parce que nous sommes les

plus forts? Mais c'est une véritable injustice. Nous employons toutes sortes de moyens pour leur abattre le courage; les forces seraient égales si l'éducation l'était aussi"
(1:186). Yet Montesquieu is quite capable of satirizing women sharply, especially in
their boudoir political manipulations. He has been labeled both an early feminist
and an exemplar of the emerging patriarchal eighteenth-century doctrine of female
domesticity. It seems to me that the subtle and complex Montesquieu is most fruit-
fully approached in the context of his tactics in the wars with the monarchy and the
Church rather than in that of today's political movements.

19. According to the Koran, "Your wives are your fields," 2:223.

20. Melon, *Mahmoud le Gasnévide*, 93.

21. Melon consistently supports the principle of servitude. In his *Essai politique
sur le commerce* of 1734, he defends slavery: "L'égalité chez les hommes est une chim-
ère," (69).

22. Montesquieu, *L'Esprit des lois*, in *Oeuvres complètes*, 2:511–22.

23. Vauban, *Projet d'une Dixme Royale*, 284.

24. Arbuthnot, "An Argument for Divine Providence." A. Desrosières discusses
the sex-ratio problem in *La Politique des grands nombres*, 96.

25. Giovanni Villani, *Nuova Cronica* (1583), 11:94; John Graunt, *Natural and Political Observation upon the Bills of Mortality* (London, 1662), 92–93.

26. See the presentation and discussion of Arbuthnot's text in Jacques Dupâquier, "Document, Providence et probabilité," 117:81–99.

27. Montesquieu, *Oeuvres complètes*, 2:511.

28. Ibid., 2:1141–46. In his *Défense de l'Esprit des lois* (*Oeuvres complètes* 2:1121–68),
Montesquieu quotes and refutes Berthier's critique in the *Journal de Trévoux*, 9 October 1749.

29. "Depuis quand ces transmigrations si fréquentes ont-elles cessé? La chose est
parlante, précisément depuis que l'introduction du christianisme a fait abolir chez
toutes les nations du Nord . . . l'utile usage de la polygamie" (Le Guay de Prémontval, *La Monogamie*, 20).

30. An epistle signed by M. V. Pigeon d'Osangis de Prémontval prefaces the
work, dedicated to "the ladies, by the wife of the author. Here is a book where the
rights of our sex are defended by the arms of virtue and probity as well as those of
religion." By her endorsement of her husband's arguments, Madame de Prémontval
came as close as any eighteenth-century French woman to joining the debate about
polygamy and population. Christine Théré discusses twenty-one women writers
who comment on population in terms of such issues as family planning and maternal breast-feeding in "Limitation des naissances." There is not, however, a single
work by a French woman writer concentrating on population before the Revolution.

31. Voltaire, *Oeuvres*, 29:231.

32. Crevier, *Observations sur le livre*, 218.

33. *Lettres de M. de Mairan au R. P. Parrenin, Missionaire de la Compagnie de Jésus à Pékin* (Paris, 1759), 137.

34. Boussanelle, *Essai sur les femmes,* 56, 130.

35. Süssmilch, *Die göttlichte Ordnung,* ed. Rohrbasser, 164–72.

36. Süssmilch, *L'ordre Divin,* ed. Hecht, 2:500.

37. The Rantzau family was originally of Danish descent, but by 1600 there were six branches with more than a hundred bearers of the name among the nobility of Denmark, Sweden, Russia, and Germany, the most notable of whom being Josias, comte de Rantzau and *maréchal de France* under Louis XIII. Jorgen Ludwig Albrecht Grof von Rantzau, or Louis de Rantzau, was also the author of another curious book, a fond description of the mores and mentalities of the great international families of European nobility in the eighteenth century, the *Mémoires du comte de Rantzow.*

38. Rantzau, *Discussion si la polygamie,* 12–13.

39. "J'emprunterai bien des choses de l'auteur de l'esprit des lois, sans m'arrêter à louer la solidité de ses principes, parce que je ne peux rien ajouter à sa gloire," said Lenglet du Fresnoy (12:959). Jean Ehrard discusses the *Encyclopédie's* inconsistencies and contradictions in regard to slavery, based on two different readings of book 15 of the *Esprit des lois,* Jaucourt's and d'Alembert's, in his "Eloge de Montesquieu," *Eloges lus dans les séances publiques de l'Académie française* (Paris, 1779). "L'Encyclopédie et l'esclavage," 121–29.

40. Cerfvol, *Le Radoteur, Article sur la polygamie,* 56.

41. Linguet, *Du Plus Heureux Gouvernement,* 62.

42. Rétif de la Bretonne, *Les Gynographes,* 374–76.

43. D'Holbach, *Essai sur les Préjugés,* in *Système de la Nature* (1770), 116.

44. Dupâquier, preface to *Recherches et considérations,* ix.

45. Moheau, *Recherches et considérations,* 130.

46. *Nouvelles Recherches sur la population.* James Riley discusses Messance's findings and the question of Providence in *Population Thought,* 23–28.

47. Pilati de Tassulo, *Traité du mariage,* 5.

48. Bernardin de Saint-Pierre, *Etudes de la Nature,* 339.

49. Voltaire puts Montesquieu's errors in larger perspective in his critique of the *Esprit des lois.* After pointing out the numerous factual mistakes, misinterpretations, and flights of fancy that characterize Montesquieu's magnum opus, Voltaire concludes: "Montesquieu is almost always wrong according to the scholars because he wasn't one; but he was always right against the fanatics and against the promoters of slavery; Europe owes him eternal gratitude." *Dictionnaire philosophique,* in *Oeuvres,* 31:109.

50. In Dupâquier and Vilquin, "Le Pouvoir royal," 1:88.

51. Ibid., 1:89.

52. According to Dupâquier and Vilquin, "Il semble bien qu'en fin de compte, ce

soit l'horreur instinctive des Français pour toute espèce de dénombrement qui ait contraint le pouvoir royal à se contenter des statistiques qu'il pouvait tirer des documents existants: rôles de tailles et registres de catholicité." Ibid., 91–92.

53. Condorcet, *Arithmétique politique,* 337.

Chapter Six: Rousseau and the Paradoxes of Reproduction

1. For discussions of the eighteenth century's uneasy struggles with questions of gender, besides M. Gutwirth's previously cited *The Twilight of the Goddesses,* see Jeffrey Merrick, "Masculinity and Effeminacy"; Robert A. Nye, *Masculinity and Male Codes of Honor;* D. Outram, *The Body and the French Revolution;* and Joan Scott, *Gender and the Politics of History.*

2. The main texts in which Rousseau discusses reproductive issues are found in the *Discours sur l'inégalité; Discours sur l'économie politique; Lettre à d'Alembert sur les spectacles; La Nouvelle Héloïse; Emile; Du Contrat social;* "Lettre à Mirabeau," 26 July 1767; and *Considérations sur le gouvernement de Pologne; Projet de Constitution pour la Corse.* All references to Rousseau's work, unless otherwise indicated, can be found in *Oeuvres complètes,* vols. 1–4.

3. Mary Wollstonecroft astutely analyzed Rousseau's seductive technique and its effect on readers: "So warmly has he painted what he forcibly felt, that interesting the heart and inflaming the imagination of his readers, they imagine that their understanding is convinced when they only sympathize with a poetic writer, who skillfully exhibits the objects of sense, most voluptuously shadowed or gracefully veiled." Quoted by Mary Trouille, *Sexual Politics in the Enlightenment* 226, who discusses Wollstonecroft's accusatory critique of *La Nouvelle Héloïse* as presented in her own novel, *Maria.*

4. Jacques Derrida treated the contradictions in Rousseau's writings in general in *De La Grammatologie,* elevating the writer to the status of emblem of a fundamental tension in Western thought between two polar experiences: the overwhelming immediacy of self-perception and the distanced quality of coherent thought. Paul de Man went beyond Derrida's interpretation, offering a complex resolution to the problem in Rousseau's relation to his own ambivalence, claiming that "the paradoxical logic of a simultaneously positive and negative evaluation, whenever the movement of history is involved, could not be more consistent." "The Rhetoric of Blindness," 102–41. See also Victor Goldschmidt, *Anthropologie et politique,* 12. Raymond Trousson treats the whole problem and contending critical arguments in *Jean-Jacques Rousseau,* 2 vols (Paris, 1988–89).

5. See Starobinski, "Jean-Jacques Rousseau et le péril de la réflection," 182–84.

6. Rousseau's sad struggles with broken families have been the subject of numerous accounts and much polemic, even before the avowals contained in the *Confessions* themselves (1782, 1789). In their notes to the Pléiade edition, B. Gagnebin and M. Raymond present a substantial dossier of documents concerning Rousseau's

presumed fatherhood and the controversies surrounding it, *Oeuvres complètes,* 1:1415–23. M. Cranston discusses both the factual information and the textual reworkings in his two-volume biography, *Jean-Jacques.* and *The Noble Savage.* Connections between the impossibility of accepting the father's role and the act of writing are analyzed by Marie-Hélène Huet in "Le Défaut de l'Histoire." See also Blum, *Rousseau and the Republic of Virtue,* 74–92.

7. Trouille, *Sexual Politics in the Enlightenment,* 64.

8. Nardi, "Rousseau contredit Jean-Jacques," 41:149.

9. Locke, *First Treatise,* in *Two Treatises,* 179.

10. Jean Ehrard traces Rousseau's profound debt to Montesquieu, despite Rousseau's having probably aided père Berthier in preparing a refutation of the *Esprit des lois* for the Dupin family. "Rousseau et Montesquieu," in *Politique de Montesquieu.*

11. In Rousseau's famous formulation: "Commençons donc par écarter tous les faits, car ils ne touchent point à la question." He apostrophizes man: "voici ton histoire telle que j'ai cru la lire, non dans les Livres de tes semblables qui sont menteurs, mais dans la Nature qui ne ment jamais." *Oeuvres complètes,* 3:133.

12. See Jean Starobinski's note 1 (Rousseau, *Oeuvres complètes,* 3:1363) for a discussion of this taxonomical issue, so crucial to Rousseau's arguments. The question continues to interest anthropologists; see Jane Goodall on chimpanzees hunting and eating other monkeys in *The Chimpanzee: Living Link between Man and Beast* (Edinburgh, 1992).

13. Michel Lévy comments: "Le lien maternel et le lien paternel ne sont pas de même nature. Le lien maternel;—grossesse, accouchement, allaitment—est physique, direct, expérimental. Le lien paternel est intellectuel et n'est compris que par réflexion. 'Dis Maman, comment on fait les bébés?' La trinité père-fils-esprit est indissociable." "Le Secret de la paternité," 1.

14. Hénaff, "The Cannibalistic City," 67:9.

15. In a fragment on "L'Etat de nature," Rousseau declares categorically that "le pur état de nature est celui où les hommes seraient . . . en plus grand nombre sur la terre" (3:475).

16. Goldschmidt, *Anthropologie et politique,* 369. "La famille qui dans l'état de nature pris rigoureusement, n'existe pas, sera cependant, plus tard, 'naturelle,'" ibid. 256.

17. Rousseau, "Essai sur l'orígine des langues," *Oeuvres complètes* 5:406.

18. Rousseau's description of the passage from endogamy to exogamy, his cryptic definition of the incest taboo as "no less sacred for being of human origin," and the distinction he establishes between nature and culture have been the subject of a series of especially privileged analytical commentaries. According to Claude Lévi-Strauss, "Rousseau ne s'est pas borné à prévoir l'ethnologie: il l'a fondée" ("Jean-Jacques Rousseau," 240), which seems to endorse both his methodology and his vision of presocietal man. Derrida subjected the conceptual affinities of Lévi-Strauss and

Rousseau regarding the incest taboo to analysis in *De La Grammatologie,* which in turn was the subject of G. Benrekassa's essay "Loi naturelle." See also D. Fourney, "The Festival," 137–60.

19. Derrida, *De La Grammatologie,* 372. Derrida sees a paradox in the idea of incest: "Avant la fête, il n'y avait pas d'inceste parce qu'il n'y avait pas de prohibition de l'inceste et pas de société. Apres la fête il n'y a plus d'inceste parce qu'il est interdit," 373–75.

20. In Benrekassa's words: "speculation about the prohibition must be viewed first of all as a phenomenon of our culture, and one should refer to the appropriate ideological formations to understand it." "Loi naturelle," 117.

21. Montesquieu, *Esprit de Lois,* 2:765.

22. Goody, *The Development of the Family,* 56. Goody sees the influence of the Church as the dominant factor in maintaining the taboo, which permitted it to exercise "a large measure of control in the domestic domain." 75. For Jean-Louis Flandrin it has more to do with the ways families allied themselves through marriage: "On ne saurait en effet expliquer cette multiplication des empêchements de mariage par une simple psychose de l'inceste . . . elle révèle l'existence de solidarités parentèles . . . particulièrement la solidarité que le mariage établissait entre deux familles, même après la mort d'un des conjoints." *Familles,* 24–25.

23. Voltaire, *La Défense de mon oncle,* in *Oeuvres complètes,* 26:379. One such uncle was of course Voltaire himself, although his relations with his niece, Mme. Denis, were probably not all that inexpensive. Elsewhere he denounces the Church's traffic in dispensations from the incest interdiction as a "servitude honteuse, contraire au droit des gens, à la dignité de la couronne, à la religion, à la nature, de payer un étranger pour se marier dans son pays." *Le Cri des nations,* in *Oeuvres complètes,* 26:566.

24. Flandrin, *Familles,* 29.

25. A. Burguière traces the history of the "enigmatic" impediment and its popularity as a literary theme in "'Cher Cousin.'"

26. Toussaint, *Les Moeurs,* 241.

27. Rousseau, *L'Origine de l'inégalité,* in *Oeuvres complètes,* 3:132.

28. He does concede an occasional exception: "note: il peut y avoir une telle disproportion d'âge et de force qu'une violence réelle ait lieu, mais traitant ici d'état relatif des sexes selon l'ordre de la nature, je les prends tous deux dans le rapport commun qui constitue cet état."

Rousseau details the deviousness of women in *pretending* to yield to male force: "Soit donc que la femelle de l'homme partage ou non ses désirs et veuille ou non les satisfaire, elle le repousse et se défend toujours, mais non pas toujours avec le meme succès; pour que l'attaquant soit victorieux, il faut que l'attaqué [la femme] le permette ou l'ordonne; car que de moyens adroits n'a-t-il pas pour forcer l'aggresseur d'user de force?" Thus women deliberately feign weakness, "elles se ménagent de loin des excuses, et le droit d'être faibles au besoin" (4:695–96).

29. In a few phrases on population originally destined for the conclusion of the *Economie politique* (eventually published in volume 3 of the *Oeuvres complètes*), Rousseau makes the point even more forcefully that the multiplication of the people is a result of prosperity. "Voulez-vous savoir si un Etat est bien ou mal gouverné, examinez si le nombre de ses habitants augmente ou diminue. . . . On juge avec raison des soins du Berger par l'accroissement des Troupeaux." An isolated phrase from the text would seem to link Rousseau's natalism with his personal concerns: "Et qu'importe à la société qu'il en périsse moins par des meurtres si l'Etat les tue avant leurs naissance en rendant les enfans onéreux aux pères." This sentence is followed by a list of deaths, baptisms, marriages, and abandoned children for Paris, 1758 (*Oeuvres complètes*, 3:527–28).

30. The subsistence issues raised in Rousseau's arguments about population would seem to own much to Mirabeau, for example chapters two and three of *L'Ami des hommes*, "La mesure de la subsistance est celle de la population," and "L'agriculture qui peut seule multiplier les subsistances est le premier des arts," 1–34. On the other hand, Rousseau formally takes issue with Mirabeau's theory about prosperity encouraging the birthrate, since it contradicts his own baleful view of economic progress. In a letter of July 1767, he tells Mirabeau: "Je connais d'autant moins votre principe de population, qu'il me paraît inexplicable en lui-même, contradictoire avec les faits, impossible à concilier avec l'origine des nations. Selon vous, Monsieur, la population multiplicative n'aurait dû commencer que quand elle a cessé réellement. Dans mes vieilles idées sitôt qu'il y a eu pour un sou de ce que vous appelez richesse ou valeur disponible, sitôt que s'est fait le premier échange, la population multiplicative a dû cesser; c'est aussi ce qui est arrivé." Letter 5991, *Correspondance complète*, 33:241.

31. The complex redaction and publication of this text are traced by B. Gagnebin in the 1964 Gallimard edition (3:1883–90).

32. Rousseau insisted that he was even more fond, not less fond, of children than were other men, as he confides in the *Neuvième Promenade:* "je ne crois pas que jamais homme ait plus aimé que moi à voir de petits bambins folâtrer et jouer ensemble et souvent dans la rue et aux promenades je m'arrête à regarder leur espièglerie et leurs petits jeux avec un intérêt que je ne vois partager à personne." *Les Rêveries du promeneur solitaire*, in *Oeuvres complètes*, 1:1087.

33. Gutwirth, *The Twilight of the Goddesses*, 369.

34. For the history of this controversy and Rousseau's decisive role in it, see Gutwirth, "Infant Eros and Human Infant," in *The Twilight of the Goddesses*, 23–75, and J.-L. Flandrin, "L'Attitude à l'égard du petit enfant" P. R. Ivinski, H. C. Payne, K. C. Galitz, and R. Rand's catalogue of exposition, *Farewell to the Wet Nurse*, offers a

rich sample and discussion of the iconography generated by the nursing controversy.

35. Pierre Burgelin comments on Rousseau's nerve, considering his personal circumstances, in blaming women for the failure of French family life: "De nombreux passages parlent de la paternité avec ce qu'il faut bien appeler une vraie inconscience chez qui porterait un tels remords. D'ailleurs Rousseau tente presque toujours de rejeter sur les mères les fautes des pères." Rousseau, *Oeuvres complètes*, 4:1311, n. 263.

36. "A force d'interdire aux femmes le chant, la danse et tous les amusements du monde [le christianisme] les rend maussades, grondeuses, insupportables dans leurs maisons. Il n'y a point de religion ou le mariage soit soumis à des devoirs si sévères, et point ou un engagement si saint soit si méprisé" (4:716).

37. According to N. Fermon, however, "Rousseau is no biological determinist and does not advocate difference between the sexes as natural but imposed by convention." *Domesticationg Passions*, 121.

38. "Toute fille lettrée restera fille toute sa vie; quand il n'y aura que des hommes sensés sur la terre." *Emile*, in *Oeuvres complètes*, 4:768.

39. Trouille, *Sexual Politics*, 73. See also G. May, *De Jean-Jacques Rousseau à Mme Roland*, for the story of the complex relations between the gifted and aggressive woman at the center of Girondin politics in the Revolution and the sugar-coated misogyny of the one she called *maitre*.

40. "First Epistle to the Corinthians," 7:4. Flandrin refers to this exception to the principle of male dominance as "one of the paradoxical characteristics of Christian marriage" (*L'Eglise et le contrôle*, 128).

41. Flandrin, "L'Egalité des époux," ibid., 27.

42. Cuche, *Une Pensée sociale catholique*, 183. He further notes: "Véhicule d'un anti féminisme d'origine cléricale pendant des siècles, le christianisme porte aussi, paradoxalement, en lui-même des éléments de libération et de progrès de la condition de la femme, nés bien souvent de ses propres exigences éthiques." I. V. Hull points out that "the remarkable aspect of marital debt was its gender equality. It is one of the few instances in the history of European norms and laws where men and women were held to have exactly equal obligations and rights." *Sexuality, State*, 12. R.-J. Pothiers described the various legal rights of husbands over their wives' bodies in France in his *Traité de la puissance du mari*.

43. François-Xavier, "Lettre à père Barze."

44. Lettre V, "Réponse à la consultation de Madame la Marquise de . . . sur les devoirs & les obligations d'une femme envers son mari." Pontas, *Dictionnaire de cas de conscience*, 1:42–43.

45. Féline, *Cathéchisme des gens mariés*, 6–7.

46. Birth limitation techniques were widely practiced in Rousseau's own native Geneva, which he had so lauded in the *Contrat social* (3:111–18) for its exemplary moral climate. According to the authors of the article "Fécondité," "en Suisse, a Ge-

nève . . . d'austères huguenots découvrent aussi les voies secrètes du refus de l'enfant: la réduction de la fécondité est de part et d'autre assez similaire. Genève recourt aussi à l'élevage mercénaire des nourrissons." A. Bideau, J.-P. Bardet, and J. Houdaille, "Fluctuations chronologieques ou début de la Révolution contraceptive," in Dupâquier, ed., *Histoire de la population française*, 2:388.

47. Buffon, "Les Animaux carnassiers," *Histoire naturelle*, 7:341.

48. Buffon's own writings are not exempt from certain subjective judgments difficult to support on the basis of rational observation. He held for instance that the temperate zone, 40 to 50 degrees north of the equator, was the optimal region on earth for the "perfection" of all types of life. Further south and further north, the "species degenerated," meaning that Laplanders and Hottentots represented "degraded" varieties of men: these "deux extrêmes sont également éloignés du vrai et du beau." America produced diminished species as well; the indigenous American "n'existait pour la Nature que comme un être sans conséquence, une espèce d'automate impuissant . . . faible & petit par les organes de la génération; il n'a ni poil, ni barbe ni nulle ardeur pour la femelle." (7:380–81). Michel Duchet comments: "On mesure combien l'anthropologie de Buffon reste commandée par une image du monde et de l'homme, qui est celle de son temps." *Anthropologie et histoire*, 277.

49. See R. A. Leigh's "Note explicative" to Buffon's ironic letter to Rousseau (13 October 1765). *Correspondance*, (Letter 4724) 27:119. Otis Fellows treats Rousseau's surprising and unreciprocated reverence for Buffon and the profound influence the naturalist exercised on him in "Buffon and Rousseau."

50. Voltaire, "Homme," *Dictionnaire philosophique, Oeuvres complètes*, 19:373–85.

51. Castel, "L'Homme moral opposé," 295.

52. Ibid., 307. J.-M. Gouesse notes that bestiality was considered by eighteenth-century theologians a more grievous sin than sodomy, un "cas réversé." "Le Refus de l'enfant," 243.

53. Cerfvol, *Le Radoteur*, 17.

54. Laclos, "De l'éducation des femmes," in *Oeuvres*, 428.

55. Rouillé d'Orfeuil, *L'Alambic des lois*, 19.

56. Boissel, *Le Cathéchisme du genre humain*, 93.

57. Condorcet, *Prospectus d'un tableau historique*, 14. Along with Condorcet's endorsement of the family as natural went his well-known articulation of anti-Rousseauvian arguments for the equality of women. The inequality imposed on women is an abuse of power. "C'est vainement qu'on a essayé depuis de l'excuser par des sophismes." "Sur l'admission des femmes," 216.

58. Diderot, *Supplément au Voyage de Bougainville* [1796] in *Oeuvres philosophiques*, 495.

59. Benrekessa, "Loi naturelle." See also B. Garbouj, "Rétif conteur: l'Utopie, l'inceste, l'histoire," in *Frontières du conte*, ed. Fr. Marotin (Paris, 1982). Michel Delon discusses literary evocations of the taboo and its transgressions in "L'Inceste."

60. Benrekassa remarks upon incest in Sade's writings: "Il permet de réaliser une figure privilégiée: celle de l'homme s'exaltant et s'adorant dans sa propre création aux dépens de la création dite naturelle." Benrekassa seems to be invoking Rousseau's thesis from the *Second Discours* when he refers to the connection between man and child as merely "dite naturelle." "Loi naturelle," 144.

61. Pierre Hartman traces the theme of rape and its various nondemographic apologies in the fictions of late eighteenth-century novelists in "Le Motif du viol," *Travaux de Littérature* 7 (1994): 223–44.

62. "Article sur la polygamie," addressed to "M. le comte Louis de Rantzow à Wologda," in Cerfvol, *Le Radoteur,* 17. J.-L. Flandrin talks about the function of one kind of ritualized rape in villages where no prostitute was available. "Les viols collectifs et, en quelque sorte, publics . . . on allait chercher la victime chez elle, pendant la nuit . . . on enfoncait sa porte, on se saisissait d'elle, on la trainait dehors, on la battait, on la violait-chacun à son tour, et parfois toute la nuit-puis il arrivait qu'on la raccompagnât chez elle et souvent, on tentait de lui faire accepter de l'argent." "Prostitution et viol," in *Les Amours paysannes,* 284. One may wonder if this custom was still extant in the eighteenth century or whether sexual violence had in general become a more purely individual act.

63. P. Darmon comments that Rousseau's style is "much more direct, much more brutal and incisive" than Roussel's. This is true for many of Rousseau's assertions in his blunt, antique virtue mode, but lyrical, tender Jean-Jacques also expresses himself amply in *La Nouvelle Héloïse* and l'*Emile.* Darmon, *Mythologie,* 157. Y. Knibiehler and C. Fouquet describe the emergent discourse of femaleness as medical pathology in *La Femme et les médecins* (Paris, 1983).

64. Menassier de l'Estre, *De L'Honneur des deux sexes,* 8, 28. According to Menassier, "man makes the laws, woman inspires morals," a popular division of labor among many male writers of the pre-Revolutionary decade.

65. Mercier, *Le Tableau de Paris,* 9:172–73. John Lough notes that Mercier finds support for his approval of harshness toward women in Rousseau. "[Rousseau] a parlé des femmes avec sévérité parce qu'il les aimait" (8:195). Lough discusses Mercier's inconsistent vehemence and its similarities to the same qualities in Rousseau. "Women in Mercier's 'Tableau de Paris,'" 122.

66. Pétion de Villeneuve, *Essai sur le mariage,* 11.

67. Diderot, *Supplément,* in *Oeuvres philosophiques,* 509.

68. Withof is one of the few to praise the Hottentots, who were at the bottom of the human barrel according to numerous Enlightenment authors. Perhaps writers felt it necessary to disparage them, as they were being dispossessed by the Dutch from their habitation near the Cape of Good Hope. Describing their alleged filth and taste for spoiled meat, the *Encyclopédie* comments: "Tous les particuliers du Cap ont de ces sauvages qui s'emploient volontiers au service le plus bas et le plus sale de la maison," *Dissertation sur les eunuques* (Duisbourg, 1756), 17:763.

69. *Ephémérides du citoyen ou Chronique de l'esprit national* (Paris, 1765). The series ran from 1765 to 1772 and was continued by the *Nouvelles Ephémérides economiques,* 1774–76, 47 vols. A sort of newsletter for Physiocrats, it is described by Jean Sgard as "the official organ of Quesnay's disciples." *Dictionnaire des journaux,* 1:377–78.

70. Cerfvol, *La Gamologie,* 5.

71. In *Les Causes célèbres, curieuses et intéressantes, de toutes les cours souveraines du voyaume,* ed. Nicolas-T.-L. Desessarts (1775–79).

72. Pétion de Villeneuve, *Essai sur le mariage,* 3.

73. See Daniel Ligou in "Bertrand Barère et Jean-Jacques Rousseau," *J.-J. Rousseau (1712–1782)* (Gap, n.d.), 61–74. Leo Gershoy, *Bertrand Barère: A Reluctant Terrorist* (Princeton, 1961).

Chapter Seven: Population Politics in Revolution

1. Fage, "La Révolution française," 311.

2. Vergniaud, "Opinion de M. Vergniaud."

3. Eric Brian traces the complex history of the relations between the monarchy and the increasingly sophisticated data made available by demography and statistics in *La Mesure de l'Etat,* see especially 145–292.

4. "Il faut . . . à la Révolution une démocratie nombreuse de petits propriétaires et à la France beaucoup d'enfants pour la défendre et la servir." "Révolution et population," Dupâquier et al., *Histoire de la population,* 3:91–92.

5. Saint-Just's beliefs about the infinite expansion of population are to be found in the "Fragments sur les institutions républicaines," *Oeuvres complètes,* 2:499–501. A. McLaren traces the socialist commitment to natalism and its contradictions in France up through the early twentieth century in *Sexuality and Social Order,* 77–92.

6. *Collection générale des décrets rendus par l'Assemblée Nationale,* bk. 6, 2:1093.

7. Ronsin, *Le Contrat sentimental,* 107.

8. 27 August 1793, in Oliver-Martin, *La Crise du mariage,* 229. Another frequent if inconsistent critic of marriage was the great natalist Rétif de la Bretonne: "Pour peu qu'on réfléchisse on sera forcé de convenir que les mariages ne peuvent être que des attentats les plus formels à la liberté des hommes, surtout des femmes, qu'autant de divorces avec le reste du genre humain." *Le Pornographe,* 41.

9. See Y. Blayo, "Illegitimate Births in France," 280. Already in 1777 observers like the abbé de Malvaux were expressing alarm over the increase in fatherless children. "La France ne sera plus qu'un hôpital d'enfants trouvés; tous les français seront à peu pres bâtards." *Les Moyens de détruire,* 173.

10. Juges, *Les Mariages heureux,* 29. E.-L.-H. de Launez, comte d'Antraigues, agreed, pointing out that it is rare for a father to wish to destroy *despotisme domestique. Observations sur le divorce,* 17.

11. J. Dupâquier comments, "à la faveur de l'unanimité nationale de la Nuit du 4 août, le régime successoral féodal, le droit de masculinité et le droit de l'aînesse

avaient été abolis." "La Révolution française et la famille," *Histoire de la population française*, 3:96.

12. Hecht, "From 'Be Fruitful and Multiply,'" 546.

13. In David Weir's formulation: "It is now well known that nuptiality provided a powerful instrument of fertility control in Western European populations, at least as far back as registers of vital events can take us in the sixteenth century." "New Estimates of Nuptiality," 48:307.

14. Vovelle, *La Révolution contre l'Eglise* (Paris, 1988). See Aulard, *Le Christianisme et la Révolution française* (Paris, 1925), and Mathiez, *La Question religieuse sous la Révolution française* (Paris, 1929). Darimayou, *La Chastité du clergé devoilée, ou Procès-verbaux des Séances du Clergé chez les Filles de Paris, trouvés à la Bastille* (Rome [Paris], 1790), and *Moniteur universel*, 24 October 1790, 190: 1132.

15. Anon., *Motions adressées à l'Assemblée en faveur du sexe* (n.p., 1789), 10.

16. *Considérations politiques et religieuses* received a long, detailed review in the *Moniteur universel*, 17 October 1792, 190:1202–4, presenting the author's arguments against celibacy. "A-t-on jamais remarqué moins de compassion, de charité, dans un père de famille que dans un sombre célibataire?" (1204). Darimayou, *La chastité du clergé devoilé* (Paris, 1790), and *Moniteur universel*, 24 October 1790, 190: 1132.

17. "Ne sentira-t-on jamais la nécessité de rétrécir l'ouverture de ces gouffres, où les races futures vont se perdre?" *La Religieuse, Oeuvres romanesques*, 310.

18. *Collection générale des Décrets*, 7:211. Fr.-S. Bézard's 1793 *Rapport et projet de décrets relatifs aux prètres mariés & défanatisés* includes additional debate.

19. P. Bruno, *Le Sang du Carmel* (Paris, 1792), 97.

20. E. Rapley and R. Rapley discuss the unexpected reluctance of most nuns to embrace secularization in 1790–91 in "An Image of Religious Women in the Ancien Régime." Ruth Graham examines the experiences of a group of nuns who did leave the convent to marry in "The Married Nuns before Cardinal Caprara." See also A. Burgière, "La Famille et l'Etat."

21. Blanchet, *Les Funestes Effets*, 9–11.

22. Bézard, *Rapport et projet*, 331.

23. Dupuy, *Observations philosophiques*, 29. Dupuy had been *Secrétaire perpétuel de l'Académie Royale des Inscriptions et Belles Lettres*.

24. J. Hecht comments on the repetitive denunciations of the unmarried: "Le célibat sera ainsi la bête noire des hommes de '89." "Célibat," 7:277.

25. Duvergier, *Collection complète des lois 1788–1830* (Paris, 1854), 2:18; 2:175.

26. Attributed to "Vata" in Hecht and Lévy, *Economie et population, Bibliographie*, n. 4390.

27. For Talma's petition and the response of Durand de Maillane, see Madival and Laurent, *Archives parlementaires*, 26:186–87.

28. *Les Actes de la Commune de Paris* (12 May 1791), 4:248.

29. "Opinion sur la manière de constater l'Etat civil des citoyens, prononcée à la séance du 19 juin, 1792" *Moniteur universel,* 21 June 1792, 173:718.

30. Bert, *Des Prêtres salariés,* 7:103.

31. Adoption had been discouraged by law under the ancien régime, again largely for reasons having to do with inheritances. Garaud and Szramkiewicz discuss the minefield of considerations the legislators had to navigate in drafting laws relating to it in *La Révolution française et la famille,* 91–107.

32. Duvergier, *Collection complète des lois,* 2:18.

33. See P. Bruno, *Le Sang du Carmel* (Paris, 1992), for an account of this tragic moment, which became both a symbol of Revolutionary excess and a rallying point for Catholic reaction in the nineteenth and twentieth centuries.

34. *Moniteur universal,* 14 ventôse, an II (March 4, 1793), 8:45.

35. Blanchard, *Cathéchisme de la nature,* 148–49.

36. *Archives parlementaires,* 87:104–5.

37. *Archives parlementaires,* 111:299–301.

38. Dupâquier et al., *Histoire de la population française,* 3:71.

39. Vovelle, *La Révolution contre l'Eglise: De la Raison à l'être supreme* (Lausanne, 1988), 135. According to the abbé Grégoire's *Histoire du mariage des prêtres,* there were only two thousand marriages of clergy during the Revolution, the majority of which were occasioned by the threats of deportation or prison during the Terror.

40. R. Graham, "Les Mariages des ecclésiastiques députés à la Convention." *Annales Historiques de la Révolution française* 57, no. 4 (1985): 480–99.

41. "Il était admis que l'enfant naturel n'avait pas de lignage et qu'exclus de la famille il devait être écarté de la succession de ses pères et mères." Garaud and Szramkiewicz, *La Révolution française et la famille,* 110. In chapter two, part one, "Du 'Bâtard' à 'l'Enfant de la nature,'" the authors present the tormented discussions of legislators attempting to reconcile conflicting values of nation, tradition, and masculinity.

42. Dupâquier, *La Population française aux XVIIe et XVIIIe siècles,* 114. Illegitimacy during the ancien régime has been estimated by Y. Blayo as rising in the second half of the eighteenth century from 1.1 percent (including foundlings) during 1740–49 to 3.0 percent during 1790–99. "Illegitimate Births," 282–83.

43. Peuchet also authored several economic studies of France, making use of demographic data (1801, 1803, 1805).

44. Décembre-Alonnier, *Dictionnaire,* 1:657.

45. 20 September 1793 in A. Aulard, *La Société des Jacobins* (Paris, 1889–99), 5:409. Chabot (1756–94), a colorful defrocked Capuchin, extremist Jacobin deputy from Loir-et-Cher, and *vicaire général* under the abbé Grégoire, was an ardent supporter of equality for "natural" children and of women's right to vote.

46. *Moniteur universel,* 21 June 1792, 173:718.

47. Phan, "La Séduction impunie," 2:56.

48. Ibid., 2:61. The flexible Berlier (1761–1840), Montagnard until Thermidor, then member of the Conseil des Cinq-Cents, courtesan of Napoleon, ended up a loyal supporter of Louis XVIII.

49. Fage, "La Révolution française," 2:330. Sauvy, "Deux Techniciens," 4:693.

50. Francini, *Moralia coniugalia,* 259–60.

51. Francis Ronsin comments that authors of the Revolutionary period are conscious of the political upheaval as it plays out. "[Ils] ont oublié le ton implorant du *Cri d'un honnête homme* s'adressant à un pouvoir lointain et hautain, pour adopter celui du citoyen, volontiers emporté et impatient tant il est persuadé et fier de participer à l'oeuvre commune de rénovation de la société." *Le Contrat sentimental,* 53.

52. Berquin, *L'Ami des enfants,* 10; Juges, *Les Marriages heureux,* 29.

53. Hennet, *Du Divorce,* vi.

54. Following Hennet's method, G. de R. de Flassan based his revolutionary analysis of divorce in natural law in *La Question du divorce.*

55. In *Le Mythe de la procréation,* P. Darmon discusses concepts of female responsibility for sterility, including Nicolas Venette's claim in 1685 that "all vices and irregularities of conception come from the woman's side rather than from the man's." Venette, *La Génération de l'homme ou tableau de l'amour conjugal considéré dans l'état du mariage,* (1685; Parma, 1696), 23. Reprinted in Darmon, *Le Mythe de la procréation.*

56. In 1791 Hennet also published a *Pétition à l'Assemblée Nationale,* an annotated anthology of prodivorce arguments from prestigious sources, quoted in the debates.

57. Juges, *Les Mariages heureux,* 10–11.

58. Anon., *Réflections d'un bon citoyen,* 2.

59. *La Nécessité du divorce,* 35. Francini discusses the evidence for possible identities of this author. *Moralia coniugalia,* 1:268.

60. See Ronsin, *Le Contrat sentimental,* 74. Chapt de Rastignac (1727–92) was a Sorbonne theologian and deputy to the National Assembly.

61. Other early Revolutionary Catholic defenses of indissolubility that questioned the salubrious effects on procreation to be wrought by divorce included abbé F.-A.-E. de Courcy's *Distinctions et bornes des deux puissances* (Paris, 1790) and the Jesuit A. Barruel's refutation of Hennet's work, entitled *Lettres sur le divorce à un deputé de l'Assemblé Nationale* (Paris, 1798).

62. "La loi . . . réalisa une réforme beaucoup plus hardie que celle souhaitée par la plupart des 'divorciares' philosophes et publicistes, selon lesquels l'indissolubilité du mariage devait être la règle et le divorce un remède assez rarement appliqué," Garaud and Szramkiewicz, *La Révolution française et la famille,* 71.

63. The inequality was restored in Napoleon's *Code Civil* of 1804. The greatest doctrinal hurdle facing Catholic defenders of indissolubility was Christ's instruction to Matthew (5:32): "Whosoever shall put away his wife, saving for the cause of

fornication, causeth her to commit adultery." Since the clause of exception regarding fornication is not present in Mark and Luke, the Gospels are viewed as ambiguous on this point. See R. Phillips, "Divorce in Catholic Doctrine," *Putting Asunder,* 17–18.

D'Antraigues attempted to synthesize traditional punishment of the adulterous
woman with the good of society, patriotism, and a benign providence:

En rendant au mariage toute sa pureté il faut rendre à la loi qui punit l'adultère
toute sa séverité et à ses Ministres toute leur vigilance. Aucun peuple n'a laissé un
pareil crime impuni. Comme il détruit le lien de la société domestique, il relâche
tous les liens politiques. Qui ne peut être heureux dans ses foyers n'a plus de
patrie.

La loi qui accorde [le divorce] doit être égale entre les deux époux. Cependant
la nature en rendant les suites de la faute d'une femme presqu'irréparables, semble aussi vouloir dédommager l'époux en accordant aussi à la femme plus de patience à supporter le chagrin, plus de clémence pour pardonner des torts *(Observations sur le divorce,* 52).

64. Abundant scholarship has been devoted to women's struggles for political
equality during the French Revolution. See J. Landes, *Women and the Public Sphere;*
D. G. Levy, H. B. Applewhite, and M. Johnson, eds., *Women in Revolutionary Paris*
(Urbana, 1979); S. Melzer and L. Rabine, eds., *Rebel Daughters: Women and the French
Revolution* (New York, 1992); and M. Gutwirth, *The Twilight of the Goddesses.* See
also M.-F. Brive et al., *Les Femmes et la Révolution française,* 2 vols (Toulouse, 1988).

65. Juges, *Les Mariages heureux,* 28.

66. Antraigues, *Observations sur le divorce,* 12.

67. Ronsin, *Le Contrat sentimental,* 145.

68. Oudot, *Essai sur les principes de la législation;* see also Oudot, *Opinion,* 17:321.
In June, legislative proposals were put forth to formulate appropriate Republican
forms of family law and to remedy the plight of children of uncertain paternity. Favorable comment appeared including such popular pamphlets as W. All'ar, *L'Enfant de plusieurs pères* (N.p., 1790). For a discussion of this legislative debate, see
Garaud and Szramkiewicz, *La Révolution française et la famile,* 95–96.

69. Oudot, *Opinion,* 5.

70. Quoted by Fr. Olivier-Martin in *La Crise du mariage,* 238.

71. Ibid., 241. Inédit, Appendice 13.

72. Saint-Just, "Institutions républicaines," *Oeuvres complètes,* 984.

73. Mary Wollstonecraft, like Saint Just, favored the legalization of a kind of polygamy in 1792, insisting that the practice "is drawn from the well-attested fact, that
in the countries where it is established, more females are born than males." She attributed the sex differential to the "enervation" of men in hot climates. In Europe,
however, where there are born males and females in a "proportion of 105 to 100," the
moral and legal problem is again that of "informal" polygamy: "When a man se-

duces a woman, it should be termed . . . a *left-handed* marriage and the man should be *legally* obliged to maintain the woman and her children." *A Vindication of the Rights of Women*, 70–71.

74. Duvergier, *Collection générale*, 22:1066. Garaud and Szramkiewicz discuss the streamlining of marriage rules in 1792 and the law's silence regarding "spiritual and affinitive relatives" in *La Révolution française et la famile*, 43. See also A. Fage, "La Révolution française," 311–38.

75. 24 prairial, an II. "Discours préliminaire prononcé par Cambacérès" in Fenet, *Recueil complet des travaux préparatoires du Code Civil*, 1:156. See J.-L. Halpérin, *L'Impossible Code civil*, for discussion of this controversy and the role of Cambacérès in the eventual formulations of women's control over marital property.

76. Lakanal, "Rapport sur J.-J. Rousseau," 5–6.

77. *Archives parlementaires* (26 June 1793), 67:484.

78. See E. Van de Walle, "De la Nature à la fécundité naturelle," 13.

79. C. Capitan describes the great authority of "Nature" in Revolutionary discourse in assigning each sex its proper role: "La Nature est la *catégorie politique corollaire de celle de 'Nation'* à qui elle fournit la matière première nécessaire pour parer à ses besoins." "Construction de l'objet," 1:332.

80. Saint-Just, "De la Nature," in *Oeuvres complètes*, 944.

81. Fauchet, *La Bouche de fer*, 65. Fauchet (1744–93) had been a famous preacher before the Revolution and in fact held the office of *Prédicateur du Roi* until Louis XVI dismissed him for his radicalism. Nevertheless, once elected to the Convention he voted against the execution of the king and against the abolition of clerical celibacy. His publication was inspired by Rousseau's discussion of public opinion in *Du Contrat social*. Ruth Graham examines Fauchet's reliance on Rousseau in "The Revolutionary Bishop and the *Philosophes*."

82. Presevot, *Principes de Législation civile*, 84–85.

83. *Censure publique pour la surveillance des moeurs et la morale publique* (Paris, 1793), 111.

84. Maréchal, *Dame Nature à la barre de l'Assemblée Nationale*, 5, 45.

85. *Moniteur universel*, 21 June 1792, 173:718. The marquis de Sade was one of the few to take exception to the connection between Republics and natality. In his pamphlet, *Français encore un effort*, he maintained that as much as monarchies needed men, "Là les tyrans n'étant riches qu'en raison de leurs esclaves, assurément il leur faut des hommes," an abundant population in a Republican government is a vice. In a sentence likely to *épater la bourgeoisie* of the period as much as did his kinkiest sexual fantasies, he favored letting each individual destroy his unwanted progeny as he saw fit. "Accordez à chaque individu de se livrer . . . au droit de se défaire des enfans qu'il ne peut nourrir ou desquels le gouvernement ne peut tirer aucun secours," *La Philosophie dans le boudoir*, 150–55.

86. Louis Prudhomme (1752–1821?), *Révolutions de Paris*, 202. The forced loan of 3 September 1793 cost married citizens earning more than 10,000 francs one-tenth of their income, whereas bachelors paid the same amount after only 6000 francs. Décembre-Alonnier, *Dictionnaire*, 1:656.

87. According to the *Code civil*, the husband owes protection to the wife, and she owes obedience to her husband (article 213); women may not legally bear witness (37), declare the birth of a child (56), or have a legal abode except that of the husband (214). He can divorce her for adultery, but she can divorce him only when he brings his concubine home (229, 230). The husband who murders his adulterous wife may be excused. The husband administers the wife's personal belongings (1428), and so on. *Code civil.* In the words of J. Traer, "Articles governing the relations of the spouses in marriage provided that the wife should have no legal personality separate from that of her husband." *Marriage and the Family*, 172. G. Fraisse analyzes the dominant discourse of biologically justified political inequality in the immediate post-Revolutionary period in *Muse de la raison*.

88. Gutwirth, *The Twilight of the Goddesses*, 366. Dupâquier, *La Société au XIX siècle: tradition, transition, transformation* (Paris, 1992), 20. For Joan Landes, the dichotomy reserving the political for men and the domestic for women was necessitated by the eighteenth century's incorporation of an educated bourgeoisie into the emerging public sphere; see Landes, *Women and the Public Sphere.* Other commentators have seen less stark divisions than Landes depicts or offered explanations linking the exclusion of women to reaction against their behind-the-scenes influence upon the affairs of the ancien régime, to the psychological needs of working class men, to economic factors, and to the reemergence of a primeval fear of the female. Responses to Landes's thesis include K. M. Baker's "Defining the Public Sphere" and D. Goodman's "Public Sphere and Private Life."

89. Dupâquier, "Révolution et population," *Histoire de la population française*, 3:65, 84.

90. Hecht discusses the hypothesis of overpopulation s.v. A.-R.-J. Turgot (1766); S.-N.- H. Linguet (1767); A. N. Isnard (1781); and J. Necker (1775) in "Malthus avant Malthus," 26:69–78.

91. As demonstrated by Cl.-Fr. D'Auxiron (1728–78), in his *Principes de tout gouvernement* (Paris, 1766).

92. Burgière identifies this period as the *intercycle labroussien* referred to in Ernest Labrousse's classical study *Esquisse du movement des prix et des revenu en France au XVIIe siècle* (Paris, 1933) of the economic and social conjuncture in France before the Revolution. Burguière, "La Déstabilisation de la société française," in Dupâquier, ed., *Histoire de la population française*, 2:475.

93. Hufton, *The Prospect before Her*, 387.

94. Rothschild, "Social Security and Laissez Faire."

95. Mercier, *Le Tableau de Paris,* 85–87. A. Burguière, "La Déstabilisation de la société française," in Dupâquier, ed., *Histoire de la population française,* 2:483.

96. Gutwirth discusses the practice of wet-nursing among the working-class and describes the living conditions of the women reduced to selling their own milk in *The Twilight of the Goddesses,* 47–51.

97. Mercier, *Le Tableau de Paris,* 85–87.

98. Condorcet, *Oeuvres,* 8:465. K. M. Baker comments on the marquis de Condorcet's opposition to the convocation of the Estates General and his wish to participate instead in a top-down, structural reform of the monarchy: "L'unité de la pensée de Condorcet," 520.

99. Turmeau de la Morandière, *Appel des étrangers dans nos colonies,* 28–29.

100. Condorcet, *Arithmétique politique,* 345.

101. For a discussion of Condorcet and contraception, see André Béjin, "Condorcet, précurseur," 347–54.

102. Quoted in L. Cahen, *Condorcet et la Révolution française* (Paris, 1904), 110; 209–10.

103. Georges Cabanis, *Observations sur les hôpitaux* (Paris, 1790). Napoleon is said to have consulted Cabanis (1757–1808) about the feasibility of a man his age contributing to the propagation of the French race. Cabanis replied: "De 40 à 45 ans l'homme peut faire des enfants bien constitués, à 50 ans il en fait quelquefois, de 50 à 60 ans il en fait rarement, à 70 ans, s'il est marié à une jeune femme, il en fait toujours." Paul Vermeil de Conchard, *Trois Etudes sur Cabanis* (Brive, 1914), 37.

104. Décembre-Alonnier, *Dictionnaire de la Révolution française,* 2:141.

105. Typical of the floundering confusion regarding responsibility for children in the wake of Catholic charities was the fate of the petition of Mme Bochet-Mouret, descendant of La Fontaine and author of several works on education. Aghast at the plight of homeless children, she offered to care for and educate a dozen of them at her own expense if she might be permitted to occupy one of the abandoned convent buildings near the *Jardin des plantes.* The offer was refused because the section leaders hesitated to create a precedent. *Les Actes de la Commune de Paris,* 3 May 1790, 5:224.

106. Dupâquier, *Histoire de la population française,* 3:63–65.

107. *Moniteur universel,* 12 June 1790, 161, 412.

108. Dupâquier, *Histoire de la population française,* "For this committee, the primary cause of beggary consisted in the disproportion between population and demand for labor."

109. Hecht, "From 'be Fruitful and Multiply,'" 4:537. See also Emma Rothschild, "Social Security and Laissez-Faire," 21:711–44. *Moniteur universel,* 31 January 1791, 32:131–32.

110. *Moniteur universel,* 26 prairial, an II (14 June 1794): 165, 208.

111. Young, *Travels in France,* 1:408.

112. Dupâquier, *Histoire de la population française,* 3:64.

113. G. Babeuf, *Du Système de dépopulation,* 1–3. See Daniel Martin for a discussion of this broadside in "La Dépopulation."

114. Godwin (1765–1836), whose *Enquiry Concerning Political Justice* (1793) predicted a luminous future for the beleaguered human race, foreseeing a world where social and economic equality reigned, where marriage would be abolished, procreation unchecked, and children provided for by the entire community.

115. Six editions of the essay appear between 1798 and 1826, with the most significant revisions appearing in the 2nd (1803) and the 6th (1826).

116. Malthus, *An Essay* [1798], in *Works,* 1:73. Malthus, like Montesquieu, held that marriage was instituted to impose an "obligation on every man to support his own children," thus explaining the "superior disgrace which attends a breach of chastity in the woman than the man. It could not be expected that women should have resources sufficient to support their own children. When therefore a woman was connected with a man, who had entered into no compact to maintain her children, and . . . had deserted her," the offspring was either a dangerous parasite on proper society or a casualty (ibid.).

117. R. Binion paraphrases this argument as: "God puts us all on short rations so that we could sharpen our wits continually in contriving to take the food out of each other's mouths." "'More Men than Corn,'" 4:568.

118. E. Van de Walle comments that Malthus's view was certainly more typical of the era than Condorcet's and that "it took the visionary turn of mind of a Condorcet to think that contraception might some day tamper with the biological determinism of uncontrolled reproduction." "Malthus Today," in *Malthus Past and Present,* ed. J. Dupâquier (London, 1983), 236. Of course, as we have seen, it was not the thought itself that was new but the attribution of moral value to the practice. In the same volume see D. Heinsohn and O. Steiger for a discussion of Malthus's opposition to Condorcet and birth control. "The Rationale of Malthus's Theory," 223–32.

119. For a dicussion of the evolution of populationist thinking in the nineteenth and twentieth centuries, see Mclaren "Sex and Socialism"; J. J. Spengler, *France Faces Depopulation;* F. Ronsin, *La Grève des ventres;* Dupâquier et al., *Histoire de la population française,* vols. 3 and 4.

BIBLIOGRAPHY

Materials Published before 1800
Collections of Documents, Reports,
and Serial Publications

Les Actes de la Commune de Paris, 2d series. S. de Lacroix, ed. 9 October 1790–10 August 1792. Paris, 1905–12.

Archives parlementaires. Recueil complet des débats législatifs et politiques. J. Madival et E. Laurent, eds. 1789–99, 47 vols. Paris, 1867–96.

Ephémérides du citoyen ou Chronique de l'esprit national: bibliothèque raisonnée des sciences morales et politiques. N. Badeau and V. Mirabeau, eds. 1765–68, P. S. Dupont de Nemours, May 1768–72. Continued as *Nouvelle Ephémérides économiques.* 1774–76. 47 vols. Paris. Vols. 1, 2, "De la dépopulation." Vol. 3, "Questions politiques et morales."

Durand de Maillane, P.-T. *Rapport sur le projet des Comités ecclésiastiques et de Constitution concernant les empêchements, les dispenses & la forme des mariages,* Paris, 1790.

Duvergier, ed. *Collection générale des Décrets rendus par l'Assemblée Nationale Législative.* 78 vols. Paris, n.d.

Histoire parlementaire de la Révolution française ou Journal des Assemblées nationales de 1789 à 1815. P. J. Buchez and P. C. Roux, eds. 40 vols. Paris, 1834–38.

Journal [Mémoires] de Trévoux. P. Lallemant, G.-F. Berthier, et al., eds. 878 vols., 1701–67.

Le Moniteur universel (Gazette nationale). 20 vols. Paris, 1789–1er germinal, an VIII (1799).

Works Cited

Ambrose, Saint. *Oeuvres sur la virginité.* Père de Bonrecueil, trans. N.p., 1729.

Antraigues, Emmanuel-L.-H. de Launez, comte d'. *Observations sur le divorce.* Paris, 1789.

Arbuthnot, John. "An Argument for Divine Providence Taken from the Constant Regularity of the Births of Both Sexes." [1712]. In *The Life and Works of Arbuthnot.* Oxford, 1892.

Astruc, Jean. *Traité des peines des secondes noces.* Toulouse, 1774.

Babeuf, Gracchus [François-Noël]. *Du Système de la dépopulation.* Paris, an III (1795–96).

Bablot, Benjamin L.-N., médecin. *Epître à Zulmis sur les avantages et les obligations du mariage.* Bouillon, 1772.

Bayle, Pierre. *Nouvelles de la Republique des Lettres* (1684–87), in *Oeuvres diverses.* Hildesheim, 1965.

———. *Dictionnaire historique et critique.* 4 vols. 1697; Basle, 1741.

Bernardin de Saint-Pierre, Jacques-Henri. *Etudes de la nature.* 3 vols. Paris, 1784–1825. Reprint, Paris, 1853.

Berquin, D. *L'Ami des enfants.* Paris, n.d.

Bert, P.-C.-F. *Des Prêtres salariés par la Nation.* Paris, 1793.

Bézard, Fr.-S. *Rapport et projet de décrits relatifs aux prêtres mariés et défanatisés.* Paris, 1792.

Blanchard, [Pierre] Platon. *Cathéchisme de la Nature ou Religion et morale naturelle.* Paris, an II (III), (1795).

Blanchet, Curé. *Les Funestes Effets de vertu de la chasteté dans les prêtres.* N. p., 1790.

Blondel, Jean. *Des Hommes tels qu'ils sont et doivent être: Ouvrage de sentiment.* Paris, 1758.

Boisguilbert, Pierre le Pesant de. *Détail de la France ou Traité de la cause de la diminution de ses biens, et la facilité du remède. En fournissant en un mois, tout l'argent dont le Roy a besoin, et enrichissant tout le monde.* Rouen, 1695. Reprinted as *Détail de la France, sous le règne présent. Augmenté en cette nouvelle Edition de plusieurs Mémoires et Traités, sur la même manière.* N.p., 1710.

Boislisle, A. de. *Mémoires des intendants sur l'état des généralités.* Vol. 1, *Mémoire de la généralité de Paris.* Paris, 1881.

Boissel, François. *Le Cathéchisme du genre humain que, sous les auspices de la nature et de son véritable auteur, qui me l'ont dicté, je mets sous les yeux et la protection de la nation française pour l'établissement du véritable ordre moral et de l'éducation sociale des hommes.* N.p., 1789. 2d ed., Paris, 1792.

Boucher d'Argis, André-Jean-Baptiste. *Principes sur la nullité du mariage pour cause d'impuissance, avec le Traité du président Bouhier sur les procédures qui sont en usage en France pour la preuve de l'impuissance de l'homme, et quelques Pièces curieusess sur le même sujet.* Paris, 1776.

———. *Traité des gains nuptiaux et de survie, qui sont en usage dans les pais de droit écrit.* Lyon, 1738.

Boulainvilliers, Henri, comte de. "Touchant L'Affaire de Mrs. les princes du sang," in *Mémoires présentés à Monseigneur le duc d'Orléans, régent de France.* La Haye, 1727. 112–56.

Boussanelle, Louis de. *Essai sur les femmes.* Paris, 1765.

Brion de la Tour, Louis. *Tableau de la population de la France avec les citations des auteurs.* Paris, 1789.

Buffon, Georges-Louis Leclerc, comte de. *Histoire naturelle, générale et particulière.* 13 vols. 1749–67; abridged edition, J. Piveteau, ed. Paris, 1954.

Butel-Dumont, Georges-M. *Théorie du luxe.* Paris, 1771.

Cantillon, Richard. *Essai sur la nature du commerce en général.* London, 1755. Reprint, C. Théré and E. Brian, eds., INED. Paris, 1997.

Cassan, Jacques. *La Recherche des droits du Roy.* Paris, 1632.

Castel de Saint-Pierre, Charles-Irénée, abbé de. *Ouvrages de morale et de politique.* 15 vols. Rotterdam, 1733–49.

Castel, Père. "L'Homme moral opposé à l'homme physique de Monsieur Rxxx." Toulouse, 1756.

Cerfvol. *Cri d'un honnête homme.* [Par Mr Philbert, prêteur de la ville de Landau en Alsace en même temps héros de l'histoire]. Lunéville, 1768. Reprint, Paris, 1769 [with *Législation du divorce*].

———. *Mémoire sur la population dans lequel on indique le moyen de rétablir et de se procurer un corps militaire toujours subsistant et peuplant.* London [Paris], 1768.

———. *Législation du divorce précédée du cri d'un honnête homme qui se croit fondé en droit naturel et divin à répudier sa femme.* London, 1769.

———. *Le Divorce réclamé par Madame la Comtesse de * * *.* London, 1769.

———. *Parloir de l'abbaye de * ou Entretiens sur le divorce, par M. De V * * *, suivi de son Utilité civile et politique.* Geneva, 1770.

———. *Cri d'une honnête femme qui réclame le divorce conformément aux lois de la primitive église, à l'usage actuel du royaume catholique de Pologne, et à celui de tous les peuples de la terre qui existent ou ont existé, excepté nous.* London, 1770.

———. *L'Intérêt des femmes au rétablissement du divorce.* Amsterdam, 1771.

———. *La Gamologie.* Paris, 1772.

———. *Supplément aux Mémoires de M. Palissot, pour servir à l'histoire de notre littérature, ou Lettre à M. Palissot sur un article de ses Mémoires.* London and Paris, 1774.

———. *Le Radoteur,* Paris. 1775.

Chapt de Rastignac, Armand-Anne de, abbé, député. *Accord de la révélation et de la raison contre le divorce.* Paris, 1790.

Charron, Pierre. *De la Sagesse, trois livres.* Paris, 1606.

Chastellux, François-Jean, marquis de. *De La Félicité publique ou Considérations sur le sort des hommes.* Amsterdam, 1772.

Chaudon, Dom Louis-Mayeul. *Dictionnaire anti-philosophique, pour servir de commentaire et de correctif au "Dictionnaire philosophique" de Voltaire et aux autres livres qui ont paru de nos jours contre le christianisme.* Paris, 1767.

Condorcet, Marie-Jean-Nicolas de Caritat, marquis de, "Sur l'Admission des femmes au droit de cité." *Journal de la Société de 1789.* 5, 3 juillet, 1790.

————. *Oeuvres*, 12 vols. A. Condorcet O'Connor and François Arago, eds. Paris, 1847–49.

————. *Prospectus d'un tableau historique des progrès de l'esprit humain.* N.p. 1793. Reprint, Paris, 1984.

————. *L'Almanach anti-superstitieux.* A.-M. Chouillet, P. Crépel, and H. Duranton, eds. Paris, 1992.

————. *Arithmétique politique, Textes rares et inédits.* P. Crépel and B. Bru, eds. Paris, 1994.

Cornaro, Louis [Luigi]. *L'Art de conserver la vie des princes . . . et la santé des religieuses.* Padoue, 1558; Trans. Utrecht, 1735.

Crevier, Jean-Baptiste-Louis. *Observations sur le livre de "L'Esprit des lois"* (also attributed to Diderot). Paris, 1764.

Darimayou, Dominique. *La Chasteté du clergé dévoilée, ou Procès-verbaux des Séances du Clergé chez les filles de Paris, trouvés à la Bastille.* Rome [Paris], 1790. Review in *Moniteur universel,* 24 October 1790, 190:1132.

Décembre-Alonnier. *Dictionnaire de la Révolution française.* 2 vols. Paris, n.d.

Diderot, Denis. *Oeuvres philosophiques.* P. Vernière, ed.. Paris, 1956.

————. *Oeuvres romanesques.* H. Bénac, ed.. Paris, 1959.

————. *Correspondance.* G. Roth and J. Varloot, eds. 16 vols. Paris, 1955–70.

————. *Mémoire pour Catherine II.* P. Vernière, ed. Paris, 1966.

————. *Oeuvres complètes.* H. Dieckmann, et al., eds. Paris, 1975.

————, and Jean le Ronde d'Alembert. *Encyclopédie, ou Dictionnaire raisonné des sciences, des arts et des métiers, par une société des gens de lettres.* 35 vols. Paris, 1751–80. Reprint, 26 vols., Lausanne et Berne, 1781.

Duguet, Jacques-Joseph, abbé. *Lettres sur divers sujets de morale et de piété, par l'auteur du Traité sur la prière publique.* 10 vols. Paris, 1708–53.

Du Laurens, Henri-Joseph, abbé. *Le Porte-feuilles d'un philosophe, ou Mélange de pièces philosophiques, critiques, satyriques et galantes.* 3 vols. Cologne, 1770.

Dupuy, Louis, député. *Observations philosophiques sur le célibat, sur l'athéisme et sur l'église romaine.* Paris, an II [1794].

Dutoit-Mambrini, Philippe. *De l'Onanisme, ou discours philosophique et moral sur la luxure artificielle et sur tous les crimes relatifs.* Lausanne, 1760.

Eon de Beaumont, Charles-Geneviève. *Les Loisirs sur divers sujets importants d'administration, etc.* 13 vols. Amsterdam, 1774.

————. "Les Espérances d'un bon patriote," in "Lettre écrite à Jean Fréron," in *L'Année Littéraire* (1759): 55–68.

Expilly, Jean-Joseph, abbé d'. *Tableau de la population de la France.* N.p. 1780. Reprint, Paris, 1973.

Faiguet de Villeneuve, Joachim. *L'Econome politique: Projet pour enrichir et perfectionner l'espèce humaine.* Paris, 1763.

Fauchet, Claude de, abbé. *La Bouche de fer.* 6 January 1791.

Felice, Fortunato-Bartolomeo de. *Le Code de l'humanité, ou la législation universelle, naturelle, civile et politique avec l'histoire littéraire des plus grands hommes qui ont contribué à la perfection de ce code.* 13 vols. Yverdun, 1778.

Féline, père. *Cathéchisme des gens mariés.* Caen, 1782.

Fénelon, François de Pons de Salignac de La Motte. *A Louis XIV. Remonostrances à ce Prince,* in *Ecrits et lettres politiques.* 1694. Reprint, C. Urbain, ed., Geneva, 1981.

Flassan, G. de R. de. *La Question du divorce discutée sous les rapports du droit naturel, de la religion, de l'histoire, de la morale et de l'ordre social.* Paris, 1790.

François-Xavier, Saint. "Lettre au père Barze," *Introduction à la vie dévote.* N.p., 1610.

Galtier, Jean-Baptiste, abbé. *Les Lettres persanes convaincues d'impiété.* N.p., 1751.

Garnier, Charles-Georges-Thomas. *Code du divorce, contenant l'explication familière des moyens et de la manière d'exécuter la loi du divorce, dans tous les cas ou le divorce est permis, et les formules des actes relatifs à la pratique du divorce.* Paris, 1792.

Gauchat, G., abbé. *Lettres critiques, ou Analyse et réfutation de divers écrits modernes contre la religion.* 19 vols. Paris, 1755–63.

Goudar, Ange. *Les Intérêts de la France mal entendus dans les branches de l'agriculture, de la population, des finances et de l'industrie, par un citoyen.* 3 vols. Amsterdam, 1756.

Grandier, Urbain. *Traité du célibat des prêtres.* 1634. Reprint, Robert Luzarche, ed., Paris, 1861.

Graunt, John. *Natural and Political Observations.* London, 1662. Reprinted as *Observations naturelles et politiques,* ed. and trans. E. Vilquin, INED. Paris, 1977.

Grégoire, Henri-Baptiste, abbé. *Histoire du mariage des prêtres en France, particulièrement depuis 1789.* Paris, 1826.

Grimm, Melchior, and Denis Diderot. *Correspondance littéraire, philosophique et critique.* 17 vols. 1753–90. Reprint, Paris, 1813.

Groubert de Groubent de Linière, Marc-Ferdinand. *L'Antimoine ou Considérations politiques sur les moyens et la nécessité d'abolir les ordres monastiques en France.* Paris, 1787.

Hennet, Albert-Joseph-Ulpien. *Du Divorce.* Paris, 1789.

———. *Pétition à l'Assemblée Nationale par Montaigne, Charron, Montesquieu et Voltaire, suivie d'une Consultation en Pologne et en Suisse.* Paris, 1791.

Holbach, Paul-Henri d'. *Systeme de la nature.* London, 1770.

———. *La Politique naturelle ou Discours sur les vrais principes du gouvernement.* 1773. Reprint, New York, 1971.

———. *Ethocratie ou le gouvernement fondé sur la morale.* Amsterdam, 1776.

Hubert de Matigny, Hilaire-Joseph. *Homme en société.* N.p., 1763.

———. *Consultations sur le divorce, pour un mari [le sieur de Crosane] qui se trouve dans le même cas que Simon Sommer et qui demande si, d'après son mémoire à consulter, et la consultation de M. Linguet, il peut également requérir du St Père une dispense de se remarier* (also attributed to Cerfvol). Paris, 1771.

Hume, David. *See* Wallace, Robert.

Juges, Philippe. *Les Mariages heureux, ou l'Empire du divorce.* N.p.1789.

Laclos, Choderlos de. *Lettres inédites.* Louis de Chauvigny, ed. Paris, 1904.

———. *Oeuvres complètes.* M. Allem, ed. Paris, 1959.

Lakanal, Joseph. "Rapport sur J.-J. Rousseau, fait au nom du Comité d'Instruction publique." Paris, an II (1794). In E. Champion, ed. *J.-J. Rousseau dans la Révolution française.* Paris, 1977.

La Porte, Joseph de, abbé. *L'Esprit des monarques philosophes: Marc Aurèle, Julien, Stanislas et Frédéric.* Paris, 1764.

———. *Almanach chinois, ou coup d'oeil curieux sur la religion, les sciences, les moeurs, le commerce de l'Empire de Chine.* Paris, n.d.

Laugier, Esprit-Michel. *Tyrannie que les hommes ont exercée dans presque tous les temps et les pays contre les femmes.* Paris, 1789.

Le Guay de Prémontval, André-Pierre. *La Monogamie, ou l'unité dans le mariage, ouvrage dans lequel on entreprend d'établir contre le préjugé commun, l'exacte et parfaite conformité des trois lois de la nature, de Moise et de Jésus Christ sur ce sujet.* 3 vols. La Haye, 1751–52.

Leroy de Lozembrune, François-Claude. *Anecdotes et remarques sur l'éducation publique.* Mannheim, 1783.

Leszczynski, Stanislas. *Pensées philosophiques, morales, et politiques, ouvrage de main de maître* (with Frédéric de Prusse). Paris, 1768.

Leyser, Johan. *Polygamia Triumphatrix, id est Discursus politicus de Polygamia, Auctore Theophilo Aletheo, cum Notis Athanasii Vincentii, omnibus Anti-Polygamis ubique locorum, terrarum, insularum, pagorum, urbium, modestè, & piè opposita.* Amsterdam, 1682.

Linguet, Simon-Nicolas-Henri. *Recueil sur la question de savoir si un juif marié dans sa religion peut se remarier après son baptême lorsque sa femme juive refuse de le suivre et d'habiter avec lui.* London, 1761.

———. *Théorie des lois civiles ou Principes fondamentaux de la société.* London, 1767.

———. *La Légitimité du divorce.* Paris, 1771. Reprint, Brussels, 1789.

———. *Mémoire à consulter et consultation pour un mari dont la femme s'est remariée en pays protestant et qui demande s'il peut se remarier de même en France,* Paris, 1771. [Also attributed to Cerfvol].

———. *Du Plus Heureux Gouvernement.* London, 1774.

Locke, John. *Two Treatises of Government.* 1669. Reprint, Peter Laslett, ed., Cambridge, 1960.

Luther, Martin. *Mémoires de Luther.* Jules Michelet, trans. and ed. Paris, 1974.

Maréchal, Sylvain. *Dame Nature à la barre de l'Assemblée Nationale.* Paris, 1791.

Malvaux, J. de, abbé. *Les moyens de détruire la mendicité en France en rendant les malheureux utiles à l'Etat.* Chaalons-sur Marne, 1789.

Malthus, Thomas Robert. *An Essay on the Principle of Population.* 1798; 1803; 1826. Vols. 1, 2, 3, and 8 in *Works,* E. A. Wrigley and D. Souden, eds. London, 1986.

Marat, Jean-Paul. *De L'Homme, ou des Principes ou des lois de l'influence de l'âme sur le corps et des corps sur les âmes.* 3 vols. Amsterdam, 1775.

Melon, Jean-François. *Mahmoud le Gasnévide, Histoire orientale.* Rotterdam, 1730.

———. *Essai politique sur le commerce.* N.p., 1734.

Menassier de l'Estre, François de. *De L'Honneur des deux sexes.* Paris, 1784.

Mercier, Louis-Sébastien. *Le Tableau de Paris.* Amsterdam, 1783. Reprint, J.-Cl. Bonnet, ed., Paris, 1995.

Merlin, Charles, père. "Dissertation sur la polygamie des Patriarches, où l'on réfute les calomnies que M. Bayle fait à ce sujet contre le Père Fenardent Cordelier, contre St. Augustin & les autres Saints Pères." In *Journal de Trévoux,* 1736.

Meslier, Jean. *Oeuvres.* R. Desné, ed. Paris, 1970.

Messance, Louis. *Tableau de la population de la France et nouvelles Recherches sur la population de la France avec . . . Effets des recherches publiées en 1766, contre le système de la dépopulation.* Lyon, 1788. Reprint, Paris, 1973.

Michaud, *Biographie universelle.* 45 vols. Paris, 1854–65.

Milton, John. *The Doctrine and Discipline of Divorce: Restor'd to the Good of both Sexes, From the Bondage of Canon Law, and Other Mistakes, to the True Meaning of Scripture, in the Law and Gospel Compar'd.* London, 1644.

Mirabeau, Victor Riqueti, marquis de. "Extrait des Eloges des hommes à célébrer." Stockholm, 1774. Reprint in *Boisguilbert parmi nous.* J. Hecht, ed. Paris, 1989, 380–440.

———. *L'Ami des hommes ou Traité de la population.* 2 vols. Avignon, 1756–58.

Moheau, Jean-Baptiste. *Recherches et considérations sur la population de la France.* Paris, 1778. Reprint, Eric Vilquin, ed., Paris, 1994.

Montesquieu, Charles-Louis de Secondat. *Oeuvres complètes.* 4 vols. R. Caillois, ed. Paris 1949–51.

Morin, H. *Histoire critique du célibat.* In *Mémoires de l'Institut National de France,* vol. 4. Paris, 1723.

Mouslier de Moissy, Alexandre-Guillaume. *Le Célibataire détrompé.* Amsterdam, 1770.

Moy, Charles-André-Alexandre, abbé de. *Discours qui a remporté le prix d'éloquence . . . sur ce sujet: Combien le respect pour les moeurs contribue au bonheur d'un Etat.* Paris, 1776.

Moyens proposés pour prévenir l'infanticide. N.p., 1781.

Observations de deux soeurs célibataires sur la discussion du décret du célibat. Paris, n.d.

Oudot, Ch.-Fr. *Essai sur les principes de la législation des mariages privés et solennels, du divorce et de l'adoption, qui peuvent être déclarés à la suite de l'acte constitutionnel.* Paris, June 1793.

————. *Opinion sur le mode de constater les naissances.* Paris, 1792.

Palissot de Montenay, Charles. *Mémoires.* Geneva, 1775. S.v. Phil[i]bert.

Pétion de Villeneuve, Jérôme. *Essai sur le mariage considéré sous ses rapports naturels, moraux et politiques, ou moyens de faciliter et d'encourager les mariages en France.* Genève, 1785; Paris, 1789.

Petty, William. *Political Arithmetick, or a Discourse Concerning the Extent and Value of Lands, People . . . .* London, 1683.

[Philibert], *Cri d'un honnête homme.* Par Mr Philbert, prêteur de la ville de Landau en Alsace en même temps héros de l'histoire. Paris, 1769, with *Législation du divorce* (also attributed to Cerfvol and Palissot).

Pichon, Thomas-Jean, abbé. *Mémoire sur les abus du célibat dans l'ordre politique et sur le moyen possible de les réprimer.* Amsterdam, 1776.

Pilati di Tassulo, Ch.-Antoine. *Traité du mariage et de sa législation.* La Haye, 1776.

Plumart de Danguel [John Nickolls]. *Remarques sur les avantages et les désavantages de la France et de la Grande Bretagne.* London, 1754.

Pontas, Jean. *Dictionnaire de cas de conscience, ou Décisions des plus considérables difficultés touchant la morale et la discipline ecclésiastique.* In Migne, J.-P., *Encyclopédie théologique.* 78 vols. Paris, 1844–64.

Pothiers, Robert-Joseph. *Traité de la puissance du mari sur la personne et les biens de la femme.* Paris, 1768.

Presevot, Joseph. *Principes de Législation civile.* Dijon, 1791.

Prudhomme, Louis. *Révolutions de Paris.* Paris, 10 ventôse, an II (12 June 1789).

Puffendorf, Samuel. *On the Duty of Man and Citizen according to Natural Law.* Lund, 1673. Michael Silverthorne, trans., James Tully, ed. London, 1991.

Puisieux, Madeleine d'Arsant de. *Les Caractères.* London, 1750.

Rantzau, Louis. *Discussion si la polygamie est contre la loi naturelle ou divine, tant de l'ancien que du nouveau testament, de ce qui a donné lieu de l'interdire aux chrétiens; si les souverains chrétiens sont autorisés de la réintroduire dans leurs états, et de quelle manière ils pourront s'y prendre sans occasionner des désordres dans les ménages.* St. Petersburg, 1774.

Réflections d'un célibataire en faveur du divorce. Paris, n.d.

Réflections d'un bon citoyen en faveur du divorce. Paris, 1789.

Réflections philosophiques sur le plaisir, par un célibatairs. Lausanne, 1784.

Rétif de la Bretonne, Nicolas Edmé. *Le Pornographe, ou idées d'un honnête homme sur un projet de règlement pour les prostituées, propre à prévenir les malheurs qu'occasionne le publicisme des femmes.* Paris, 1769.

————. *Les Gynographes, ou idées de deux honnêtes femmes sur un projet de règlement proposé à toute l'Europe pour mettre les femmes à leur place et opérer le bonheur des deux sexes, avec notes historiques et justificatives.* La Haye, 1777.

————. *Andrographe ou Idées d'un honnête homme sur un projet de règlement proposé à toutes les nations de l'Europe pour opérer une réforme générale des moeurs et par elle le bonheur du genre humain.* La Haye, 1782.

──────. *Monsieur Nicolas, ou le Coeur humain dévoilé. Paris,* 1796. Reprint, *Paris,* 1883.

Richard, Jérome, abbé. *Réflexions critiques sur le livre intitulé "Les Moeurs."* Aux Indes [Paris], 1748.

Robert, Louis-Joseph-Marie. *De l'Influence de la Révolution française sur la population.* 2 vols. Paris, 1802.

Rouillé d'Orfeuil, Augustin de. *L'Alambic des lois, ou Observations de l'ami des Français sur l'homme et sur les lois.* Hispaan, 1773.

Rousseau, Jean-Jacques. *Oeuvres complètes.* 4 vols. B. Gagnebin, M. Raymond, eds. Paris, 1959–69.

──────. *Correspondance complète.* 50 vols. R. A. Leigh, ed. Oxford, 1967–91.

Roussel, Pierre, docteur. *Système physique et moral de la femme.* 1775. Paris, 1809.

Sabatier, André-Hyacinthe. *Odes nouvelles et autres poésies précédées d'un discours sur l'ode.* Paris, 1766.

Sade, Donatien-Alphonse-François, marquis de. *La Philosophie dans le boudoir.* Paris, 1795. Reprint, Amsterdam, 1965.

Saint-Just, Louis-Antoine. *Oeuvres complètes.* M. Duval, ed. Paris, 1984.

Saint-Lambert, Jean-François de. *Les Saisons et les jours, poèmes.* N.p., 1764.

Sarpi, P. *Histoire du concile de Trente.* Amsterdam, 1751.

Saxe, Herman-Maurice, maréchal de. *Réflexions sur la propagation de l'espèce humaine dans "Mes Rêveries," ouvrage posthume.* Dresde, 1757

Suchon, Gabrielle. *Le Célibat volontaire ou la vie sans engagement.* Paris, 1700. Reprint, S. Auffret, ed., Paris, 1994.

Süssmilch, Johann Peter. *Die göttlich Ordnung in der Veranderungen des menchlichen Geslechts.* Berlin, 1741. Selections translated as *"L'Ordre divin" aux origines de la démographie.* 3 vols. Jacqueline Hecht, trans. and ed., Paris, 1979. A second volume of translated selections, *L'Ordre divin dans les changements de l'espèce humaine, démontré par la naissance, la mort et la propagation de celle-ci.* J.-M. Rohrbasser, trans. and ed. Paris, 1998.

Tissot, S. T. *De L'Onanisme ou Dissertation sur les maladies produites par la masturbation.* Lausanne, 1760.

Toussaint, Fr.-V. *Les Moeurs.* Paris, 1749; facsimile, Amsterdam, 1972.

Turmeau de la Morandière, Denis. *Appel des étrangers dans nos colonies.* Paris, 1763. Reprint, Paris, 1973.

Vauban, Sébastien le Prestre, maréchal. *La Méthode Générale et facile pour faire le dénombrement des peuples.* N.p., 1686.

──────. *La Description de l'election de Vézelay.* N. p., 1696.

──────. *Projet d'une Dixme Royale, suivi de deux écrits financiers.* N.p., 1707. Reprint, Paris, 1933.

Venette, N. *La Génération de l'homme ou tableau de l'amour conjugal considéré dans l'état du mariage.* Parma, 1696. Reprint, no. 23 in *Le Mythe de la procréation à l'âge baroque.* Paris, 1981.

Vergniaud, Pierre-Victorin. "Opinion de monsieur Vergniaud sur le mode de constater les naissances, mariages et décès." *Assemblée nationale législative, rapports, opinions,* 9 April 1792.

Verzure, Mme de. *Réflexions hazardées d'une femme ignorante qui ne connaît les défauts des autres que par les siens et le monde que par relation et par oui-dire,* Paris, 1776.

Voltaire. *Oeuvres.* A. J. Q. Beuchot, ed. Paris, 1829–34.

——. *Oeuvres complètes.* 52 vols. L. Moland, ed. Paris, 1877–85.

——. *Correspondence.* T. Besterman, ed. Vols. 85–135 in *Complete Works.* Geneva, 1968–77.

Wallace, Robert. *Dissertation historique et politique sur la population des anciens temps, comparée avec celle du nôtre, dans laquelle on prouve qu'elle a été plus grande autrefois qu'elle ne l'est de nos jours. On y joint quelques Remarques sur le Discours politique de M. Hume sur la population des anciens temps.* M. Eidous, trans. Amsterdam, 1769.

Withof, Ph.-Laurent. *Dissertation sur les eunuques.* Duisbourg, 1756.

Wollstonecraft, Mary. *A Vindication of the Rights of Women.* London, 1792.

Young, Arthur. *Travels in France.* London, 1792.

Materials Published since 1800

Baker, Keith M. "Politics and Public Opinion under the Old Regime: Some Reflections." In *Press and Politics in Pre-Revolutionary France.* J. R. Censer, J. D. Popkin, eds. Berekley, 1987. 204–46.

——. "L'Unité de la pensée de Condorcet." In *Condorcet, mathématicien, économiste, philosophe, homme politique.* P. Crépel, C. Gilain, eds. Montrouge, 1989. 515–24.

——. "Defining the Public Sphere in Eighteenth-Century France: Variations on a Theme by Habermas." In *Habermas and the Public Sphere.* Craig Calhoun, ed. Cambridge, 1992. 181–211.

Barny, Roger. "Rousseau dans la Révolution." *Dix-Huitième Siècle* 6 (1974): 59–98.

——. "Les Aristocrates et J.-J. Rousseau dans la Révolution." *Annales Historiques de la Révolution française* 50 (1978): 534–68.

Béjin, André. "Condorcet, précurseur du néo-mathusianisme et de l'eugénisme républicain." *Histoire Économique et Sociale* 7, no. 3 (1988): 347–54.

Benrekassa, Georges. "Loi naturelle et loi civile: L'Idéologie des Lumières et la prohibition de l'inceste." *Studies on Voltaire and the Eighteenth Century* 87 (1972): 115–44.

Bernos, M. *Le Fruit défendu, les Chrétiens et la sexualité de l'antiquité à nos jours.* Paris, 1985.

Bernstein, Michel. "Sur la Diffusion des oeuvres de Boisguilbert et de Vauban de 1695 a 1713." In *Boisguilbert parmi nous. Actes du Colloque international de Rouen.* J. Hecht, ed. Paris, 1989. 163–65.

Binion, Rudolph. "'More Men Than Corn': Malthus versus the Enlightenment," in "Forum," C. Blum, ed. *Eighteenth-Century Studies* 32, no. 4 (1999):564–69.

Blayo, Yves. "Illegitimate Births in France, 1740 to 1829." *Bastardy and Its Comparative History.* London, 1984.

Bloch, Marc. *Les Rois thaumaturges.* Paris, 1961.

Blum, Carol. *Rousseau and the Republic of Virtue: The Language of Politics in the French Revolution.* Ithaca, 1986.

———."Une Controverse nataliste en France au XVIIIe siècle: la polygamie." Henri Léridon, ed. *Population* 1–2 (1998): 93–112.

Boislisle, A. de. *Mémoires des intendants sur l'état des généralités: 1. Mémoire de la généralité de Paris.* Paris, 1881.

Brian, Eric. *La Mesure de l'Etat: Administrateurs et géomètres au XVIIIe siècle.* Paris, 1994.

Burguière, André. "Réticences et intégration pratique du remariage dans la France d'Ancien Régime, XVIIe-XVIIIe siècles." In *Marriage and Remarriage in Populations of the Past.* J. Dupâquier, E. Hélin, P. Laslett, M. Livi-Bacci, and S. Sogner, eds. London, 1981.

———. "La Famille et l'Etat. Débats et attentes de la société française à la veille de la Révolution," *La Famille, la loi, l'Etat de la Révolution au Code Civil.* I. Thery and C. Biet, eds. Paris, 1989.

———. "'Cher Cousin': Les Usages matrimoniaux de la parenté proche dans la France du XVIIIe siècle." *Annales Histoire Science Sociale* 6 (1997): 1339–60.

———, and Eric Vilquin. "Le Pouvoir royal et la statistique démographique." *Pour une histoire de la statistique,* vol. 1. Paris, 1978.

Cairncross, John. *After Polygamy Was Made a Sin: The Social History of Christian Polygamy.* London, 1974.

Capitan, Colette. "Construction de l'objet et univers du sens en histoire." In *Les Femmes et la Révolution française.* 2 vols. M.-F. Brive, ed. Toulouse, 1988. 1:331–37.

Capitani, François de. "The *Encyclopédie* in Switzerland." In *The Encyclopédie and the Age of Revolution.* Cl. Donato and R. Maniquis, eds. Boston, 1992.

Charbit, Y., and Béjin, A. "La Pensée démographique." In *Histoire de la population française,* J. Dupâquier, ed. 3:465–501.

Cuche, François-Xavier. *Une Pensée sociale catholique: Fleury, La Bruyère, Fénelon.* Paris, 1991.

Connor, R. E. "'Can You Apply Arithmetick [sic] to Everything?': Moll Flanders, William Petty, and Social Accounting." *Studies in Eighteenth-Century Culture* 27 (1998): 169–94.

Corvisier, A. "Célibat et service militaire au XVIIIe siècle." *Mesurer et comprendre;*

Mélanges offerts à Jacques Dupâquier. J.-P. Bardet, Fr.Lebrun, R. Le Mée, eds.. Paris, 1993.

Cranston, Maurice. *Jean-Jacques, the Early Life and Works of J.-J. Rousseau, 1712–1754.* Chicago, 1982.

———. *The Noble Savage, Jean-Jacques Rousseau, 1754–1762.* Chicago, 1992.

Darmon, Pierre. *Le Mythe de la procréation à l'âge baroque.* Paris, 1981.

———. *Mythologie de la femme.* Paris, 1981.

Darnton, Robert. *Gens de lettres, gens du livre.* Paris, 1990.

———. *The Literary Underground of the Old Regime.* Cambridge, Mass., 1982.

Décembre-Alonnier, P. *Dictionnaire de la Révolution française.* 2 vols. Paris, 1866–68.

Delon, Michel. "Un Monde d'Eunuques." *Europe* 55 (1977): 79–88.

———. "L'Inceste: Horreur et séduction." *Magazine Littéraire* 301 (1992): 22–26.

———. "The Priest, the Philosopher, and Homosexuality in Enlightenment France." In *Unauthorized Sexual Behavior during the Enlightenment. Eighteenth-Century Life.* R. P. Maccubbin, ed. 1985. 3:122–31.

Delumeau, Jean, and Roche, Daniel. *Histoire des pères et de la paternité.* Paris, 2000.

De Man, Paul. *Blindness and Insight: Essays in the Rhetoric of contemporary Criticism.* Minneapolis, 1983.

Derrida, Jacques. *De La Grammatologie.* Paris, 1967.

Desrosières, Alain. *La Politique des grands nombres, Historie de la raison statistique.* Paris, 1993.

Dittgen, Alfred. "Les Mariages civils en Europe: Histoires, contextes, chiffres." *Droit et Société.* 36–37 (1997): 309–29.

Dobie, Madeleine. *Foreign Bodies: Gender, Language and Culture in French Orientalism.* Stanford, 2000.

Duchet, Michel. *Anthropologie et histoire au siècle des Lumières.* Paris, 1971.

Dumézil, Georges. "Le Rex et les Flamines maiores." *The Sacral Kingship.* Leiden, 1959.

Dupâquier, J. *La Population française aux XVIIe et XVIIIe siècles.* Paris, 1979.

———. "Document, Providence et probabilité." *Revue de Synthèse* 117 (1985): 81–99.

———, and M. Dupâquier. *Histoire de la démographie.* Paris, 1985.

———, and E. Vilquin, "Le Pouvoir royal et la statistique démographique." *Pour une Histoire de la statistique.* Paris, 1978. 1:83–101.

———, et al. *Histoire de la population française.* Vol. 2, *De la Renaissance à 1789.* Vol. 3, *De 1789 à 1914.* Vol. 4, *De 1914 à nos jours.* Paris, 1988.

Ehrard, Jean. *Politique de Montesquieu.* Paris, 1965.

———. "*L'Encyclopédie* et l'esclavage: deux lecteurs de Montesquieu." In *Enlightenment Essays in Memory of Robert Shackleton.* G. Barber and C. P. Courtney, eds. Oxford, 1988.

Esmonin, E. "*Les Mémoires* des intendants pour l'instruction du duc de Bourgogne." *Bulletin de la Société d'Histoire Moderne* 55 (1956): 12–21.

Fage, Anita. "Les Doctrines de population des Encyclopédistes." *Population* 3 (1951): 610–24.

———. "La Révolution française et la population." *Population* no.1 (1955): 311–38.

Farge, Arlette. *La Vie fragile, Violence, pouvoirs et solidarité à Paris au XVIIIe siècle.* Paris, 1986.

Fauve-Chamoux, Antoinette. "Le Surplus urbain des femmes en France préindustrielle." *Population* (1998), nos. 1–2:359–76.

Fellows, Otis. "Buffon and Rousseau: Aspects of a Relationship." *PMLA.* 65 (1960): 184–96.

Fermon, Nicole. *Domesticating Passions: Rousseau, Women and Nation.* London, 1997.

Flandrin, Jean-Louis. *L'Eglise et le contrôle des naissances.* Paris, 1970.

———. "L'Attitude à l'égard du petit enfant et les conduites sexuelles dans la civilisation occidentale." *Annales de Démographie Historique* (1973): 143–210.

———. *Les Amours paysannes, Amour et sexualité dans les campagnes de l'ancienne France.* Paris, 1975.

———. *Le Sexe et l'Occident.* Paris, 1981.

———. *Familles, parentés, maison, sexualité dans l'ancienne société.* Paris, 1986.

Foucault, Michel. *Histoire de la sexualité,* Vol. 1, *La Volonté de savoir.* Paris, 1976.

Fourney, Diane. "The Festival at the Water-Hole: Rousseau, Freud, and Derrida." *The Eighteenth Century: Theory and Interpretation* 2 (1990): 137–60.

Fraisse, Geneviève. *Muse de la raison: La Démocratie exclusive et la différence des sexes.* Paris, 1989.

Francini, Giacomo. *Moralia coniugalia ou de l'impossible sacralité, du mariage à l'époque de la raison.* Unpublished doctoral dissertation, Ecole des Hautes Etudes en sciences Sociales. Paris, 1998.

———. "Il Divorzio nella Francia des XVII secolo: ingerenza o rinuncia istituzionale?" *Richerche Storiche* no. 1 (1995): 35–60.

Frazier, James. *The Golden Bough: The Dying God.* New York, 1968.

Garaud, M., and R. Szramkiewicz. *La Révolution française et la famille.* Paris, 1978.

Goldschmidt, Victor. *Anthropologie et politique: Les Principes du système de Rousseau.* Paris, 1974.

———. "Public Sphere and Private Life: Towards a Synthesis of Current Historical Approaches to the Ancien Régime." In *History and Theory: Studies in the Philosophy of History* 31, no. 1 (1992).

Goody, Jack. *Death, Property and the Ancestors.* Stanford, 1962.

———. *The Development of the Family and Marriage in Europe.* Cambridge, 1983.

Goubert, Pierre. *Louis XIV et vingt millions de Français.* Paris, 1966.

Gouesse, J.-M. "Le Refus de l'enfant au tribunal de la conscience." *Annales de Démographie Historique* (1973): 231–61.

Graham, Ruth. "The Revolutionary Bishop and the *Philosophes.*" *Eighteenth-Century Studies* 16 (1983):117–40.

————. "The Married Nuns before Cardinal Caprara." In *Pratiques religieuses, mentalités et spiritualités dans l'Europe révolutionnaire.* B. Plongeron. Paris, 1988.

Grosrichard, Alan. *Structure du sérail.* Paris, 1979.

Gutton, J.-P. *Domestiques et serviteurs dans la France de l'Ancien Régime.* Paris, 1981.

Gutwirth, Madelyn. *The Twilight of the Goddesses: Women and Representation in the French Revolutionary Era.* New Brunswick, 1992.

Guy, Basil. *The French Image of China Before and After Voltaire.* Geneva, 1963.

Habermas, Jurgen. *The Structural Transformation of the Public Sphere: An Inquiry into a Category of Bourgeois Society.* T. Burger and F. Lawrence, trans. Cambridge, Mass., 1989.

Hajinal, J. *European Marriage Patterns in Perspective.* D. V. Glass and D. E. C. Eversley, eds. London, 1965.

Halpérin, Jean-Louis. *L'Impossible Code civil.* Paris, 1992.

Hanley, Sara. "Engendering the State: Family Formation and State Building in Early Modern France." *French Historical Studies* 16, no. 1 (1989): 4–27.

Hasquin, Hervé. "Voltaire démographe." *Etudes sur le XVIIIe siècle* 3 (1976):133–48.

————. "Politique, économie et démographie chez Diderot: Aux Origines du libéralisme économique et démocratique." In *Thèmes et figures du siècle des Lumières.* Genève, 1980.

————. "Le Débat sur la Dépopulation dans l'Europe des Lumières." In Moheau, *Recherches et considérations sur la population de la France,* E. Vilquin and H. Léridon, eds. Paris, 1994. 397–424.

Hecht, Jacqueline. "La Vie de Pierre Le Pesant, seigneur de Boisguilbert." *Pierre de Boisguilbert ou la naissance de l'économie politique.* Paris, 1966.

————. "L'Idée de dénombrement jusqu'à la Révolution." In *Pour une Histoire de la statistique.* INSEE. Paris, 1978. 1:21–81.

————. "Malthus avant Malthus: Conceptions et comportements prémalthusiens dans la France de l'Ancien Régime." *Dix-Huitième Siècle* 26 (1994): 67–98.

————"Célibat, stratégies familiales et essor du capitalisme au XVIIIe siècle: Réalités et représentations." In *Ménages, familles, parentèles et solidarités dans les populations méditerranéennes.* AIDELF. Paris, 1996. 7:257–84.

————. "From 'Be Fruitful and Multiply' to Family Planning: The Enlightenment Transition." in "Forum: Demographic Thought and Reproductive Realtities: From Montesquieu to Malthus." C. Blum, ed. *Eighteenth-Century Studies* 32, no. 4 (1999): 536–51.

————, and Claude Lévy. *Economie et population: Les Doctrines françaises avant 1800. Bibliographie générale commentée.* Institut National d'Etudes Démographiques. Cahier no. 28. Paris, 1956.

————, and A. Sauvy. "Le Grand Homme du 'Grand Siècle': Vauban." *Les Cahiers Français* 15 (1957):30–34.

Hénaff, Marcel. "The Cannibalistic City: Rousseau, Large Numbers, and the Abuse of the Social Bond." *Substance* 67 (1992): 3–23.

Henry, Louis, and Jacques Houdaille. "Célibat et âge du mariage au XVIIIe et au XIXe siècles en France." *Population* no. 2 (1964): 267–90.

Houdaille, Jacques. "La Noblesse française, descendance 1600–1900." *Population* no. 3 (1989): 501–513.

Huet, Marie-Hélène. "Le Défaut de l'histoire: Ecriture et paternité chez Rousseau." *Modern Language Notes* 104, no. 4 (1989): 804–18.

Hufton, Olwen. "Women without Men: Widows and Spinsters in Britain and France in the Eighteenth Century." *Journal of Family History* 9 (1984): 310–25.

———. *The Prospect before Her: A History of Women in Western Europe, 1500–1800.* London, 1995.

Hull, Isabel V. *Sexuality, State and Civil Society in Germany, 1700–1815.* Ithaca, 1996.

Ivinski, P. R., H. C. Payne, K. C. Galitz, and R. Rand. *Farewell to the Wet Nurse, Etienne Aubry and Images of Breast-Feeding in Eighteenth-Century France.* Catalogue of exposition. Williamstown, Mass., 1998.

Kantorowicz, Ernst. *The King's Two Bodies: A Study in Medieval Political Theory.* Princeton, 1957.

Kates, Gary. *Monsieur d'Eon is a Woman: A Tale of Political Intrigue and Sexual Mascarade.* New York, 1995.

Kenshur, Oscar. "Pierre Bayle and the Structures of Doubt." *Eighteenth-Century Studies* 21, no. 3 (1988): 297–315.

Keohane, Nannerl. *Philosophy and the State in France. The Renaissance to the Enlightenment.* Princeton, 1980.

Knibiehler, Yvonne. "Le Célibat. Approche historique." In *La Famille. L'Etat des savoirs.* François de Singly, ed. Paris, 1992.

Kors, Alan. *D'Holbach's Coterie: An Enlightenment in Paris.* Princeton, 1976.

Kra, Pauline. "The Invisible Chain of the *Lettres persanes.*" *Studies in Voltaire and the Eighteenth Century* 102 (1973): 121–41.

Landes, Joan. *Women and the Public Sphere in the French Revolution.* Ithaca, 1988.

Laqueur, Thomas W. "Masturbation, Credit, and the Novel during the Long Eighteenth-Century." *Qui Parle* 8, no. 2 (1995): 2–20.

Legeard, C. *Guide de recherches documentaires en démographie.* Paris, 1966.

Leibacher-Ouvrard, L. "L'Eunuque anathème et prétexte. Economie libidinale et construction de l'hétérosexualité." In *Sexualité, mariage et famille au XVIIIe siècle.* O. B. Cragg and R. Davison, eds. Quebec, 1998. 11–26.

Le Roy Ladurie, Emmanuel. *L'Ancien Régime.* Paris, 1991.

Levy, Darline G. *The Ideas and Careers of Simon-Nicolas Linguet: A Study in Eighteenth-Century French Politics.* Urbana, 1980.

Lévy, Michel. "Le Secret de la paternité: des Dix Commandements au Code Civil et à la Sécurité Sociale." In *Ménages, familles, parentèles et solidarités dans les Populations méditerranéernes.* AIDELF, Paris, 1995. 1–6.

Lévi-Strauss, Claude. "Jean-Jacques Rousseau, fondateur des sciences de l'homme." *Anthropologie structurale* 2 (1973): 45–56.

———. *Tristes Tropiques.* Paris, 1975.

Lough, John. "Women in Mercier's 'Tableau de Paris.'" In *Women and Society in Eighteenth-Century France.* E. Jacobs et al, eds. London, 1979.

Martin, Daniel. "La Dépopulation au service de l'idéal social Robespierriste." In *La Légende de la Révolution.* C. Croisille, J. Ehrard, and M.-C. Chemin, eds. Clermont-Ferrand, 1988. 201–14.

May, Gita. *De Jean-Jacques Rousseau à Mme Roland.* Geneva, 1964.

Maza, Sarah. *Servants and Masters in Eighteenth-Century France.* Princeton, 1983.

———. "Women, the Bourgeoisie, and the Public Sphere: Response to Daniel Gordon and David Bell." *French Historical Studies* 17, no. 4 (1992):935–50.

McLaren, Angus. *Sexuality and Social Order: The Debate over the Fertility of Women and Workers in France, 1770–1920.* New York, 1983.

Merrick, Jeffrey. "Domestic Politics: Divorce and Despotism in Eighteenth-Century France." In *The Past as Prologue.* C. Hay and S. Conger, eds. New York, 1995. 373–86.

———. "Masculinity and Effeminacy in the 'Mémoires secrets.'" *The "Mémoires secrets" and the Culture of Publicity in Eighteenth-Century France.* J. D. Popkin and B. Fort, eds. Oxford, 1998. 129–42.

———. "The Religious Police of the Ancien Regime and the Secularization of Jurisprudence in the Eighteenth Century." *Proceedings of the Nineteenth Annual Consortium on Revolutionary Europe: 1750–1850,* forthcoming.

———, and B. T. Ragan, eds. "The Marquis de Villette and Mademoiselle de Raucourt: Representations of Male and Female Sexual Desire in Late Eighteenth-Century France." In *Homosexuality in Modern France.* Oxford, 1996.

Miller, Leo. *John Milton Among the Polygamophiles.* New York, 1974.

Milton, John. *Treatise on Christian Doctrine,* In *Works of John Milton,* vol. 15. New York, 1933.

Murphy, Antonin. *Richard Cantillon: Entrepreneur and Economist.* Oxford, 1986.

Nardi, Emma. "Rousseau contredit Jean-Jacques." *Annales de la Société J.-J. Rousseau* 41 (1997): 131–51.

Nye, Robert A. *Masculinity and Male Codes of Honor in Modern France.* New York, 1993.

Oliver-Martin, Fr. *La Crise du mariage dans la Législation intermédiare, 1789–1804.* Paris, 1901.

Outram, D. *The Body and the French Revolution: Sex, Class, and Political Culture.* New Haven, 1989.

Pappas, John. *Berthier's 'Journal de Trévoux' et les philosophes. Studies on Voltaire and the Eighteenth Century* 3 (1957).

Perrot, Jean-Claude. "Les Economistes, les philosophes et la population." In *La Population française.* J. Dupâquier, ed. 2:499–551.

Phan, Marie-Claude. "La Séduction impunie ou la fin des actions en recherche de paternité." In *Les Femmes et la Révolution française.* Toulouse, 1988. Vol. 2.

Pison, Gilles. "La Démographie et la Polygamie." *Population* no. 1 (1986): 93–122.

Phillips, Roderick. *Putting Asunder: A History of Divorce in Western Society.* Cambridge, 1988.

Poumarède, Jacques. "Le Droit des veuves sous l'Ancien Régime (XVIIe-XVIIIe siècles) ou comment gagner son douaire." In *Femmes et pouvoirs sous l'Ancien Régime.* D. Haase-Dubose, E. Vienot, eds. Paris, 1981.

Quérard, J.-M. *La France littéraire ou Dictionnaire bibliographique des savants, historiens et gens de lettres de la France, ainsi que des littérateurs étrangers qui ont écrit en français, plus particulièrement pendant les XVIIIe et XIXe siècles.* Paris, 1827–39.

Rapley, Elizabeth, and Robert Rapley. "An Image of Religious Women in the Ancien Régime: The *Etats* des Religieuses of 1790–1791." *French History* 11 (1997) 4: 387–410.

Rebelliau, A. *Vauban.* Paris, 1962.

Rétat, Pierre. "Luxe." *Dix-Huitième Siècle* 26 (1994): 79–88.

Riley, James. *Population Thought in the Age of the Demographic Revolution.* Durham, S.C., 1985.

Roche, Daniel. *France and the Enlightenment.* Cambridge, Mass., 1998.

Ronsin, Francis. *La Grève des ventres. Propagande néomalthusienne et baisse de la natalité française.* Paris, 1980.

———. *Le Contrat sentimental, Débats sur le mariage, l'amour, le divorce, de l'Ancien Régime à la Restauration.* Paris, 1990.

Rothkrug, Lionel. *Opposition to Louis XIV: The Political and Social Origins of the French Enlightenment.* Princeton, 1965.

Rothschild, Emma. "Social Security and Laissez-Faire in Eighteenth-Century Political Economy." *Population and Development Review* 21, no. 4 (1995): 711–44.

Rousseau, George S. "The Pursuit of Homosexuality in the Eighteenth Century: 'Utterly Confused Category' and/or Rich Repository." In *Unauthorized Sexual Behavior during the Enlightenment, Eighteenth-Century Life*, R. P. Maccubbin, ed. Vol. 3 (1985):132–68.

———, and R. Porter, eds. *Sexual Undergrounds of the Enlightenment.* Chapel Hill, N.C., 1988.

Sauvy, Alfred. "Deux Techniciens précurseurs de Malthus: Boesnier de l'Orme et Auxiron." *Population* no. 4 (1955): 691–704.

———. "Some Lesser-Known Demographers of the Eighteenth Century." *Population Studies* no. 1 (1965): 3–22.

Schulte van Kessel, Elisja. "Vièrges et mères, entre Ciel et terre." In *Histoire des femmes en Occident*, vol. 3. G. Duby and M. Perrot, eds. Paris, 1991.

Scott, Joan. *Gender and the Politics of History*. New York, 1988.

Sgard, Jean. *Dictionnaire des journaux, 1600–1789*. 2 vols. Paris, 1991.

Sollers, Philippe. *Le Nouvel Observateur*. 8–14 August 1996, 7.

Spengler, J. J. *French Predecessors of Malthus: A Study of Eighteenth-Century Wage and Population Theory*. New York, 1965.

———. *France Faces Depopulation, 1936–1976*. Durham, N.C., 1979.

Starobinski, Jean. "Jean-Jacques Rousseau et le péril de la réflection." *Annales Jean-Jacques Rousseau* 34 (1956–58): 139–73.

———. *Jean-Jacques Rousseau, La Transparence et l'obstacle*. Paris, 1971.

Thau, Etienne. *Raison d'Etat et pensée politique*. Paris, 1966.

Théré, Christine. "Limitation des naissances et émancipation des femmes au XVIIIe siècle." *Les Modes de régulation de la réproduction humaine*. AIDELF, Paris, 1994. 6:425–40.

Tomaselli, Sylvana. "Moral Philosophy and Population Questions in Eighteenth-Century Europe." *Population and Resources in Western Intellectual Traditions*. M. S. Teitelbaum and J. Winter, eds. Cambridge, 1989.

Traer, James. *Marriage and the Family in Eighteenth-Century France*. Ithaca, 1980.

Trouille, Mary S. *Sexual Politics in the Enlightenment, Women Writers and Rousseau*. Albany, 1997.

Van de Walle, Etienne. "De La Nature à la fécundité naturelle." *Annales de Démographie Historique*. 1988. Paris, 1989. 14–15.

Van der Cruysse, D. "De Bayle à Raynal: Le Prophète Muhammad à travers le prisme des Lumières." In *Orient et Lumières*, ed. A. Moalla. Grenoble, 1987. 85–96.

Van Roosbroeck, G. L. *Persian Letters before Montesquieu*. New York, 1972.

Venturi, Franco. *Italy and the Enlightenment*. London, 1972.

Viguerie, Jean de. "Une Forme nouvelle de la vie consacrée: Enseignantes et hospitalières en France au XVIIe et XVIIIe siècles." *Femmes et pouvoirs sous l'Ancien Régime*. Paris, 1981.

Vilquin, Eric. "Vauban, inventeur des recensements." In *Annales de Démographie Historique* (1975): 207–57.

Walter, Eric. "Le Complexe d'Abélard ou le Célibat des gens de lettres." *Dix-Huitième Siècle* 12 (1989): 147.

Weinreb, Ruth P. *Eagle in a Gauze Cage: Louise d'Epinay, Femme de Lettres*. New York, 1993.

Weir, David R. "New Estimates of Nuptiality and Marital Fertility in France, 1740–1911." *Population Studies* no. 48 (1994): 307–31.

INDEX